"Ajahn Buddhadāsa spent more than sixty years in the forest in southern Thailand engaged in meditations, reflections, study of the words of the Buddha, living close to the elements, and teaching. He revealed an exceptional range of realizations throughout his life. *Seeing with the Eye of Dhamma* embraces the expanse of his teachings, rich with insights, suitable for daily life. Readers will find reflections on cultivation of the mind, inquiry into the self/ego, superstitious beliefs, and the importance of the observation of life, as well as explanations of the Buddha's core teachings on mental suffering, conditionality, dependent arising, the elements, mental concoctions, voidness, the goal, and *nibbāna*. A profound book provides a mind-opening reading experience: *Seeing with the Eye of Dhamma* falls into this category."

—CHRISTOPHER TITMUSS,
author of *The Explicit Buddha*

"*Seeing with the Eye of Dhamma* introduces the reader to one of the most important figures of modern Buddhism. Ajahn Buddhadāsa, together with the Dalai Lama, is one of the foremost thinkers who has worked to adapt Buddhism to the modern world by putting forth interpretations of the tradition that are rooted in the Buddha's teachings while at the same time new and provocative. This book offers an opportunity to meet this great mind, who has been an inspiration for thousands of modern Buddhists, including myself."

—GEORGES DREYFUS,
author of *The Sound of Two Hands Clapping*

"Ajahn Buddhadāsa was a teacher ahead of his time. Dispensing with the metaphysics of rebirth and other realms of existence, he envisioned the Dhamma as a way of life here and now that can be realized by everyone, lay and monastic alike. Delivered half a century ago in rural Thailand, the refreshing and informal lectures collected in *Seeing with the Eye of Dhamma* open a window onto an extraordinary Buddhist teacher, whose message may be even more relevant today than when it was first delivered."

—STEPHEN BATCHELOR,
author of *After Buddhism*

OTHER BOOKS BY

BUDDHADĀSA BHIKKHU

Buddha-Dhamma for Inquiring Minds

Christ-Dhamma, Buddha-Dhamma

Dhammic Socialism

Disadhamma: Mankind's Pathway Dhamma

First Ten Years of Suan Mokkh

Handbook for Mankind

Heartwood of the Bodhi Tree: The Buddha's Teachings on Voidness

Keys to Natural Truth

Me and Mine

Mindfulness with Breathing: A Manual for Serious Beginners

Single Bowl of Sauce: Teachings beyond Good and Evil

Under the Bodhi Tree:
Buddha's Original Vision of Dependent Co-arising

EBOOKS

An expanding list of free distribution ebooks, poems, and articles can be found at www.suanmokkh.org. Extensive audio offerings in translation are available on SoundCloud.

SEEING WITH THE EYE OF DHAMMA

THE COMPREHENSIVE TEACHING OF

BUDDHADĀSA BHIKKHU

Translated by

DHAMMAVIDŪ BHIKKHU AND SANTIKARO UPASAKA

SHAMBHALA

Shambhala Publications, Inc.
2129 13th Street
Boulder, Colorado 80302
www.shambhala.com

Cover art: *Phra Buddhadāsa,* an oil on canvas by Tongdee Panumas.
From the Buddhadāsa Indapañño Archives collection (Ref. BIAF-OB8.3-2/37).
Interior design: Claudine Mansour Design

9 8 7 6 5 4 3 2

Printed in the United States of America

♾ This edition is printed on acid-free paper that meets the
American National Standards Institute z39.48 Standard.
♻ Shambhala Publications makes every effort to print on recycled paper.
For more information please visit www.shambhala.com.
Shambhala Publications is distributed worldwide by
Penguin Random House, Inc., and its subsidiaries.

Library of Congress Cataloging-in-Publication Data

Names: Phra Thēpwisutthimēthī (Ngư̄am), 1906–1993, author. |
Upasaka, Santikaro, 1957– editor.
Title: Seeing with the eye of Dhamma: the comprehensive teaching
of Buddhadāsa Bhikkhu / translated by Dhammavidū Bhikkhu and
Santikaro Upasaka
Description: Boulder: Shambhala, 2021. |
Includes bibliographical references and index.
Identifiers: LCCN 2021011799 | ISBN 9781611807660 (trade paperback)
Subjects: LCSH: Dharma (Buddhism)
Classification: LCC BQ4190 .P7388 2021 | DDC 294.3/4432—dc23
LC record available at https://lccn.loc.gov/2021011799

CONTENTS

THE DALAI LAMA

I had the privilege of meeting the Venerable Buddhadāsa when I first visited Thailand in 1967 and also at his forest monastery, Suan Mokkh, some years later. He was my senior spiritual brother, and conversations with him revealed what a learned and accomplished practitioner he was.

In rigorously serving the Dhamma and teaching it to lay-people as well as monastics, he lived a deeply meaningful life. I welcome the publication of this new compilation of his work: *Seeing with the Eye of Dhamma.*

With my prayers and good wishes,

August 18, 2021

PREFACE

A great blessing and joy in my life are the hundreds of hours of one-on-one Dhamma conversation I was honored to have with Venerable Ajahn Buddhadāsa Bhikkhu. These encounters began in October 1985 and continued until the months of his final illness in 1993. Like many others before me, I met him outdoors, under the trees of Suan Mokkh, the Garden of Liberation he founded. Any evening that he wasn't otherwise occupied, or ill, I was free to bring my questions to his compound—library, outdoor office, and dwelling—at the base of Golden Buddha Hill. If he was sitting on his usual stone bench out front or in his rocking chair sheltered from the rain, I was welcome, as were various dogs, fish, humans, and chickens—the latter occasionally standing on his crossed legs or pecking at the table that held my tape recorder. These interviews were an education for me and provided a certain amusement for him as he fielded the questions of a curious, opinionated, sincere *farang* (person of European extraction). I also had the privilege of sitting next to him during dozens of live translations, as Dhamma flowed through him—and me. My spirits continue to be lifted by the beautiful words that were enticed from my mouth.

At times I abused the privilege. Ordination doesn't magically erase the *kilesas* of young men; alas, I amply proved that fact. When something in the monastery irked me, usually the perceived misbehavior of someone, I felt entitled to take my complaint to the top. As I rattled on with my irritation and arrogance, he sat quietly, occasionally nodding, perhaps smiling wryly. If I got overly carried away, he would clear his throat more loudly, cough, maybe even grunt—cues I took a while to recognize. Usually, however, my words and ire, not meeting with opposition or acceptance, dissipated into the evening air, perhaps drowned out by roosters crowing or the drone of cicadas. He didn't argue, he didn't help me see reason, and he didn't sympathize or egg on. He was empty of such egoistic impulses. Hence, my floundering ego embarrassed itself, wilted, and petered out. Afterward, he might admit I'd been stupid. Then we could discuss the Dhamma of clinging and letting go. I came to see the wordless embodiment of emptiness as his greatest teaching.

Mapping the Journey of Life

Human life is at heart a contemplative journey of deepening wisdom, kindness, ethics, and freedom. For Ajahn Buddhadāsa, this journey starts with the recognition that spiritual cultivation has a central place in our lives. The meditation this involves goes far beyond "sitting," or any particular technique. In his teaching in *Seeing with the Eye of Dhamma*, he examines the capacities required for the journey and maps a progression of increasingly subtle inquiries that extend into all aspects of life. He describes how one can mature through ever more satisfying realizations of "the best that life has to offer."

This book is the teaching of a Buddhist thinker, practitioner, informal scholar, poet, photographer, amateur archaeologist, and innovative preacher. He was a teacher who emphasized practice and spiritual experience while deeply revering the Pali suttas, the thousands of discourses from the Buddha as recorded by early Buddhism. To read these pages is to discover insights into a mind dedicated to Buddha-Dhamma and its purpose, thus a mind that grappled with issues with which we all must grapple. The words and style may be his—or of his culture, or of Theravada Buddhism—but the fundamentals are humanly universal.

Ajahn Buddhadāsa invites us to think carefully, inquire deeply, and look courageously in order to discover Dhamma in the suffering we concoct, the path we cultivate, and the peace of nonconcocting to be realized. He makes extensive use of teachings drawn from the early record of the Pali suttas and arranges them in order to highlight their contemplative core. He shows us how to use these timeless texts as guides that awaken Dhamma within us. An active, curious intellect is necessary for the journey, along with willingness to make space for quiet reflection.

Buddhadāsa Bhikkhu's Early Life and the Founding of Suan Mokkh

Born Ngeuam Panich, Buddhadāsa Bhikkhu lived almost all his life in the Ban Dorn Bay watershed, where the Tapi River drains the southern Thai heartland and flows into the Gulf of Siam. This area has a long Buddhist history going back to the Srivijaya maritime empire (ca. seventh through twelfth centuries C.E.). Buddhist temples abound in and around Chaiya, the main town, along with a few mosques and ruins from the Srivijaya period. Srivijaya was an important commercial and cultural power located in the Malay Peninsula, Sumatra, and Java, controlling the main trade route between India and China. There, Hindu, Mahayana, Vajrayana, and Theravada influences intertwined. This ancient heritage had a lifelong role in Buddhadāsa Bhikkhu's life and was probably a factor in his creative openness to other religions, as well as "Buddhayana," his term for the core of liberating Dhamma that runs through all genuine Buddhist traditions.

Ngeuam was born in Phum Riang, a small coastal market town where his family kept a store. From the age of eight until ten, he lived as a temple boy and received an all-around education in life. He grew up helping at his family's shops in Phum Riang and Chaiya, near the railroad. Following Thai custom, he ordained in 1926 at the age of twenty. He found monastic life meaningful and became active in the Dhamma life of the community. A couple years later, an uncle arranged for him to be tutored in Pali by a leading Pali scholar in Bangkok. Learning the scriptural language was the accepted avenue for monastic advancement in Thailand at that time. Some aspects of life in the "Venice of Asia," as it once was, nurtured him. The noise and corruption did not. After excelling in the first year's Pali examinations, he crashed out in the following year. Having taken the radical step of reading the Pali suttas and Vinaya discipline for himself, he found he could no longer parrot back the expected answers during the exams. He knew well what the answers were but didn't think them in the spirit of the Buddha's actual message. Realizing that his path required a lifestyle more like that of the original Sangha, he left the big city and returned home.

With his family's support, in 1932 he founded Suan Mokkh amid an overgrown temple on the outskirts of Phum Riang. He was able to borrow a Tipiṭaka, the traditional "three baskets" of Discourses, Discipline, and Abhidhamma, and continue his studies in the forest. Living alone for a couple of years, he began his "scientific experiments" with Dhamma lifestyle and practice, including traditional ascetic practices and fasting. During a rains retreat of strict silence, children from the nearby village teased him as "the crazy monk." He kept a detailed journal of the effects within his body and mind.

The year 1932 also saw Thailand become a constitutional monarchy, and in that same year, he and his brother, Dhammadāsa, launched *Buddha-Sāsanā Quarterly*, through which they developed their writing skills. Along with articles on Dhamma and practice, each issue included translations from the Pali suttas. This was an important change, since little of the Tipiṭaka was available in accessible Thai at that time. The journal brought him to the attention of Buddhist intellectuals, including Somdet Phra Buddhaghosajahn (Jaroen Ñāṇavaro), the acting Supreme Patriarch. Buddhadāsa Bhikkhu's translations were both accurate and readable, which gave credibility to the thinking of this backwater southern monk. The Somdet became an important confidant and patron. He provided support when certain high-ranking monks were offended by Ajahn Buddhadāsa's use of the Buddha's words to question their lavish lifestyles in rich Bangkok temples. The young monk's simple way of living and his loyalty to the Buddha's original teachings were an inspiring contrast.

After his innovative teachings attracted monks who wanted to study with him, he relocated Suan Mokkh to larger quarters farther inland. His family purchased uncultivated land around Golden Buddha Hill, on which the foundations of an ancient stupa were found. He shifted his activities to this new Suan Mokkh toward the end of the Second World War. This is where he remained for the rest of his life.

Buddhadāsa Bhikkhu's mission was in clarifying the wise, skillful understanding that guides the ennobling path. He maintained that anyone with sufficient understanding of "the heart of the Buddha's teachings" would know what and how to practice and could use the suttas to monitor themselves. He forthrightly maintained that everyone with basic intelligence and sincerity should have access to fundamental Buddhist principles and the liberating teachings of Buddhayana, such as the noble eightfold path, emptiness, dependent co-arising, and thusness. He believed that sincere Buddhists deserve more of their teachers than exhortations to merit making and quietism.

Over the next decades, Ajahn Buddhadāsa taught throughout southern Thailand, and he often traveled to Bangkok and Chiang Mai in the North. He became a powerful and progressive voice in Thai Buddhism through many publications, influential lectures at important venues in Bangkok, special trainings for university students, and creative use of new communication technologies. In 1954 he represented Thailand at the historic Buddhist Council in Rangoon. In 1955 he made a pilgrimage to India and collected photographs of ancient Buddhist art to replicate on buildings at Suan Mokkh. For a decade, beginning in 1956, he provided ethical training and Dhamma teaching to all new judges in Thailand, which made a lifelong impression on many of them.

As the Cold War ramped up in Southeast Asia and the region saw increasing violence, Ajahn Buddhadāsa became a leading advocate of a Buddhist middle way between the secular materialisms of capitalism and communism. Never part of the conservative monastic power structure, he wasn't prone to ideological radicalism either. He observed that Buddhism and the early Sangha had more in common with socialism than capitalism, although the Buddha's socialism was based in Dhamma, not economics and freedom for the kilesas. Ajahn Buddhadāsa called this "Dhammic socialism." He believed that Thailand should seek a social path true to its own causes and conditions rather than the dictates of foreign powers. Such a path would be based in Buddhist ethics and Dhamma. He challenged Buddhists to think for themselves, be true to their roots, and aspire for more than happy rebirths in the next life. He also was an early voice for ecological conservation, again as a natural expression of Buddhist ethics, compassion, and wisdom. He inspired students, activists, and government officials to work for a society of ethics, nonviolence, and interreligious cooperation. Suan Mokkh became a spiritual haven for many seeking just responses to the polarizing changes of the 1960s and 1970s.

Dhamma Proclamation Lectures

In 1971, Ajahn Buddhadāsa instituted a regular series of Saturday afternoon lectures at Suan Mokkh. He planned a thorough reexamination of Theravada teachings that addressed what he saw as a crisis in Buddhism and the need to respond to modern realities. Along with lectures to specific groups—teachers, judges in training, medical students, resident monks—these became a major component of his life's work and were published within his Dhamma Proclamation Series (eighty-one volumes to date). In the foreword to the first published set of the weekly lectures, he announced,

> The aim of this series is to produce manuals for examining and comparing the many Dhamma principles and practices that have become increasingly problematic due to erroneous interpretations, being inappropriate with the times, and a growing diversity in the backgrounds of Buddhists. Courage is needed in our thinking and interpretation, rather than dogmatically holding to overly literal and customary beliefs. These amount to a crisis within Buddhism, which I have observed for many decades and watched increase year by year until feeling that it's time for a thorough and critical reexamination for the benefit of ordinary Buddhists in this era.
>
> —SANDASSETABBADHARMA,
> *lectures from January to March 1971, collectively published in 1973*

A new style of teaching was needed, better suited to modern education and communications, that broke with traditional Thai sermonizing. Each series of lectures took place on Saturday afternoons for three months. There were three series per year, each named after a major Buddhist holiday, and a three-month pause during the southern Thai rainy season. This timeframe supported a systematic reflection on a wide variety of themes and teachings.

Ajahn Buddhadāsa sought to reshape how his compatriots understood the Buddha, his Dhamma, and the Buddhist religion they were born into. For him, *nibbāna* was a living possibility to be experienced in this life. "Supreme reality *dhammas*"—such as *idappaccayatā* (conditionality), *tathatā* (thusness), *suññatā* (emptiness), *paṭiccasamuppāda* (dependent co-arising), and *ariya-sacca* (ennobling truth)—were shared with all thoughtful Buddhists rather than a narrow elite of monastic scholars. In his understanding, all aspects of Buddhism, if true to the Buddha, can be linked to these core themes, and all of these major threads of Buddha-Dhamma are found to support one another. He creatively followed them through the wide variety of concerns faced by modern Buddhists.

Ajahn Buddhadāsa was a creative teacher whose way of life exemplified Dhamma even in seemingly mundane matters. His teachings for university students, professionals, government officials, and social workers rethought ethics in the modern world and advised approaches to meditation that didn't require retiring to a monastery. He touched on social realities in ways highly unusual for a senior Thai monk. While not entirely dismissive of traditional exposition, which was based on a group of medieval Singhalese commentaries, he wasn't afraid to critique them when they confused what is found in the original suttas. However, as his purpose remained practical, he never attempted a comprehensive scholarly treatise.

Audience, Setting, and Approach

Ajahn Buddhadāsa's talks were regularly attended by *sahayadhammas*, Dhamma comrades. The lectures of this particular series took place from January through March 1983, during the southern Thai cool and dry season. Along with the monks, nuns, and other residents with whom Ajahn Buddhadāsa interacted more or less daily, the audience was a mix of local farmers, merchants, and civil servants, as well as middle-class students from nearby provinces. Some traveled by overnight train all the way from Bangkok, six hundred kilometers to the north. These regulars, including visiting monks and nuns among the householders, had a basic education in Buddhist teachings, influenced by long-standing orthodoxies and popular beliefs. Yet they were interested in reexamining that legacy and focusing on the heart of the teachings. Many of the regulars were well educated. Some, however, were local villagers who may have tended rubber plantings or worked for hire. It wasn't unusual for locals with limited formal education to understand Ajahn Buddhadāsa as well as or better than intellectuals from Bangkok, especially when the former were regulars and the latter spotty in their interest or overly sophisticated. These were Buddhadāsa Bhikkhu's supporters in proclaiming the good Dhamma. They came together for the sake of the right understanding that guides the path and realizes the end of *dukkha*.

From the age of sixty onward, Ajahn Buddhadāsa vowed to remain at Suan Mokkh. Consequently, talks such as those in this book took place under the trees and upon the sands of its outdoor Dhamma amphitheater among the kinds of Dhamma comrades listed above. A comprehensive teaching composed in this way is not organized the way a Western thinker might organize a book. Nor is it organized like a series of special lectures at a university or a collection of papers given at various times and places. A set of teachings like this unfolds with themes gradually introduced, revisited from lecture to lecture, fleshed out more thoroughly in a particular talk or two, and then available for reference in the following talks. This style of teaching involved a built-in review of the major themes and explorations as they developed over three months—and throughout a lifetime.

Readers of this translation will be best served when they approach it with the spirit in which the talks were given—allowing the teachings to unfold through patient study, reflection, and contemplation. This English version reduces the repetition to some extent without changing the basic character of Ajahn Buddhadāsa's teaching style, in which he introduces and weaves themes within a larger fabric of Dhamma.

A Little Dhamma Book

By the time of the lectures that became this book, Ajahn Buddhadāsa had delivered more than thirty such series, most of which were published within a few years. Tape recordings also circulated. Thus, by then, those who followed his efforts had a solid intellectual foundation to guide their lives and practice. Now he recognized a new problem: assimilating and integrating the wealth of teachings into a coherent understanding. Practitioners needed a comprehensive vision of the path that tied it all together. Therefore, he conceived of a single volume that would bring together essential Dhamma teachings found in the Pali suttas and reveal the threads of progressive cultivation running through them. He named it *Little Dhamma Book*. As he explained in the first lecture of the series,

> The intention behind this series of lectures is to meet the need for a comprehensive single volume, a "little Dhamma book," to aid people in their study and practice. The required information is scattered about in an enormous number of publications and can be difficult to track down. Our intention, here, is to produce a single yet complete book for general use. These talks will proceed step by step, covering those themes necessary for study by non-specialists. We'll talk about human beings for the sake of reaching our highest potential as humans.

Note that he was not speaking only to specialists or monks. Rather, he spoke to everyone interested in an intellectually cogent understanding of Buddha-Dhamma that they could center their lives in.

A *little* Dhamma book? Readers might wonder what is so little about a book that's twice the size of previous works by Ajahn Buddhadāsa published in the United States. By "little" he was indicating this book's nature as a single volume focused on unifying threads—comparatively quite different than the expansive tendencies of the many themes covered in earlier volumes of his teaching. Further, Thai Buddhists accustomed to hearing about the forty-five volumes of the Thai Tipiṭaka would be relieved to have a coherent contemplative map in one place.

While the situation in the English-reading Buddhist world is in many ways different from that of Thai Buddhism fifty years ago, there are commonalities. The profound influences of science, materialism, consumerism, individualism, and social fragmentation rearranged Thai society during Ajahn Buddhadāsa's lifetime, as they had already done and continue to do in English-reading countries. An ever-expanding marketplace of Buddhist teachings and practices, sometimes incongruous, befuddled Thais as they do elsewhere. Around the world, the increasing pressures of modern life have diminished space for quiet reflection and living with nature. As we cope with a world tied together by markets, social media, and shared existential crises, Ajahn Buddhadāsa's systematic clarity can only help us in navigating the plethora of influences and pressures.

Outline of the Contemplative Journey

The central theme of this book is "life as cultivation of mind." This incredibly simple thesis is explored and emphasized throughout the book, with various subthemes that support it in different chapters. All of these are drawn from Theravada teachings, for the most part as found in the Pali suttas. Because the early record is given primacy over later developments, you will find interpretations that challenge certain mainstream Theravada beliefs. Ajahn Buddhadāsa's audience members were interested in this reevaluation of Buddhist teaching, even when the challenges were uncomfortable.

While this book is comprehensive in its way, Ajahn Buddhadāsa wanted the themes concerning practice to stand out from those concerning theory. Here, his exposition of practice doesn't emphasize practice as one or another of the well-known meditation techniques that have often come to mean "practice" in most Western convert communities at the expense of a more rounded consideration including ethics and wisdom. In these talks, he barely mentions *ānāpānasati*, the system of meditation traceable to the Buddha, which Ajahn Buddhadāsa practiced all his life and taught in great detail and depth. Rather, here he is concerned with the practice of inquiry and contemplation more broadly, in its multiplicity of forms within the activities of quotidian life. For this purpose, he poses many questions, provides examples of how to pursue them, and leaves much for students to uncover themselves. Each chapter of this book maps a stage of this journey and how it relates to the final purpose of our lives. He elaborates themes little by little, in stages rather than all at once, and returns to them organically. The insights of previous chapters are incorporated as new avenues of inquiry open. His listeners at the time could then carry on the inquiry over the following weeks. Readers, now, can do the same.

The central theme is developed through the book's chapters as follows. Ajahn Buddhadāsa starts with an inquiry into the nature of human life and sketches the themes that will be elaborated as we go. From the beginning, he emphasizes the dilemmas of the sense media—hearing, touching, seeing, smelling, tasting, and thinking—without which experience can't happen and through which all suffering occurs. He explores the ongoing dynamic of body and mind fabricating each other—usually, but not necessarily, as suffering, depending on whether ignorance or wisdom is in charge. When insight is lacking, clinging to "me" and "mine" occurs. Focused contemplation leads to the understanding that all aspects of life are fundamentally empty of "me" and "mine," of any abiding self we can cling to, possess, or control. Body and mind are "just so."

The suffering of the world teaches us the dangers of ignoring spiritual cultivation. So we begin to awaken. Our ordinary wishes for happiness and well-being lead us to the recognition that the central role of mind requires its development and maturation. Such psycho-spiritual training unfolds through stages that reveal deeper layers of life and mind's reality. This meditation and contemplative cultivation require courage in facing afflictions and hindrances, as well as skill in both serenity and clarity. When practice is sincere and consistent, thusness and emptiness are progressively realized; nobility and refuge are internalized.

The life of mind has inherent potentials that make cultivation possible. Still, ignorance remains and superstition—misguided understanding and practice—occurs. Uncovering the many superstitions that still influence us is a necessary aspect of the journey. Correctly practiced, the contemplative path lifts us out of ignorance and superstition as insight and wisdom grow. Ajahn Buddhadāsa gives the essential elements of Buddhology, the science of awakening, by providing wisdom perspectives that challenge misunderstanding, unquestioned beliefs, assumptions, and confusion and open us to the wise, skillful understanding that ends dukkha.

It was important to Ajahn Buddhadāsa to use language and examples that would resonate for his listeners. For instance, he often used farming examples. While modern urban readers tend to be increasingly distant from the sources of our food, spiritual traditions regularly draw on agricultural similes and symbols. This is especially appropriate in Buddhism, where Dhamma means "nature." Further, a book dedicated to *bhāvanā* can't escape the food production roots of "cultivation." I hope that these local flavors of teaching will inspire postmodern readers to reconnect with the natural world.

Samādhi, the gathering together and unification of mind, is another essential ingredient in the contemplative journey. Samādhi can mean "meditation" and the "themes of meditation." More centrally, it is the very gathering and unifying that lead to the nondistraction, simplicity, and inner stillness that are essential to contemplation. Mindfulness and other factors are also crucial, but they lack strength and don't see deeply when samādhi is weak. Ajahn Buddhadāsa serves the Buddha in echoing the great importance the suttas give to samādhi, attributing insight to samādhi rather than mindfulness.

Instead of promoting one or the other unilaterally, it's best to emphasize how the two work in partnership. When they do so successfully, it makes insight possible within ordinary life and not just in specialized settings.

The Buddha gave us maps of the journey that we can use to assess what lies ahead, how far we have grown, how we might backslide, and characteristics that need to be strengthened. The contemplative journey observes the myriad forms of egoistic rebirth, the recycling of *saṃsāra*, and the fabricating of mind-body aggregates. It discerns the wholesome potentials from among destructive habits and increasingly intuits the possibility of pausing the needless busyness of modern existence. So, we must study the sense media and what arises from them—the territory where life is lived. When we wander without true understanding, we concoct the life of clinging to "me" and "mine," the so-called aggregates of clinging.

To let go of clinging, we must see that life is mind with body. Awareness, consciousness, and mind are at the heart of embodied life. Ignorant thinking isn't satisfied by the simplicity and naturalness of mind with body. Expecting more, it fabricates additional layers and narratives, especially regarding "me" and "mine," along with "you," "him," "her," and "them." So we contemplate the life happening through the senses to discover it's all just mind. This is how mind wakes up from sleep and realizes *anattā*, "not-self."

Seeing the basic qualities and elements of experience undermines the habits of clinging and affliction. The more contemplation sees the compounding of such elements, the basic stuff of experience, the more we recognize an alternative to fabricating egoistic suffering. We have glimpses of a rather unique element, nibbāna, that doesn't concoct more trouble. The more cultivation of mind—not really of "me" or "you"—sees how all things are simply natural elements behaving impermanently, the less compelling is the "somebody" to be the center of it all. In the space between egoistic constructs, mind's pristine luminosity awakens, sloughing off ignorance and superstition. The life of cultivating mind-heart-psyche culminates in the end of concocting.

Pali Terms and Suttas

Ajahn Buddhadāsa took care to explain Pali terms to his Thai audiences. He thought that serious students of Buddha-Dhamma would be happy to learn important Pali terms, especially when available translations aren't satisfactory, or popular interpretations obscure the original meaning. For this reason, readers will find an abundance of Pali terms in this text. I recommend that readers pause to become familiar with them, aided by endnotes and glossary entries. Learning these terms can be a valuable aspect of contemplation, especially when they challenge our comfortable word associations and concepts. They add clarity and provide a sense of how the Buddha and early Buddhists understood Dhamma. Learning the nuances of an unfamiliar word opens our understanding when the word is relevant to our inner world. Often, simple English equivalents are merely a starting point for understanding.

The Pali terms found here are treated in various ways. Well-known proper nouns such as Buddha, Dhamma, and Sangha occasionally have parenthetical explanations. When an accurate and understandable English equivalent is available, the Pali is mentioned sparingly. Frequently used terms such as *dukkha*, *nibbāna*, *citta*, *bhāvanā*, and *saṅkhāras* are best learned with aid of parenthetical explanations, the glossary, and the index. With terms such as *samādhi* that have a complex cluster of concepts and meanings that no single English equivalent can capture, the richness of meaning gradually accumulates with regular reflection. When familiar translations—"mindfulness" for *sati* and "feeling" for *vedanā*, for example—are limited by common usage, the Pali appears alternatingly as reminders. The other editors and I hope you will make liberal use of the glossary.

The Thai language contains many words borrowed from Pali and Sanskrit, but with quite different grammar. To fit the many Pali terms included in this translation, I have adapted them to English grammar. Whereas Thai usage tends to be ambiguous as to number, I've employed an anglicized plural to better fit with English grammar.

Besides that, I've used standard Pali spelling rather than following Thai pronunciation or spelling.

Key Concepts and Terms

The main audience for these talks was familiar with the concepts Ajahn Buddhadāsa regularly used. Here, I'll introduce certain concepts and themes central to this work.

Study, *Sikkhā*

Throughout his teaching, and prominently here, Ajahn Buddhadāsa speaks of study and training (*sikkhā*). In this context, study means more than reading books and is different than modern institutionalized learning. Although he benefited from mentors and tutors, he was largely self-taught, with nature and the Tipiṭaka being his most important teachers. Nature, for him, meant both his surroundings at Suan Mokkh and the nature within as explored through Dhamma investigation. Famously, he honored dogs and fish as teachers too. Study encompasses all forms of learning, including those referred to as practice, training, meditation, and contemplation. He once explained, "Sikkhā is to observe oneself in order to see oneself in order to let go of oneself and be free."

Mind, *Citta*

These talks, and Buddhism more broadly, emphasize the centrality and importance of citta, "mind." The vast majority of things discussed here happen in or are activities of mind. The related terms *heart*, *awareness*, *consciousness*, and *psyche* are encompassed by "mind," which better suits Ajahn Buddhadāsa's usage than the alternatives. As none of these terms have precise definitions, be open to the various aspects and functions described as mind. Most importantly in this work, mind is that which can be cultivated and is able to realize "the best thing that we ought to receive." In the absence of such realization, mind suffers.

Concocting, *Saṅkhāra*

"Concocting," the English translation of the Thai *prung-taeng*, Ajahn Buddhadāsa's translation of the Pali *saṅkhāra*, appears throughout this work. *Prung* is "to cook and season," *taeng* is "to dress and decorate." "Concoct," from Old French, meaning to cook together, is a good fit. The variants "concoct," "concoction," and "concocted," as well as the synonyms "fabricating" and "creating," are also used. Concocting is implicit in every stage of this journey. For example, cultivation is a form of concocting (chapter 2), *vaṭṭasaṃsāra* is another (chapter 8), and so is the compounding of elements (chapter 12). Concocting and its opposite are front and center in the final stage of the journey (chapter 13). As everything is a saṅkhāra, it behooves us to understand the range of meaning of this nuanced word and its importance for life and death.

Afflictions, Corruptions, *Kilesas*

Kilesas, the hurtful aspects of concocting, have great importance and weight in Thai Buddhist teachings. Not playthings to be pooh-poohed with trendy euphemisms, the kilesas are serious concerns due to the profound harm these unruly concoctions cause. The cruder kilesas are reactive emotions that cause countless problems and ruin lives. Ajahn Buddhadāsa's explanations emphasize how kilesas tarnish, pollute, afflict, and corrupt citta, hence "corruptions" and "afflictions." The categories of kilesas should be named properly in order to capture the grosser forms of pollution and harm, rather than softer terms that fail to jar our postmodern sensibilities. First, *lobha*, "greed," is the flagship of the category of kilesas that grasps and pulls things toward us. In the modern economy, greed is ubiquitously promoted and has become banal. Second, *dosa* is the category of kilesas that react against things. Though many Thais associate it with anger (properly *kodha*), hatred is dosa's full manifestation, along with rage and wrath. While we experience these extreme forms less often, we frequently express the moderate and milder forms such as aversion, irritation, annoyance, and resistance. Third, *moha*, "delusion," is the category of kilesas that wobble and spin around their objects. Vastly diverse, moha includes confusion, doubt, expectation, longing after the past, envy, shame, and the many subtleties of conceit. Fear and worry could be a fourth category of kilesas; otherwise, they are included under moha.

Right, Correct, *Sammā*

Rightness and correctness (Thai, *kwaam-tuk-dong*; Pali, *sammatta*) is an omnipresent theme in Ajahn Buddhadāsa's teaching and refers to the middle way of eight sammattas that leads to the end of dukkha. Rather than being opposite to "bad" or "wrong," "right" means being in harmony with the law of nature. Out of sympathy to readers impatient with repetition, I alternate among the English adjectives "right," "correct," and "proper," with connotations of "accurate" and "true" (not false). Clinging to goodness isn't the middle way and it fosters suffering, so it cannot be *sammā*; to be right and proper is to contribute to ending and preventing suffering.

Cultivation, Development, *Bhāvanā*

Cultivation makes the contemplative journey possible, as we develop the capacity to see more deeply into the heart of life. *Citta-bhāvanā* is cultivation of heart and mind, while *paññā-bhāvanā* is the cultivation of intelligence, wisdom, and insight. These two aspects of bhāvanā are loosely equivalent to meditation. Ajahn Buddhadāsa took pains to distinguish the Buddhist understanding of bhāvanā from the material and economic "development" promoted by the Thai government and the World Bank, as well as the competing ideology of communist materialism. A spiritual understanding of development based in mental clarity, compassion, and inner freedom chooses wisely among the enticements of material development.

"Self," *Attā*

The suffering of clinging to "me" and "mine" is central to Ajahn Buddhadāsa's teaching, along with the antidotes anattā and suññatā. None of these can be understood without addressing *attā*. While this crucial term is central to understanding Buddhism, its translation is problematic. While "self" is a somewhat better translation than "ego" or "soul," confusion with how "self" is used in Western psychology and popular speech causes more trouble than with any other word used to translate Buddhist teachings. When the anattā teachings are read through the lens of attā, thus assuming the reality of "me," "self," "personality," "identity," and "other," they can never "make sense." This can lead to extreme ideas about "no-self." The Buddha's pragmatic, nondogmatic teachings are skillful means that serve letting go and nonclinging. A metaphysical view such as "there is no self" goes too far. To reference attā, the text contains the expediencies of adding adjectives (*permanent*, *separate*, *lasting*), explainers in endnotes, and helping phrases.

Superstition, *Sayasāstra*

Throughout the book, Ajahn Buddhadāsa points out how misguided approaches to meditation go astray. He challenges us to examine received beliefs and assumptions to verify that they fit with path and fruit. His concept of *sayasāstra*—"sleepology," the science of sleeping, superstition—includes subtleties that might not come to mind with the English word *superstition*. His meaning encompasses all knowledge, beliefs, and behaviors arising from ignorance. Starting with the most obvious superstitions, we learn to notice the distortions that turn legitimate knowledge into superstition. For example, scientific knowledge—imperfect and subject to revision—can become dogmatic, especially when used for purposes of power and pride.

Chapter 7 is full of examples from Thai Buddhist culture, some of which may be foreign to readers in English, so I have added explanations to make his points clear. I also added notes to encourage readers living outside Southeast Asia to consider parallels in their own cultures and forms of Buddhism. After all, Ajahn Buddhadāsa was encouraging people to think and explore for themselves, anything else being sayasāstra. Here are a few examples of current beliefs that he would have considered forms of superstition: You can be whoever you want to be. You can have it all. The wisdom of the market. Rugged individualism.

Some modern superstitions are patently foolish and blatantly dangerous, such as racism and other forms of bias, weaponizing "the right to life," and conspiracy theories of right and left. No culture is immune to this human tendency, which at times can have a positive role, up to a point. Still, many superstitions are more deleterious than beneficial. We transcend "sleepology" with Buddhology, the science of awakening.

Path, Fruit, and Nibbāna, *Magga-Phala-Nibbāna*

These quasi-technical terms, derived from post-sutta schemes, illustrate an important feature of Ajahn Buddhadāsa's teaching. The monastic elite construed many Pali terms and teachings to be beyond the capacity of ordinary people. Ajahn Buddhadāsa disagreed and sought both to clarify the original meaning and bring them down to earth for the practical benefit of his audience. He usually deemphasized the technical interpretations of the commentaries that accrued many centuries after the Buddha. He wanted sincere practitioners to understand the noble path, its fruit, and the reality of freedom from dukkha as genuinely possible in their lives without waiting for benefits after death. He preferred simple, down-to-earth examples to foster understanding of the most profound teachings of Buddhism, such as emptiness, thusness, and nibbāna. Compassion dictates that these teachings be made available to all sincere aspirants.

Dhamma Language

Ajahn Buddhadāsa distinguished two kinds or levels of language needed in Dhamma teachings. He referred to the ordinary, conventional, literal use of language as "people language," the language of everyday business and the stories we tell about ourselves and each other. The literal, conventional meaning of words cannot adequately convey the depths of Dhamma, which requires a nonpersonal language, one that speaks in terms of phenomena, processes, and conditionality rather than the persons of "people language." In Dhamma language, the language of liberation from "me" and "mine," words such as *birth* and *saṃsāra* refer to more immediate realities than their literal meanings. Basic Buddhist terms are used in both ways, for instance *dukkha* as pain and as the suffering arising from clinging. Wise readers are mindful of both levels of meaning.

CONTRIBUTIONS AND ACKNOWLEDGMENTS

Originally I was reluctant to take on this project. The original translation was by a friend, with whom there inevitably would be differences concerning the many thousands of choices that go into translating, editing, and publishing. I had a series of long conversations with colleagues at the Buddhadāsa Indapañño Archives (BIA)—which manages Buddhadāsa Bhikkhu publications on behalf of Suan Mokkh and brokered this project—and with Shambhala Publications, which wanted to publish a major work by Ajahn Buddhadāsa. Eventually I realized that I could take this on only if I had complete freedom to shape, edit, and retranslate as I saw best for meeting our main objectives: conveying Ajahn Buddhadāsa's Dhamma faithfully and accurately in accessible language for non-Thai readers of English. With Ven. Dhammavidū having started the Dhamma ball rolling, and with the encouragement of BIA, I agreed to take on what became a deeply meaningful personal journey.

To start, I was brought in as senior editor, which entails supervising translations on behalf of BIA and Suan Mokkh. By the end, however, I have done much more than supervise. I retranslated many sentences and paragraphs, not just occasional words and phrases, and I translated passages that weren't in the original translation. I worked with Shambhala and BIA editors to rearrange the lecture material into a publishable book. Therefore, the title of cotranslator was added to senior editor. These roles are rooted in thirty-five years of study under Tan Ajahn Buddhadāsa Bhikkhu, practicing accordingly, and learning the blessings of Dhamma, however Dhamma presents in my life, which have been varied and provocative.

Pondering the phrases, sentences, paragraphs, and structure of the Thai lectures and the original translation has been a wonderful Dhamma journey. As the themes of this little Dhamma book came together in my understanding, their meaning became real—that is, not merely words and ideas. Tracing Ajahn Buddhadāsa's development of these themes, and how he wove them together, built and echoed in me. Whenever hardships arose, all connected with "me" and "mine," this work constantly drew my attention to profound Dhamma teachings that fostered recognizing and relaxing such "me" and "mine."

Time constraints played a role too. I am slow in such work, prone to nitpicking and obsession. Inspired by this unfolding of Dhamma, with Covid-19 in the air and travel put on hold, I've been able to sustain attention on the project through to its completion in 2021. Thus the themes of *Seeing with the Eye of Dhamma* have been a major support during the isolation brought on by the pandemic and have informed my online teaching. This impetus for sustained Dhamma contemplation has been a powerful, most-rewarding gift.

I am immensely grateful to those who invited me into this project. To Ajahn Buddhadāsa for this teaching as well as decades of guidance. To my Thai aunts and uncles who transcribed and published the lectures. To Ven. Dhammavidū for his interest in the lectures and the work of his original translation. To the Buddhadāsa Indapañño Archives in Bangkok for taking on the project and bringing me into it; in particular to Dr. Bunchar Pongpanich for his connections and support, and to Kittisak Rungrueangwatthanachai, Cindy Stewart, and Sante Vichitbandha for important contributions. To Nikko Odiseos and Shambhala Publications for their flexibility regarding Thai concerns and for facilitating publication. To Matt Zepelin and the editorial team, who have been wonderful companions in shaping the manuscript. To François "Paco" Merigoux for countless felicities, meticulous reading, and delicate management.

Finally, following Ajahn Buddhadāsa's example, I am grateful for the opportunity to serve the Buddha, Dhamma, and Sangha.

The translators, editors, sponsors, and publisher hope you will enjoy Ajahn Buddhadāsa's distinctive style and voice and his unwavering focus on the essentials of spiritual practice. May readers embark on this path wholeheartedly and experience profound change.

—SANTIKARO UPASAKA
Kevala Retreat
April 2021

SEEING WITH THE EYE OF DHAMMA

INTRODUCTION

The intention behind this series of lectures is to create something special to meet the need for a comprehensive single volume, a "little Dhamma book," to aid people in their study and practice. The required information is scattered about in an enormous number of publications and can be difficult to track down. Our intention here is to produce a single yet complete book for general use. As this is a journey of looking successively more deeply into life and Dhamma, we're calling this collection *Seeing with the Eye of Dhamma*.[1]

These talks will proceed step by step, covering those themes necessary for study by nonspecialists. On this first occasion, the topic is the ordinary or normal condition of human life. We'll talk about human beings for the sake of reaching our highest potential as humans. To do that, we'll need to consider life in a way that results in a comprehensive and fundamental understanding of the nature of human life, how it can be developed, and how far that development can go. Our intention is that all who sincerely study and practice will develop their lives prosperously in Dhamma and ultimately meet with the highest success—that is, to be human beings without any problems.

Other than that, we really don't have much to do. Ordinary people have plenty of problems, one after the other without end. However, humans can lift themselves above all of those problems—to be precise, they can be *arahants* (worthy ones), who are complete, having fulfilled the purpose of human life.[2] However, saying so makes people nervous. They are afraid of being arahants because they think that's too good, too elevated, and not really useful. Suggest becoming an arahant and few show interest because they see it as beyond them or as too much trouble. Consequently, they remain stuck fast in the midst of trouble and strife, always entangled in their problems.

The human world has plenty of problems. Ascend to the heavenly worlds and there will be problems there too. Reach the worlds of *brahma* gods and there will still be problems. Mind in such heavenly and godly conditions is not beyond problems.

The biggest problems of all are those of "me" and "mine." The ignorant understanding that there is a "me" and things that are "mine" brews up almost endless desires for things that cause new and strange problems. People have endless problems to deal with, but that's claimed to be normal, to be human nature.

With the ending of our problems, life becomes trouble-free, which is the ultimate realization. Then our struggles are over. This realization is the culmination of the system of practice known as *brahmacariya* (the supreme way of living). After this, it isn't necessary for us to deliberately practice for any improvement. This culmination can only be known when becoming arahant, one who has completed the main task of life, because there aren't any problems left. This means that life has been freed from all the forms of *dukkha* (distress, disease, suffering) directly and indirectly.

If you're interested in this and not afraid that it will be too good for you, perhaps we can consider it together and come to an understanding. If it's too much for you, your mind won't be interested, which means that it doesn't want to be interested. We might talk anyway, but that would be a waste of time for both speaker and listeners.

This problem challenges us a lot these days, particularly me, who as Buddhadāsa, "servant of the Buddha," has had the duty of explaining Dhamma to you all these many years. It seems we haven't been able to lead people to the high level of realization that solves all their problems. I attribute this failing to the reasons already mentioned: the majority see it as too goody-good, unpalatable, boring, and not entertaining. Such people can't resist the ups and downs of the baser activities of life.

Even many of the people who don't live so coarsely understand brahmacariya as not suitable for them. The best thing Buddhism has to offer doesn't interest them, whether they are monks or laypeople. Observe the monks in their monasteries: Some of them show little genuine interest; their minds aren't wholly focused on the Dhamma that can raise them to the highest level of having ended all problems. Although they endure listening to Dhamma talks, they pay little attention, let their minds wander, or doze off. Hardly any of them are interested in following with subtlety and care; they are more interested in fooling around. Look at the books some of today's monks invest in and read. Most aren't about the quenching of dukkha, about ending the corruptions. You will find a lot of reading for pleasure, along with books on general knowledge unconnected with quenching dukkha. They would rather be scholars and philosophers, famous in special areas of knowledge. Or popular preachers. Hence, genuine Dhamma, Dhamma on the highest level, is wasted these days. The genuine teachers are looked at as crazy, talking about things that people listening don't want to hear.

Encountering these problems all the time, we aim to create a book able to solve them. We will deliver this series of lectures in this spirit. Whether we are successful or not remains to be seen. I'm not yet certain that we'll be successful, so let's see how this journey turns out.

1

THE ORDINARY CONDITIONS OF HUMAN LIFE

Now we'll begin by looking at the basic nature of ordinary human life and the issues that we ought to be aware of. I'll endeavor to speak in terms that will be easy to grasp and study.

Causes and Conditions Shape Life's Many Forms

The very first topic is that this life can take many forms depending on the prevalent causes and conditions. Life as each of us normally lives it, as already exists and is known by us, has causes and conditions that lead to our particular manners of living. Other ways of living can come about in the same way. For instance, a life that is worse than ours can easily be had by anyone who behaves accordingly, just as our way of living comes easily to us. A more elevated way of life, which improves and excels until reaching that of arahant, also can be cultivated. The arahant form of life comes about easily for those who are on track to be arahant. We have the capacity to choose among the causes and conditions that will create and shape the life we aspire to.

Ordinarily we don't understand this and just allow life to meander according to fate. We let fate determine our lives while we give in to our momentary needs and passing desires. For instance, young monks ordain without knowing what they really want, so they let things happen according to passing circumstances. They see friends studying for the Dhamma examinations, so they do the same. Seeing friends studying Pali, they do the same. They don't know why they are studying. They assume it will be good and beneficial somehow. In reality, such monks don't know why they do what they do, although they have undertaken a way of life supposedly dedicated to Dhamma.

People who don't leave home for the sake of Dhamma, who remain in the life of home and city, also allow things to be carried along by fate, by circumstances. The little desires arising from the daily kilesas (afflictions and corruptions of mind)[1] lead them along because they don't understand the whole story of life. Their knowledge isn't complete, so they can't get to the heart of the matter and focus on what's best. They don't see that the best is available. If one truly understands the causes and conditions of whatever way of life one may choose, one can create the causes and conditions for that life.

Please be certain that life can take many forms depending on its causes and conditions. We can choose the best possible form for us if we know how to choose and how to aspire. We need not surrender to circumstances and fate.

To sum up, we don't know why we were born and what we were born to do. Lacking this knowledge, we allow life to be carried along by fate. We let fate or destiny choose our forms of life for us, which is so unwise it's beyond crazy. I sympathize with all those in this plight. Hence, I try to point out the fact that there are causes and conditions that can create the life that we truly deserve. So take an interest and study matters that the Buddha revealed, then choose the most appropriate form of life. Choose with appropriate and sufficient understanding rather than mere daydreaming or following along. We could have the best and most appealing sort of a life, but we won't if we don't know how to make it happen.

Satisfaction Can Be Part of Whatever We Do

We can live a life full of happiness and enjoyment, a life without any dukkha, if we know how to work with mind. Buddha-Dhamma can make mind smart, bright, and clear, and thus able to know things as they truly are so that there's none of the clinging that makes life burdensome and causes suffering. Whatever is considered by people to be dukkha, to be unpleasant, is seen as "just like that." For instance, any duties that we must carry out are understood as good, appropriate, and excellent; thus we're satisfied with them. We can make our livings with contentment. When we know how to manage life so that we're happy in doing our work, there's no dukkha involved in such activities.[2]

I once watched people working in the mud. They were catching fish, and the work was dirty, sweaty, and stinky, full of thorns and other obstacles. Yet they thoroughly enjoyed themselves because they really liked getting the fish. They were happy with every fish they caught. No matter how difficult, dirty, and dangerous, they had a great time of it. Our lives are the same. If we know how to enjoy everything we must do, we will never suffer. For instance, if we're disappointed with something, instead of getting upset, we recognize how this is the nature of things and don't bother suffering about it. If we're tired, if life is being difficult, again we understand it as being "just like that, just how it is." If we can look on the bright side, as it were, seeing whatever good or benefit is to be found, we can be happy in our labors and get the results and benefits for our lives.

In general, people don't think like that. Instead, they consider such work tiring, difficult, and troublesome. They prefer other methods—such as theft, extortion, or trickery—that don't require so much effort and hardship. They want to make millions quickly, even if dishonestly. With such attitudes there's no willingness to endure the hard work and difficulties of rowing a river taxi, pulling a rickshaw, sweeping streets, cleaning sewers, and the like. Nobody likes such work because they don't know how to improve their minds in order to like it.

We need to study Dhamma enough to be able to improve mind so that we enjoy our tasks and duties, no matter what they are, and can do them properly. We can improve our minds to be satisfied in any work—however sweaty, wearisome, and troublesome—so that there's no dukkha in it.

In comparison, consider the butterfly. It makes its living by gathering nectar from flowers while spreading pollen where it's needed and helping to make nature beautiful. The butterfly operates in such a way that it has no dukkha. We, too, can operate and perform our tasks without dukkha, but to do that, we need to know how to improve mind first. We can't just mimic butterflies and do our duties instinctually. As humans, we'll need to understand how to improve our minds before we can do so. This is important, it's the way to survival, so please take interest.

A hired laborer, such as a launderer or dishwasher, doesn't need to look on their work as difficult and troublesome. Then, just by looking on tasks in the right way, we can perform them without having to be the "me" who is bitter, resentful, or disappointed.[3] If we're employed to wash dishes, clean house, do laundry, or cook and prepare food, anything that we must do can become an art form and be enjoyable. We can begin to understand such things like sweeping the house, the floors, and the yard as making things clean and tidy, so that we sweep and clean with love. When cleaning is an art form, we find satisfaction in each movement. When reminding ourselves of this every time we clean the bathroom or take out the trash, we are content the whole time—not just when the job is over. If we're content while we're actually doing something, we turn our work into an art of enjoyment.

Generally speaking, people aren't properly mindful of their work. Their minds wander and they aren't able to pay attention to the task at hand. Perhaps the work being done is looked down on, judged to be plebeian, slavish, and beneath one's dignity. However, if we know the truth, that there isn't anything that is common or base, then no matter what kind of work is done, it's accepted as something that helps feed us and sustains life. It all depends on our minds anyway.

If we're smart enough, we can find satisfaction in doing any kind of work, so long as it is ethical. This is the right way to consider all kinds of work. Some people see certain kinds of work as lowly and thus for "inferior people" to do. However, if we don't have the knowledge to advance us in the workaday world, we have to find a way to be happy with what we've got. Eventually we may accumulate knowledge and thus earn our living by performing better, less physically demanding, and more elevated tasks. But whatever we do, we need to learn to do it in such a way that breeds satisfaction. If we have this attitude in how we approach everything we must do, working will be a kind of paradise for us.

Choose Wisely among the Many Forms of Life

To sum up briefly, life can take many forms and develop in many ways, some of them quite amazing and wonderful, even involving miraculous power. The miraculous power contained in them is that they all lead to the most excellent satisfaction, if only we know how to uplift mind. Of course, we aren't talking about dishonest activities here; delinquents have their own satisfactions because of the state of their minds. Here we mean the satisfaction of persons of quality that's derived from performing their work in right and proper ways, producing good results here and now, and not causing any problems later on.

So make up your mind. Of the many forms life can take, that we can choose from, don't be so foolish as to make the wrong choice. We should always try to choose the form that best suits our station in life. Don't bother complaining about how clever or slow you are, about your fate or misfortune. If we can be satisfied with what we are and what we have at any given time, we can be happy. We can all have good fortune in our different ways.

If we all uphold this principle, nobody will do evil, there won't be any hooligans and thugs, and nobody will be without employment. Everybody will have work to do and with pleasure. Everyone will be happy in their labors, and the liquor shops, opium dens, cinemas, and cabarets will all close. They will disappear when nobody wants such things, when they're happy with their lives, work, and duties. People won't feel the need to spend extravagantly for escape, excitement, and stimulation. Consequently, people would be able to dwell in sufficiency, peace, and happiness. When tired, rest; once rested, work. When resting or relaxing, there will be happiness; when working, there will be happiness too. What more could anybody want? Everything is taken care of when people find satisfaction in every activity.

Our nature gives us the ability to choose, but mostly people aren't wise enough to do so. In fact, they never manage to choose, and won't know how to, when they can only think in shallow ways. Consider this example: By making offerings and prayers to spirits, one will receive great rewards without having to do anything tiring. There are those who do such things in the hope of getting rich. They buy lottery tickets hoping for riches, but they never get rich that way, except in the sense of being rich in psychological problems, which is where such beliefs lead.

This is the first item for you to be interested in: among the many different ways we can choose to live our lives, whatever form we choose has its necessary causes and conditions that we must bring about correctly.

Heaven and Hell Arise at the Senses

The next topic I want you to understand is another crucial aspect of nature—that is, the sense media. Because each of us has two eyes, two ears, a nose, a tongue, a body, and a mind, all sorts of things happen and there are difficulties and problems. Don't be careless where the senses are concerned as they're the central factor in almost all of life. Our six senses are each the basis of intense sensations capable of concocting everything under the sun, which leads to all manner of problems. This wouldn't happen with rocks because they lack eyes, ears, nose, tongue, body, and mind. People, however, aren't rocks, and we are equipped with all six senses, each of which has its particular function and its vast sphere. The eyes have their visual function, which doesn't overlap with the functions of the ears and nose. The eyes create innumerable problems concerning forms, while the ears create innumerable problems concerning sounds. The other senses create problems particular to their functions.

We are living animals, sensate beings. All our problems arise from having eyes, ears, a nose, a tongue, a body, and a mind. If we didn't have sense media, there wouldn't be any problems. If our senses were less important, we would have fewer problems to deal with.

That's probably the case with trees, for instance, which don't have discernable sense organs. Animals have the same array of sense organs as human beings, but with less psychological functionality and impact, hence their problems are also less. Human senses, however, have broad capabilities that we have enhanced even more. As the spheres of experience for the eyes, ears, nose, tongue, body, and mind have greatly expanded, people the world over enjoy the increased opportunities for stimulation, thereby increasing their problems. We create all kinds of delicious, attractive, and amusing objects to stimulate the senses and then thoroughly indulge these things. This creates the extreme selfishness that behaves violently and coldheartedly kills people around the world. When our thinking is deluded by personal advantages, we fight with anything that gets in our way. We now have wars going on all over the world and nobody thinks it strange. That's how the sense media drag life into our many messes and problems, and with increasing violence.

The Buddha said that the origin of our problems is *phassa* (sense contact), right here with impressions via the eyes, ears, nose, tongue, body, and mind. The *āyatanas*, the sense media both inner and outer, are the source of all things because when they are impacted, sensations and experiences occur. For example, with sense media we naturally acquire more knowledge with each passing day. Once we're born, the eyes, ears, nose, tongue, body, and mind increasingly perform their duties. Each day, children come to know more, grow in cleverness, and expand their experiences because the senses encounter new and different things. Correct understanding arises from sense contacts. However, wrong thinking and understanding (*micchādiṭṭhi*) also arise from sense contacts. Some occasions of phassa happen without any chance for intelligence and clear knowing, which leads to misunderstanding and increases the storehouse of wrong understanding. Earlier, there wasn't so much micchādiṭṭhi. Now, however, it increases because contacts through the eyes, ears, nose, tongue, body, and mind aren't wisely restrained and increasingly turn the wrong way.

When we act wrongly, the corresponding results (*kamma-vipākas*) follow. Both *kamma* (intentional action) and *vipāka* come from contacts via the eyes, ears, nose, tongue, body, and mind.[4] Hence, heaven and hell are right here. Hell occurs with contacts via the eyes, ears, nose, tongue, body, and mind. Heaven occurs with contacts via the eyes, ears, nose, tongue, body, and mind. However, this isn't how we usually talk and teach. We prefer to imagine places we don't actually see, and therefore we don't observe hell and heaven in the eyes, ears, nose, tongue, body, and mind. Even the study and realization of nibbāna, the ultimate purpose and benefit in Buddhism, requires careful attention to the contacts taking place at the senses. But we prefer to look elsewhere and place our faith in nebulous things. We wander ever further from truth and end up with speculations, foolishly following the opinions of others.

If we know how to use the senses most skillfully in our studies, we'll know everything, because everything is gathered in the sensations and experiences of the eyes, ears, nose, tongue, body, and mind. Ignorant of this fact, we learn about all sorts of other things. Reality, however, is with the senses, which is wasted and has no real benefit if we aren't interested.

The ABCs of Buddhist Study

Anyone who wants to understand Dhamma first of all has to be interested in studying everything concerning the sense media. If asked what the ABCs of Buddhism are, reply, "The senses." Begin your study at the basic ABC level with a study of the senses. The Buddha, Dhamma, and Sangha can keep for later. They aren't the origin of our problems. Dukkha lies in wrongdoing concerning the eyes, ears, nose, tongue, body, and mind. The Buddha can't help us create dukkha or directly help us to quench dukkha. He can only advise us in how to manage our reactions to sense experience. In revealing dukkha and its quenching, he points to the eyes, ears, nose, tongue, body, and mind, which means that the teaching is really all about getting to know the senses in order so that we can regulate our responses to them such that dukkha doesn't arise. The story ends right where no sufferings can arise.

Therefore, this little volume of *Seeing with the Eye of Dhamma* encourages you to be interested in matters of the eyes, ears, nose, tongue, body, and mind as being the most important for human beings to know. Otherwise you won't be able to solve any of the problems in your mind.

The senses are the root of everything that happens in life and with our minds. They are the doors through which mind contacts the outer and inner worlds. Mind connects everything together. If there wasn't mind, there wouldn't be anything. Because there is mind, everything exists. All experiences—feelings of pleasure and pain, well-being and distress, life and death, anything and everything—happen because there is mind. Mind, however, can't do anything without the five physical senses. The eyes, ears, nose, tongue, and body are the five communication media that allow mind to know the external world. The eyes communicate with visual forms, the ears communicate with sounds, the nose communicates with odors, the tongue communicates with flavors, and the skin communicates with tangible sensations. If these didn't exist, there would be almost nothing, and if there wasn't mind, there would be nothing at all.

Generally, people aren't much interested in the realities of mind and show more interest in superficial matters, in the variety of sights, sounds, odors, flavors, and bodily sensations. This interest manifests as troubling desire for the fun, stimulating, and pleasurable experiences available through these senses. Driven by distorted desire, we worship and sacrifice to the senses rather than caring about the *sukha* and dukkha, the well-being and distress, of mind itself. When we're interested only in superficialities and deceptive appearances, we are easily infatuated with loving and hating, which expand into fear, anxiety, longing, jealousy, envy, and the like. We don't look into the sources of all these problems, and we don't see that they come from mind's ignorance interacting with forms, sounds, odors, flavors, tangibles, and mental phenomena.

These matters are the ABCs of life and of our study. Yet some pundits say it is *paramattha* (ultimate meaning and purpose) and thus isn't appropriate for ordinary people, who are warned against studying it. Really? People don't need to study ultimate meaning and purpose? Children don't need to know this? In truth, if we go back to the original Pali texts, at what the Buddha himself taught, we find that he pointed to the sense media and sense contacts as the starting point for Dhamma study and training. They are studied as paṭiccasamuppāda, the dependently co-arising process through which dukkha arises. What a shame that this teaching is suppressed by those who arrogantly claim it's too elevated and distant.

I implore you to get interested in the sense media—the eyes, ears, nose, tongue, body, and mind—as the first subject that you need to know about and understand. When we know all about them we'll understand other things too. We'll know how to behave as human beings. Nobody will need to tell us that we shouldn't kill other beings, take what isn't given, and abuse sexuality. Ethics come naturally when we understand the reality underlying our experiences. At present, lacking genuine knowledge we go astray; even if warned not to do something, we don't listen. We act wickedly toward ourselves and others because we don't know how to live as human beings. Consequently, please rethink and reexamine your life according to how a complete understanding of the sense media is essential for understanding Dhamma deeply enough to get the most benefit from it. For the sake of fulfilling our great human potential, and thereby quenching dukkha, please remember this important theme: practice in order to know the eyes, ears, nose, tongue, body, and mind thoroughly.

Body and Mind Don't Require a Self

Our third major topic is the possibility of having a body and mind without there needing to be a "self." This will probably sound very strange to people used to the sense that there is a self, who routinely experience a "me." This body of ours occurs as functions of a physical system, incorporating the functions of the eyes, ears, nose, tongue, and body, along with the nervous system. These physical systems wonderfully perform their various functions. There is mind, which senses things through the body. These two aspects are enough; they're all we need. Commonly known as *nāmarūpa*, they also can be called "mind with body." The Pali texts refer to them as *nāmarūpa*, and together mind and body form an intimate pair, so intertwined that nāmarūpa isn't separable into two. So we have nāmarūpa, mind and body, which is sufficient. There's no need for a third member, an *attā*, or "self." If we assume there is a self, a third something that is the owner of the body and mind and that controls them, that's just ignorance.[5]

The Buddha had a different teaching than what others taught before him, in that he taught that there wasn't anything that could be properly considered "self" (*attā*, a lasting entity with separate, independent existence). The natural phenomena of mind and body, *nāma* with *rūpa*, are all that's needed. Thoughts of self are misunderstandings, products of wrong thinking when mind is mistaken about contact made with outside objects via the body's senses. This wrong mental apprehension has caused us big trouble repeatedly and will continue to do so right up until we die. This is what stops us from quenching dukkha and genuinely improving things in our lives.

Before going any further, grasp this basic principle: we have body and mind without requiring a self. These two components together compose what we think of as a person. We suppose that there is someone, but in truth there is just body and mind pooling their resources to carry out the operations of life in accord with the promptings of nature. The body is the physical part, the structure and shell, that supports. Mind is the part that experiences and feels, rather like an overseer controlling the body. There is a body because there is mind, and there is mind because there is a body. Performing their different functions, they work together for life to continue. Whenever they fail to cooperate, both die.

All things are concoctions of nature. Certain concoctings make up body, others make up mind. None of them are lasting realities or essences. Although they aren't enduringly real, they can do what they need to do according to their conditions. Even with their changeability and uncertainty they have influences and effects.

Please consider how bodies and minds have experienced all sorts of strange and amazing things through countless generations of human beings. After many tens, or perhaps hundreds, of thousands of years, what are human beings capable of? Consider the wonderful, seemingly miraculous things that humankind has accomplished, such as modern electronics and space travel. The ancients couldn't dream of such things. And who taught us all these marvelous accomplishments? It was the eyes, ears, nose, tongue, body, and, of course, mind. The senses saw and experienced ever more broadly and deeply, expanding steadily and gathering it all together as accumulated knowledge; expanding and innovating into areas seemingly divine or miraculous, such as flying through the air.

None of those accomplishments required an attā, a lasting self. Simply bodies with minds as nature intended, combining, concocting, naturally developing, and progressing. There's no need to cling to them as anything more amazing, special, or superb than they really are. It's all quite ordinary. We cling to nothing when it's all realized as natural, ordinary, and "just like that."

Usually, however, our minds aren't like that. They fall in love with things, become infatuated, and get lost in clinging. Tricked by knowledge, they cling to knowledge. Tricked by work, they cling to work. They are tricked and deluded by wealth, fame, pleasure, stimulation, and delight. Such delusions and infatuations may go to extremes. Don't look at others; after all, we ourselves are deluded with our own concerns and may take them to extremes. Consequently, our actions and work disturb and trouble others, which is a worldwide problem at present. Some, thinking only of their own benefits and because they have the power, cause trouble for others. Hence, this world is divided between left and right, which struggle against each other endlessly. This struggle between those in power and those without power will continue for a long time as they seek control of the various resources and temptations of the world, the bait that hooks and reels in the people of this world.

Again, there is simply the body and mind without any real need for attā, or self, for some special ingredient or essence that's in control or at the center of it all. The one fundamental principle to be aware of is that nāmarūpa, mind and body, is enough for everything that happens and needs to happen. Attā isn't required for quenching dukkha and realizing nibbāna. Body and mind are trained and improved through contact with and experience of the world, which fosters growing intelligence. We develop ourselves through experience, bringing about real intelligence.

At first, people didn't have any knowledge of nibbāna. After experiencing a lot of suffering, they began to search for clues to nibbāna. After repeatedly meeting with trouble and strife, they discovered that the suffering comes from our minds being poorly maintained and wrongly directed. Starting over and looking in a new direction, they realized that suffering didn't occur when they didn't make up self. Actually, because mind behaves wrongly or rightly all by itself, there's no need for self, God, or anything from anywhere to be added.

In this body-mind combination, mind is most crucial. Mind is the heart of the matter. The body is like the outer skin or shell, while mind is the most important component. Hence, we really need to understand mind much more than the body. As anything and everything is experienced by mind, and the important results occur in mind, we need to make a particular study of it. The body is a supporting structure, and however much we study it, we must study mind exponentially more.

The Nature of Mind Is Essentially Untroubled

Our fourth topic is crucial for understanding mind. Natural mind is without corruptions (*kilesas*) and troubles of greed, aversion, and delusion. Mind is a natural element: mind element (*citta-dhātu*), or perhaps formless element (*arūpa-dhātu*), as you like. It's a natural element in the same sense that earth, water, fire, and wind are natural elements. However, this particular element concocts itself and becomes the "mind" we speak of. Mind, on the most fundamental level, isn't good or bad. It's without any form of affliction or trouble and is therefore described as "luminous," like the clear, sparkling radiance of a diamond or the bright radiance of the sun. Of course, this luminosity is formless, immaterial.

The nature of this luminous mind is to be unpolluted and uncorrupted by kilesas, yet it can concoct troubles superficially. The eyes, ears, nose, tongue, body, and mind can stimulate the arising of kilesas that temporarily overwhelm mind, obscuring its luminosity for a time. However, once the conditions supporting kilesas change and end, that affliction withers away and luminous mind reemerges. Mind is like this; this is its true nature. It's naturally luminous until the wrong kind of concocting creates troubles that cloud and obscure its natural luminosity. While luminous, mind is empty of dukkha and trouble-free. When no longer luminous and thus polluted, it's distressed, confused, turbulent, and suffering. The important observation is that originally and fundamentally mind isn't afflicted or corrupt. The kilesas are just passing occurrences, created when mind reacts carelessly to stimulation via the eyes, ears, nose, tongue, body, and mind. Mind is taken over by kilesas when it is confused by the senses.

When seeing very clearly that body (the senses) and mind can be distinguished, mind knows that it can be taken over by kilesas—or just as well, not be taken over. The corruptions aren't mind, which means that they can be prevented. Mind can be managed so that it stays trouble-free and preserves its luminosity. This is the meaning of *vipassanā*: meditation and mental training that lead to insight.

Training or cultivating mind (*citta-bhāvanā*) means developing it so that nothing can tarnish, dull, or afflict it. It has been much too easy for things to stimulate corruption, darken the luminosity, and create dukkha. Now, we'll cultivate mind through calming meditation, insight meditation, and other skillful practices. When this bhāvanā is carried out fully, mind can't be darkened anymore. Because it's more intelligent, sharper, and fully capable, the troubles can't rearise in mind. Then this condition is protected, preserved, and improved, not allowing anything to soil or corrupt it again.

Experiencing this, we understand the nature of mind, know it as it is, and thus know that mind can be trained. We now have complete confidence that we ourselves are capable of such training. We are happy to study for the sake of such training. With this delight in mental training, citta-bhāvanā occurs naturally in those who truly understand that mind can be trained.

At present, we probably don't see mind's nature clearly enough, and so we remain unconvinced that we can train mind. We may try to meditate, but we can't quiet mind instantly and so we give up easily. People who come here to Suan Mokkh often ask how long it takes to train mind. Encountering mental restlessness and distraction, they can't take it even for a little while; they give up in defeat. We see many who are like this. Hardly anybody persists in their struggle to train mind, to increasingly bring it under their power until mastery is accomplished, until the subtlest troubles and distractions no longer can arise in mind. Instead, surrender comes far too easily, and they accept defeat. So don't give up! Struggle on twenty times, thirty times, fifty times, even a hundred times.

Know that the nature of mind is essentially uncorrupted; troubles are stirred up only when things impact mind. Therefore we can separate corruption from mind through the simple method of acting rightly in regard to whatever provokes it. This method is known as *citta-bhāvanā* (mental cultivation). Whether we speak in terms of *vipassanā* or *samādhi* (concentration, meditation), they are collectively referred to as "mental cultivation" or "psycho-spiritual training." This is something we must understand.

Misunderstanding Gives Rise to Superstitious Belief

The fifth thing you need to understand is that mind is difficult to understand and, consequently, we don't understand it truly and properly. We misunderstand mind and, for instance, take it to be a ghost, spirit, or something too mysterious to understand. We speak of it in strange, bizarre, or supernatural terms, whatever pleases us at the time—all of which should be categorized as superstition (*sayasāstra*).[6] Superstition believes in the incomprehensible and irrational, and it occurs because we don't understand the true nature of mind. If we understood mind as it really is, superstitious beliefs wouldn't occur—nobody would ever think and believe in such ways. At present, we don't know mind as it actually is. It's a mystery to us, so we concoct speculations and blindly follow the claims of others. We place our faith in superstitious, unreasonable knowledge that is based in blind belief, which has led to a profusion of ideologies and sects.

Sayasāstra is very powerful, even after our many scientific advances. These beliefs arose tens and hundreds of thousands of years ago and persist powerfully to this day. Superstition arose when human beings first began to think about mind and misunderstood its nature. Such belief has the advantage of not having to be logical and not needing to be explained. It's all about believing, which has a strong appeal. Sayasāstra is seductive. The more mysterious such beliefs are, the more people take to them. When something is transparent and can be frankly, clearly explained, people don't accept it so easily. But the more something smacks of mystery and is incomprehensible, the more people willingly take it in. Such is superstition's big advantage. Even more ridiculous is that practically everybody is fond of how cheap it is. Superstitious beliefs involve very little investment: a pig's head, perhaps, or a bottle of liquor offered to the spirits or gods. Such advantages have kept sayasāstra alive and kicking right down to the present day.

Such superstitions are born of our instinct for ignorance, which makes them compatible with any foolish instincts we still have. For example, take the desire to have others help us rather than helping ourselves. Sayasāstra will offer immediate help, and people buy it because it fits their instinct to have others help them. Children, once they are born, receive all kinds of help from parents and other caregivers and can lose the strength of character needed to help themselves. They repeatedly rely on help from others until the habit becomes well entrenched and they can't get by without help from others. This is to superstition's advantage. Once such people don't know how to help themselves, they must rely on spirits, angels, and gods instead.

Taking this superstitious path obstructs truth, which fits with weak-minded intelligence. This world has many fools, people lacking in wisdom, who prefer sayasāstra to Dhamma and reality. Consequently, superstition is popularly received and firmly established in our world. Don't think that there aren't any superstitious beliefs and practices in developed, prosperous countries. We find it there, too, according to their cultural traditions, such as misunderstandings about God and calling on God for assistance. These beliefs will persist as long as ignorant human beings, no matter where they are, have an instinctual preference for the easy way, to let somebody else do for them what they should do for themselves. In the end, it's all mixed up and confused, and the sayasāstras that people create come back to be their lords and masters. Superstitions created by their own ignorance come back to rule them. How ridiculous is that?

Such superstition needs to be understood clearly. When we misunderstand and react wrongly regarding mind, we create systems for more foolish credulity. These systems of superstition are opposed to truth and reality. Those of a superstitious inclination have insulted and reviled me until exhausting their vocabulary, but I remain undaunted and continue to point to the truth of these matters. Essentially, if we know mind as it really is, all sayasāstra will dissolve of its own accord.

Nowadays, superstitious beliefs have reached an amazing level. As an example, people dab ritual marks on Buddha images to bestow them with the powers of a Buddha. Images are cast in a foundry but can't be used until someone comes along to apply the auspicious signs. Only then can they be Buddhas. Think about this: Common people create Buddhas just by making special marks on metal and stone images. That's a lot of Buddhas! Among the superstitious, that little mark is good for life. Merely take some powder, add holy water, bless it, and dab a little on the forehead, and that's good for life. You can see for yourself whether this is truly good or not.

Misunderstanding of truth, reality, Dhamma, and mind creates systems of sayasāstra. If we surrender to the power of superstition, we won't be able to connect with Dhamma and Dhamma will be worthless for us. We won't benefit from Dhamma because we misunderstand the facts of nature, especially concerning mind. Misunderstanding and faith in superstition create a great obstacle that keeps people from connecting fully with Buddhology (*buddhasāstra*, the science of awakening). Superstition inhibits, suppresses, opposes, and prevents realization of truth. If humanity doesn't understand these matters, sayasāstra will increasingly dominate and this world will become increasingly ridiculous. Dukkha isn't quenchable when the true nature of mind and body are misunderstood, which is a predicament of our own creation. So study the deep and complex mechanisms of the eyes, ears, nose, tongue, body, and mind adequately, then you'll know the truths and realities we speak of as "ultimate Dhamma." Through this highest Dhamma, you will realize path, fruit, and nibbāna,[7] so that you're able to live above dukkha and mind won't be afflicted anymore. Mind will be luminous all the time.

We Worship the Kilesas as Good

From our beginnings in the wombs of our mothers, we naturally lack correct knowledge; we don't have right knowledge that accords with nature. This mind that only superficially knows sense contacts via the eyes, ears, nose, tongue, body, and mind lacks deeper understanding of what truth is. It doesn't know release through the power of mind and release through wisdom (*cetovimutti* and *paññāvimutti*). It doesn't know what dukkha is, what the causes of dukkha are, what the quenching of dukkha is, or how the way of quenching dukkha works. Mind lacks this sort of knowledge from before birth. Once born, each child is surrounded by a plethora of things that lead it away from truth (*sacca*). It thus grows up in the midst of falsity and delusion regarding what it experiences through the sense media. Ignorance of reality increases: it doesn't know the way of survival—that is, the path for realizing nibbāna.

This is our "original sin." While other religions have their particular concepts of original sin, we Buddhists understand it to be the misunderstanding sparked by all the things encountered after emergence from the womb. Those who raise us bring delicious things for us to eat and we become infatuated with the delicious. They bring lovely and beautiful things, encouraging us to fall for beauty. Soon we're hooked into clinging to "me" and to "mine" and then clutching at selfishness. We go ever further astray, which doesn't decrease as we grow into adolescence. We carry such wrong views until we're old and gray.

Observe and examine yourself to see whether the misunderstanding that's been with you all along has ever decreased with the passing of time. Actually, it only increases, becomes firmer and stronger, and becomes extremely difficult to remove. When we can't get rid of it, we must bear its dukkha, and endure it until we awaken the aspiration to be free of it. Then, with wise aspiration, we commit to turning things around, to resolving our dilemma. Hence, if we've been lucky enough to realize this, we know that the misunderstandings and their suffering can be solved. Convinced that we can do so, we apply ourselves, make the necessary adjustments, and steadily lessen the dukkha we endure. We come to know life without suffering.

Personally, there's no need to suffer. Socially, there's no need to suffer. Families need not suffer. All peoples, communities, societies, and countries—the whole world—need not suffer. This is the ultimate purpose. How can life without suffering come about? We need to let Dhamma save the world, have Dhamma rule the world, so that it is dukkha-free.

"Lacking knowledge since in the womb" means we've arrived empty-handed. Since birth, right knowledge not being taught, we've been loaded up with misunderstandings. Who bothers to teach children about the quenching of dukkha? They're only fed, filled, indulged, pampered, flattered, and babied, until thoroughly spoiled. That's how it is. Whose sin is that? Born naturally lacking any true knowledge, emerging from the womb with nothing, then filled with misunderstandings and increasingly with selfishness, we're infatuated with delightful, stimulating sensual experiences until we worship the pleasure and fun of the senses. And we can never earn enough money to fulfill our sensual indulgences.

It's time to recognize that this problem exists and how difficulties have piled up proportionally. Through repeatedly deepening these habits, we strengthen tendencies and inclinations toward repeating them even more. These accumulated tendencies are known as *anusayas*. Every time a corruption arises, the corresponding tendency increases. Kilesas occur depending on causes and conditions. Although always temporary, activated corruptions—greed (*lobha*), anger (*kodha*), and delusion (*moha*)—build up tendencies toward further afflictions of their kind, thus promoting their reoccurrence in the future. The tendencies strengthen with each subsequent occurrence of affliction and gain the advantage. These tendencies toward troubles become thick and stubborn. We struggle to overcome the afflictions because the tendencies toward their reoccurrence are stronger than tendencies for their nonoccurrence.

Now it's time to build a Dhamma fortress so the kilesas can't happen. Combat them with mindful, clear comprehension—that is, develop the ability to be fully aware and apply the right kind of intelligent response to any potentially meaningful sense contact. Each time we prevent their arising, we decrease our familiarity with them and their corrupting power decreases. Just be careful to prevent them. Regulate them so they don't arise when provoked and their power lessens. Our habituation to them diminishes bit by bit. This is our way to survival and a healthier life. So don't give in, don't be discouraged, and you'll increasingly be able to control them. Eventually you can control them completely. Then the tendencies will disappear altogether, and kilesas won't arise again.

Here we must consider the thinking that's gone wrong—that is, appreciating and worshipping troubled acquisitions as good and beneficial. This isn't nice to hear, but we worship getting what the afflictions want as wonderful, which is much the same as worshipping the kilesas themselves. We worship the kilesas—that is, we want what the kilesas want. We desire the fun, delicious, and stimulating things of the world; we worship them as God. "God," here, means the highest reality or power that we must put faith in, must fear, and must obey. We believe in the corruptions, we fear them, and we obey their promptings. With such lifelong habits, we have the kilesas as our God.

Now it's time to change, to put our faith in the Buddha and act according to what he taught. This is difficult because we've been worshipping the God of troubles almost since birth. Our history makes it difficult to honor Dhamma and realize path, fruit, and nibbāna. Like everything in life, our ability to change depends on the necessary causes and conditions, on the right opportunities, and on wise choices. If causes and conditions come together appropriately, if there's good Dhamma teaching and skillful training, we can change and relinquish the kilesas. No longer cooperating with afflictions and troubles, our inclination is toward Dhamma and we genuinely seek to practice according to Dhamma.

Thus "light" arises. The light of survival arises when we stop worshipping the afflictions and instead honor what is real and true, that which is righteous and excellent—namely, Dhamma. We orient toward sacca, the truth of truths.

May Your Understanding Be Sandiṭṭhiko

This is how Buddhology takes charge.[8] Previously, it was all sayasāstra, "sleepology," the science of and knowledge for remaining asleep. Now we transform with the knowledge of one who is awake, whose eyes are wide open, who sleeps no more. Thus we enter into the Buddha's way and slowly, gradually, follow the path to its end, to the realization of path, fruit, and nibbāna. You should find it interesting that there is such a path.

It's vital that you experience and know all of this for yourself, directly within your own mind. To merely believe what I or anyone tells you will never be right. It's wiser and safer to follow the advice of the *Kālāma Sutta*.[9] Don't go against its tenets in anything—that is, don't just believe blindly. Believe only when clearly seeing the reality of something, then steadily change to the correct way. Respect Dhamma, the highest truth, do the right things, and realize the supreme reality, nibbāna, which is the culmination of everything.

Everything worth knowing is and must be *sandiṭṭhiko* (directly knowable and personally experienceable in mind). This word is highly significant because our Dhamma practice fails when it isn't sandiṭṭhiko; Dhamma truths must be personally experienced and understood. Many of us repeat the word daily in our chanting service without benefiting from actual personal experience.[10] It isn't sandiṭṭhiko until we experience it personally and know it directly within ourselves. Please consider the value of words merely recited without directly experiencing the truth they refer to. Let all Dhamma that we speak of or recite be intimately and directly known. If we talk about dukkha, let it be felt personally so mind directly knows how dukkha actually is. That corruptions, selfishness, and troubles are the cause of dukkha is to be known deeply and intimately within the experience of the kilesas themselves. Let everything important be sandiṭṭhiko.

The things that need to be sandiṭṭhiko—personally experienced and seen—before anything else are the eyes, ears, nose, tongue, body, and mind, plus their external counterparts and partners: the forms, sounds, odors, flavors, tangible sensations, and mental objects. Based in these, contact, feeling tones, and further experience arise. All of this has to be personally seen to be really useful as genuine knowing. The Buddha declared the senses and their objects to be the starting point of the supreme way of living (*brahmacariya*). In the intellectual study and exploration of Dhamma, the senses have to be tackled first. In practice, these sense media come first. And the result of practice, the penetration of truth, requires direct sandiṭṭhiko experience of the senses and their modes of operation.[11]

Entering the refuges—personally realizing the Buddha, Dhamma, and Sangha—is harder than you think. The ways they are widely misunderstood get in the way. Direct experience of the eyes, ears, nose, tongue, body, and mind is easier, because we can see them working. To know intangible Buddha, Dhamma, and Sangha before they are understood and seen is difficult. So we begin with merely reciting the words and receiving the refuges in the ordinarily ritualistic way. Although doing so is akin to superstition, we'll have to let it pass for now and continue to accept the Buddha, Dhamma, and Sangha as our refuge, although they aren't yet understood. Subsequently, through proper study and practice, understanding increases until the Buddha, Dhamma, and Sangha become sandiṭṭhiko experiences too.

Quench dukkha for once and know the real Buddha, Dhamma, and Sangha in that mindful experience. We must quench dukkha in our own hearts first to know what quenching dukkha really is. Then we see the Buddha who understands dukkha's quenching, the Dhamma that quenches dukkha, and the Sangha of those who consistently quench dukkha. Merely hearing and reading about the qualities of the Buddha, Dhamma, and Sangha aren't sandiṭṭhiko knowledge. Our intellectual level of sandiṭṭhiko isn't yet the real thing, but it can be useful as principles and maps.

So, it's "*Buddhaṃ saraṇaṃ gacchāmi, dhammaṃ saraṇaṃ gacchāmi, saṅghaṃ saraṇaṃ gacchāmi*" for now: "To the Buddha for refuge I go, to the Dhamma for refuge I go, to the Sangha for refuge I go." Then we gradually approach and discover the real refuges. When mind quenches suffering, when first experiencing that there isn't any dukkha, we know just how Buddha is. All Buddhas are just this, just as when our minds quench dukkha. This is how we really know the Buddha that realizes, the Dhamma that quenches, and the Sangha that practices. Right here is sandiṭṭhiko experience of Buddha, Dhamma, and Sangha.

I'm afraid that for many years our understanding of Buddha, Dhamma, and Sangha hasn't been sandiṭṭhiko, and that, consequently, we'll be ignorant of them until the days we die. The monks and novices shouldn't carelessly boast—they don't have direct, personal knowledge of the Buddha, Dhamma, and Sangha either.

Householders shouldn't carelessly depend on them. Friends, don't be distracted and slothful by neglecting what's needed for Dhamma and the teachings to be sandiṭṭhiko.

My next words will probably be criticized as presumptuous: Once we quench dukkha, when we truly understand and put an end to distress, at that time we are Buddha. Some will take this as an affront to the Buddha, but it's the simple truth of what happens. Mind takes on a little of the character of the Buddha and becomes a little Buddha. Mind that quenches dukkha and experiences the quenching of dukkha is itself Buddha. Whether we describe this as "mind realizes Buddhahood" or "mind has Buddha nature" amounts to the same thing. Having the characteristics of Buddhas, this mind is Buddha.

Be most industrious for the sake of dukkha and its quenching being sandiṭṭhiko. All the *dhammas* (realities) supporting the quenching of dukkha must be sandiṭṭhiko too—that is, seen clearly by and within oneself. They also must be characterized as being *akāliko*, "timeless," beyond the realm of time; as being *ehipassiko*, "inviting one to come and see"; as being *opanayiko*, "leading one ever deeper into truth"; and finally, as being *paccattaṃ veditabbo viññūhī*, "directly experienceable by the wise," not requiring an intermediary.

These are the first things we need to know concerning Dhamma, concerning our understanding of Buddhism, necessary for our comprehensive "seeing with the eye of Dhamma." I will do my best to continue in this vein in order to compile a single volume that covers the essentials of Dhamma. My aim is to give readers a single source for their necessary understanding of Buddha-Dhamma.

✳

This first chapter has focused on the nature of life, which has its secrets and profundities. The nature of life has many dimensions, which I have considered one by one. We will continue with this approach to clarify what we must practice so there will be greater certainty in realizing the fruits of such practice. Thus our understanding of Dhamma principles and techniques will be correct and Dhamma will be of genuine benefit for us.

2

TO CULTIVATE MIND IS TO DEVELOP LIFE

Having considered the natural conditions of human life, this chapter will consider what we ought to do with our humanity. We will examine life's development (*pattana*) through the cultivation of mind (*citta-bhāvanā*).

Cultivating mind means making mind progress and thrive, which is the same as making life progress. Developing life means making it better and healthier. When the progress or increase isn't for the better, that really shouldn't be called "development" at all.[1] Progress can be right or wrong; when wrong, it progresses without wise direction. There is, for instance, worldly progress that brings problems in its wake—trouble, strife, oppression, and dukkha. There is progress in the field of education, but of the kind that doesn't bring truly beneficial results, so that we still have delinquents and criminals throughout society, and more of them than ever. Among the educated classes, too, we have well-educated criminals. Clever people make clever crooks, creating long-lasting troubles for society. Such things happen when progress is wrong. If there is to be the right kind of progress, it must always move in the direction of well-being and fulfillment.

Cultivating (*bhāvanā*), much the same as *developing* (*pattana*), means to advance progress. *Cultivating* is used in the temples, and still has its ancient meaning, which has hardly changed at all, while *developing* is used outside of the temples and concerns the whole world, where its meaning has changed in accord with worldly trends, such as the emphasis on economics. Here, the term *mental cultivation* will be used when mind develops and makes progress wisely. Mental cultivation will necessarily develop life too, causing life to progress. Why is this so? Well, in reality, everything is connected with mind, everything arises with mind as captured in this Pali verse:

> *Jivitaṃ attabhāvo ca sukhadukkhā ca kevalā*
> Everything, including life, self-image, well-being, and pain,
> *Ekacittasamāyuttā*
> Occurs together with this single mind.
> *Lahuso vattate khaṇo*
> Moments of time pass rapidly.[2]

The whole experience of being alive is put together by mind, as if everything is created by mind. Suppose that people didn't have minds, would they be able to do anything? We would be rather like logs of wood or chunks of rock, unable to do anything at all. Because there is mind, all sorts of things happen. Mind thinks, thus things happen.

Everything Happens Because There Is Mind

Mind is a wonder. If the body were without mind, there would be no life. Only because there is mind can the body operate at all. Mind functions by way of the senses, the media between the inner and outer worlds. These sense media are the eyes, ears, nose, tongue, body, and mind, which are paired with forms, sounds, odors, flavors, tangibles, and mental objects. The inner and outer worlds are connected through them, with mind becoming active in the moment of sense contact. Mind wouldn't have any means to operate if we lacked eyes, ears, nose, tongue, and body. It couldn't function without them, as if there wasn't any mind at all. Hence, comprehend the importance of the senses in making it possible for mind to function normally. It's able to make contact with the outer world, with forms entering through the eyes, with sounds entering through the ears, with odors through the nose, with flavors through the tongue, with touches by way of body surfaces, and with mental objects and sensations occurring in mind itself.

These interactions are sense contacts (*phassas*), through which feeling tones (*vedanās*) arise. Pleasant and unpleasant feeling tones happen because mind is the connecter at the moment of sense contact. When feeling tones arise and mind is ignorant, there's liking when the feeling is pleasant and disliking when the feeling is unpleasant, thus afflictions (*kilesas*) such as greed, anger, and delusion also arise. Kilesas arise with both pleasant and unpleasant vedanās, so don't blithely assume one kind is good and the other bad. Because these scenarios are repeated over and over again during life, they become habitual. The repetitive arising of kilesas develops familiarity with them—an inclination or tendency toward them happening again. These underlying tendencies toward afflictions are the anusayas.

The next aspect of kilesas to consider is *taṇhā* (craving, ignorant desire). There are two kinds of desire. One kind arises in conjunction with mindfulness and wisdom and shouldn't be confused with craving. Taṇhā, however, is ignorant desire, wanting at odds with reality. For example, apprehending something as agreeable gives rise to liking. Lovable things are loved, and annoying things are disliked. Both cases are ignorant and create their concomitant desires: craving to get, craving to be, craving to get rid of, and craving to not be. Because they're all happening in ignorance, such desires are taṇhā. Mind itself desires and feels taṇhā. Without mind, there wouldn't be anything that craves.

When desire arises within ignorant mind, it naturally concocts thinking of the kind called *upādāna* (clinging). Immediately following the desire is an assumption that "I desire," that "I'm the one who gets," "I'm the one who doesn't get," "I'm the one who is affected," and so on. Ignorant desire begets upādāna, ignorant clinging. We subsequently develop tendencies to cling and attach: to cling as "being me," to cling to things as "mine," to cling to sensuality, to cling to views and opinions, and to cling to foolish traditions and empty behaviors. Clinging creates mental entanglement and permeates the subconscious of each and every person.

Because we live our lives under the power of ignorance, we're a problem for ourselves and others. Distress, oppression, and harmfulness occur on all sides, because our lives are full of such ignorant desire and clinging. All this is possible solely because of mind.

The preceding paragraphs demonstrate how anything and everything arises with mind, comes together with mind, and is connected with mind. Whatever state mind is in will dictate how events are understood and dealt with; therefore, it's our duty to train mind, to make it advance and grow in the right way, to stop it from being foolish and making mistakes, to keep it from doing wrong and causing problems—in short, to prevent it from spreading dukkha.

Sense Media Are the ABCs of Buddhism

A proper study of Buddhist teachings starts with the sense media (*āyatanas*). These ABCs of Buddhism need to be understood before anything. The Buddha taught that feelings of pleasure and pain (*sukha* and *dukkha*), and cravings and corruptions, are concocted in reaction to the six senses. Hence, we should find out how it is that the eyes, ears, nose, tongue, body, and mind, along with their counterparts—forms, sounds, odors, flavors, tangibles, and mental objects—give rise to feeling tones, craving, and clinging, and thus to kilesas and their bitter fruit of dukkha. If we lack clear knowledge of how this happens, our understanding will be secondhand and we'll have trouble understanding Buddhism properly. When there's no real understanding, there's no clear seeing and no real benefit to our study. Therefore, first of all, get to know the eyes, ears, nose, tongue, body, and mind.

The Pali language of the Buddha-Dhamma has a couple words whose usage may seem strange to you and whose significance you may not have grasped: *uppāda* (arising) and *nirodha* (quenching). Eyes arise and eyes quench, ears arise and ears quench, noses arise and noses quench, tongues arise and tongues quench, bodies arise and bodies quench, and minds arise and minds quench. Do you understand this unfamiliar Dhamma language? In the language of Dhamma, it's said that the eyes arise only when they do the work of seeing, the ears arise when they function in hearing, the nose arises when it does the work of smelling, and so on. When the senses aren't performing their respective duties, they are said to quench. In everyday language, we don't put it in Dhamma terms; rather, we think that we are always in possession of eyes, ears, nose, tongue, body, and mind, regardless of what is happening. We assume that the senses are always around. This, unfortunately, is an overly superficial understanding.

In Dhamma language, when the senses perform their duties, they are said to arise; when their duties are over, they are said to quench. Investigating further, we see that mind (*nāma*, mentality) arises and quenches, and that form (*rūpa*, physicality) also arises and quenches. This means that the body arises when the body functions somehow and quenches when that's over. It is said to have arisen when functioning and to have quenched when that function finishes. For example, the eyes aspect of body arises when it functions as seeing and quenches when that seeing ends.[3]

Further, the physical elements of earth, water, fire, and wind also arise and quench. When the elements mingle together as the body and are active, at that time, at that moment, they are described as having arisen. The earth, water, fire, and wind elements arise performing their functions as properties of an active body. The elements arise and quench dependent on the body, while mind—another element—also arises and quenches dependent on the body. Everything, without exception, is in the process of arising and quenching. When something does its duty, performs its function, that is called "arising," and when its duty is done and passes away, that is called "quenching."

To understand arising and quenching properly will be highly beneficial because Dhamma is just this way. That is, all things are *saṅkhāras* (conditioned things that arise in dependence on conditions), and to arise and quench is the nature of such things. There isn't anything that won't arise and quench. Hence, since the six senses arise, they also quench. Comprehend this by experiencing the arising of eyes, ears, and other senses. Don't let your knowledge be mere memorization of something read or heard. The senses and their modes of operation are the ABCs, the starting point, for the study of Buddhism, just as the alphabet is the starting point for the study of a language. This is why we need to give attention to the sense media first of all.

Now, the eyeballs are made of tissue, which is primarily earth element; there's temperature, fire element; there's liquid, water element; and there's movement, wind element. Further, there's the nervous subsystem connected with the eyeballs, which is the basis of visual consciousness, the conduit through which mind functions regarding the eyes. These are the functions involved in the seeing of a form; when a form meets the nervous system at the eyes, seeing occurs—that is, eye consciousness arises and does its duty. The functioning of eye consciousness represents the eye seeing whenever a visual form interacts with the eyes. These three things working together are contact (*phassa*).

When there is contact, the experience is felt as vedanā, which will be pleasing, unpleasant, or indifferent to the eyes. Every conscious experience is felt in one of these ways, along a spectrum of pains and pleasures. Once there is vedanā, desire is conditioned by the power of that vedanā. Visual pleasure leads to desiring, such as to acquire. Visual displeasure leads to desiring to avert, get rid of, to destroy, and the like. These feeling tones stimulate craving, taṇhā. Then the sense that there is a "me, the desirer"—or a "me" to be pleased or displeased, someone to get or to miss, someone who will win or will lose, or whoever—appears right then and there. Many "me's" can occur, shaped by craving.[4]

The World Arises with the Senses

The world, according to Buddhist understanding, arises at the eyes, ears, nose, tongue, body, and mind. *World* as studied in modern education is the planet Earth, the physical world that is divided into continents, countries, and various parts. If we're aware of this, we can use *globe* instead, which has a different meaning to *world*. *Globe* implies the body of Earth, while *world* implies Earth as well as all the creatures on and in it that have life, mind, and feelings. However, the "world" in Dhamma language, in the language of Buddha-Dhamma, is said to arise, or occur, when the eyes, ears, nose, tongue, body, and mind connect with forms, sounds, odors, flavors, tangibles, and mental objects.

More subtly, the Buddha said that there is sensory hell (*āyatanika-naraka* or *āyatanika-niriya*) whenever mind is "hot" as a result of experiencing contacts between the eyes, ears, nose, tongue, body, or mind and their respective objects. Along with this kind of hell, there is sensory heaven (*āyatanika-sagga*) whenever there is mental ease, satisfaction, or joy arising with sense contact. Please contemplate these heavens and hells of the Buddha. The Buddha didn't talk about heavens and hells in the old ways: heavens somewhere up in the sky and hells underground, that we go to, one or the other, after we die. He didn't object to that explanation but related something more amazing and interesting: heavens and hells occur at the eyes, ears, nose, tongue, body, and mind. All the realms or worlds are accessible to us because of the way mind responds to particular sense experiences.

You must take interest! The entrances to all the worlds are at the sense doors, and even nibbāna appears in connection with the eyes, ears, nose, tongue, body, and mind. The realization of nibbāna is found in acting correctly where the senses are concerned because it's here that quenching and coolness appear.

Hence, this single topic of the eyes, ears, nose, tongue, body, and mind is relevant to everything. Understanding them leads to understanding everything, just as we must learn our ABCs to access all the world's literature. The āyatanas are everything. Whether or not there will be sukha or dukkha, happiness or distress, depends on how we behave toward the things we see, hear, smell, taste, touch, and know. Behave correctly and there's no dukkha; behave incorrectly and dukkha occurs immediately.

Everything Happens through Mind

Of all the phenomena arising with the six senses, the most important factor is mind (*citta*). Citta has the duty of perceiving and thinking, hence it creates all kinds of things. If we couldn't think, mind wouldn't create anything and nothing would happen. Everything is created by mind's ability to think and imagine. When mind functions through thinking and creating, it's called *citta*; when it knows or senses, it's called *mano*; and when it cognizes at the senses, it's called *viññāṇa*. Citta, mano, and viññāṇa—which can be translated as "mind," "mind-sense," and "consciousness"—distinguish important aspects of mind. To keep from getting too complicated, just take it that mind functioning one way is known as *citta*, while another way of functioning is known as *mano*, and a third is known as *viññāṇa*. Don't let this be mere bookish knowledge; get to know citta, mano, and viññāṇa as they are, through observing mind's operations. Unwise people study Dhamma from notes, but smart people will study it within themselves. If we write down *citta*, *mano*, and *viññāṇa* on paper, we can memorize the terms. But if we're smart, we'll actually know each one as experienced in awareness: thinking and related mental activity (mind), experiencing inner objects (mind-sense), and sense consciousness.

I believe that Dhamma study must be done from experience, from actual things and events, as with scientific studies. Thus we directly know mind when functioning as citta, when functioning as mano, and when functioning as viññāṇa. If we study philosophy or logic, our studies are based on hypotheses more than on actual experience. When we study scientifically, we take real things to observe, research, and experiment with. If we study Dhamma from books, through intellection, it won't actually be Buddha-Dhamma.[5] To be Buddha-Dhamma, our studies must be scientific. Considering the eyes, we observe actual eyes in operation. Similarly with functioning ears, the actual nose as it smells, and so on. Along with them, the forms, sounds, odors, flavors, tangibles, and mental objects that impact the senses are actual experiences too. When there is a sense impact and consciousness arises at one of the senses, this sense cognition (*viññāṇa*) is to be known as it happens, not just ruminated over as a series of memorized names. Then the arising of sense contact, although it happens very quickly, also must be known as it actually is. When there is phassa, there will be vedanā, a feeling tone of satisfaction, dissatisfaction, or ambiguity. When a vedanā arises, ignorant desire (*taṇhā*) also arises, in line with the arisen feeling tone. From this comes the ignorant idea of "me," the one who desires. The ignorant citta creates such feelings of "me" and "mine," which is the central problem because the "me" and "mine" creates dukkha. All afflictions rest on a "self" that has been concocted through ignorance. The kilesas originate in illusions of self and put down deep roots in such self when it's established in ignorant mind.

We'll say more about these details later. Now we'll summarize the main issue in just six words: eyes, ears, nose, tongue, body, and mano. I encourage everyone to study them carefully. Remember, look out for chances to observe and understand the senses and their operations. This subject is huge—it's the "All," the beginning and the end of our problems.

Consider this example. Delinquents commit crimes because they don't understand sense contacts and the feeling tones arising from them. Thugs give too much meaning to such things, hence they waste their money on them and then commit more crimes to get more money. Their foolishness is much more than is ordinary, so they rob and perhaps even kill. If they could see contact and feeling as they are, as ordinary, they wouldn't be provoked into acting in the ways that they do. Afflictions and foolish cravings, all the evil in this world, happen because the senses and their objects aren't properly understood.

Be heedful that, in this day and age, people are often short of money because they use what they have to buy "bait," to buy what sensually attracts and lures them. The mere mention of this may be hard for you to take, yet it gets to the heart of the matter. Please explore this personally: how we buy more bait to indulge in the stimulation of the eyes, ears, nose, tongue, body, and mind. No matter how much we buy, it's never enough. However much we consume, it's never enough. Hence, our salaries aren't sufficient to satisfy our desires.

To manage the senses, we need to know their master well, which means we need to know how to manage mind. Mind is the overseer, with the duty of interpreting and responding to the promptings of the five physical senses as well as to its own internal operations. To talk of managing the senses is all right but somewhat indirect; if we talk of managing mind, we'll be spot on. Hence, we get to know mind well so that when it operates at the eyes, ears, nose, tongue, body, and mano, there's awareness and it's managed well. Don't let citta go astray and act ignorantly, with stupidity and confusion. Stop it from being foolish and infatuated, and from misunderstanding things. When citta goes wrong, there is dukkha. When we manage it correctly, there's no dukkha.

Buddhism Is Living Wisdom, Rather Than Bookish Philosophy

Now we want to point out that strenuous efforts to study Buddhism, when wrongly directed, are unsuccessful and unbeneficial. Success lies in personally understanding the eyes, ears, nose, tongue, body, and mano: how they operate, how the afflictions arise from their operations, and thus how dukkha arises dependent on them. However, for people who prefer to regard Buddhism as a field of general knowledge, as a subject for debate, or as a European-style philosophy, there will never be a day when they actually know it. Please don't treat Buddhism as a Western-style philosophy.

What a shame that we Thais have clumsily borrowed the Indian term *prajñā* to translate the Western term *philosophy*. The Sanskrit term *prajñā* actually means *paññā* (wisdom) and is most appropriate for discussing Buddha-Dhamma, but we make a mess by confusing it with Western philosophy or something worked out through logic. We need to discover truth in actual experience of the eyes, ears, nose, tongue, body, and mind as they function—from the reality of contact, feeling, and craving, and from the personal experience of dukkha. Such Dhamma knowledge is sandiṭṭhiko.

This is what we mean by saying it's all about the citta—about experiencing, managing, and cultivating mind properly. We're interested in natural facts rather than philosophical hypotheses. Bear this in mind while studying the Buddha's system: everything comes together at the eyes, ears, nose, tongue, body, and mano. When we stray from this base, there's no point to such studies because they won't have any benefit. Be it heavens, hells, nibbāna, or anything we might experience, it will always be connected with the senses. If we look in the right places, we will understand this.

We've taken a long time to help you realize just one thing: that everything comes together with mind (*citta*). All matters and all teachings come together with mind, which carries out its duties at the eyes, ears, nose, tongue, body, and mind itself.

By restraining the senses, we can regulate mind. Further, when we regulate mind, which is the source of all things, we automatically manage the senses. So we'll cultivate mind—that is, we'll train it to function properly—by not allowing it to respond to sense experience in its naturally ignorant ways. If we allow mind to carry on naturally, without really understanding it, we will operate under the power of ignorance. We'll say that again: if we just let things take their natural course, whatever happens will happen in ignorance. The six senses are paired with their sense objects—for example, the first pair is eyes and form. The eyeballs and the optic nerves are the basis for mind arising to perform its cognizing functions, which happens when an external form impacts the eyes. The form and the eyes interact in performing their respective functions and are said to have arisen. When the form has yet to impact the eyes, the two aren't functioning yet and haven't arisen. Once the eyes arise, the form arises; they meet, and the eyes then see—eye consciousness (*cakkhu-viññāṇa*) occurs. Through the appearance of cakkhu-viññāṇa there is a triple arising of eyes, form, and eye consciousness and their interaction is called *phassa* (contact).

Phassa is the most formidable of occurrences. Everything and anything is a consequence of phassa, of contact. On the arising of phassas, feeling tones (*vedanās*) quickly appear. Satisfying feelings are *sukha-vedanās*; uncomfortable feelings are *dukkha-vedanās*; and indeterminate feelings are *adukkhamasukha-vedanās*.[6] These feelings play a dominant part in the drama of life, and the ways they dominate mind are naturally unwise. As was previously mentioned, children don't have knowledge when they are born. They don't know about the quenching of dukkha, about liberation through mental calm and wisdom. They lack such knowledge, and won't, in the normal course of events, acquire it during this life either. Hence, when feelings of satisfaction occur, there's liking; when feelings of dissatisfaction arise, there's disliking; and when indeterminate feelings arise, there's doubt and confusion.

Remember this word *vedanās*. The vedanās are almost as formidable as phassa. Phassa is the most dangerous core of experience, but it's when there are vedanās, feeling tones, that trouble arises. When phassas are allowed to happen naturally, they happen in ignorance. This gives rise to ignorant vedanās—that is, feeling tones that aren't understood as they really are. The ignorant mind naturally likes pleasant vedanās and dislikes painful vedanās, and experiences doubt and confusion when faced with neither-painful-nor-pleasant vedanās. Because of ignorance, unwholesome desires follow, the kinds of desire that shouldn't happen. These are followed, in turn, by infatuation, anxiety, anger, and so on. This is the natural result of just letting things follow their course. This is the basic pattern for everyone.

With this natural flowering of ignorant habits, we should get to know ourselves well by studying every point of Dhamma from the realities within this mind-body. Don't rely on books, notes you've taken, and other external sources as anything more than pointers and aids to memory. The real learning is from the living reality within.

Do we understand that allowing things to follow their natural course amounts to ignorance? Can we see the imperative to train mind for wisdom—to provide it with genuine knowledge? Hence, we practice for mind to be aware when experiencing phassas and vedanās; otherwise, ignorance will be in control. We train mind in direct knowledge so that it won't fall into liking the agreeable, disliking the disagreeable, or being confused by the ambiguous. It then will be out of danger and not prone to fall into infatuation, anger, fear, anxiety, longing after past things, jealousy, envy, shame, and other afflictions.

Training Mind to Know Its Unobstructed Luminosity

How should we train mind? And do we see training mind as important? If mind isn't trained, the flow of mental concocting naturally follows the path of ignorance. We train mind to give it the knowledge to manage the mental flow. When insight is in charge of all sense contacts, dukkha doesn't happen. When something comes to stimulate contact and some sort of feeling arises, we can be aware of it as "just like that." Then we don't fall into liking and infatuation, no matter how enticing the experience may be. Nor will we fall into aversion or fear, even though we're experiencing something apparently hateful or fearsome. Consequently, we'll be safe and out of danger.

Do you now see how important cultivating mind is? If it wasn't so important, I wouldn't spend so much time on it. We talk about mental training as being vital and crucial to encourage the understanding that it's something we all need to do, because cultivating mind is also about developing life, which isn't just for a few special people.

Can this training of mind be accomplished? Can you do it? Don't respond hastily or you will probably give the wrong answer. People generally don't know whether it can or can't be done, so they just go along with others who say that it can. Such vagueness undermines conviction. The Buddha says something very significant on this point: he observes that mind is naturally luminous (*pabhassara*). This perspective makes training mind possible, as we learn that it is naturally without afflictions or corruptions. However, this luminous mind is obscured, gloomy, and muddled whenever visiting kilesas take over. When does this happen? It happens at contact; with the arising of phassas and vedanās, ignorance can also slip in and dominate mind so that greed, anger, confusion, and more arise.

Mind that would have been luminous and pristine has become afflicted, dark, and gloomy.

The true nature of mind is luminous—that is, radiant, bright, and resplendent. According to the Buddha, anyone who clearly sees the essential luminosity of mind is fit for psycho-spiritual cultivation. One knows that luminosity returns once the adventitious kilesas pass, along with their supporting causes and conditions. No matter what, we can look forward to mind's unobstructed luminosity reappearing. Those who believe that the nature of mind is to always be clouded have no opportunity for successful cultivation. When we know the reality, we see for ourselves that cultivating mind is definitely possible. We know that the developed mind can manage the flow of phassa, vedanā, taṇhā, and the rest so that there's no dukkha. Hence, we have the interest and the motivation to do the job.

3

SAMĀDHI WITHIN THE PATH OF CULTIVATION

With regard to mind's training, I want to consider something that is poorly understood and seldom heard. When teachers discuss the cultivation process as *sīla* (ethics and virtue), *samādhi* (meditation for unification and stability of mind), and *paññā* (intelligence and wisdom), they commonly say that sīla, being about behavior, doesn't directly concern mind, while samādhi and paññā do. But that's not right; such understanding is superficial. To cultivate mind, all three aspects—sīla, samādhi, and paññā—are needed.

To begin with, upholding the five sīla precepts, our basic ethical trainings, requires that mind have correct understanding of this fundamental level of Dhamma. It knows it mustn't kill, steal, sexually transgress, lie, or consume intoxicants. Mind must be sufficiently elevated to be able to abstain from such harmful actions; otherwise, skillful abstinence won't be possible. For instance, mind must be restrained and trained so that it comes to abhor and fear drinking liquor. Once its attitude toward alcohol changes, when it no longer entertains the drinking of liquor, nor of killing, stealing, adultery, or lying in any of the many ways possible, mind is then elevated sufficiently. We train the sīla mind well so that we can keep the sīla precepts and avoid breaking them in any way. This is mental cultivation on the sīla level.

Mental Cultivation through Sīla, Samādhi, and Paññā

Next is the samādhi aspect of citta-bhāvanā (mental cultivation). Mind that has become used to weakness, doesn't rest in its own strength, and is cluttered with the *nīvaraṇas* (hindrances, disturbing moods and attitudes) is now retrained. Simply put, make it fit enough to be above its enemies. Let it be collected and concentrated. From there, the wisdom aspect of citta-bhāvanā cultivates genuine knowledge of phenomena as they actually are. It's necessary to train mind in mastering everything it needs to comprehend.

Citta-bhāvanā works on these three distinct levels: the sīla level of training mind, so that it can keep the ethical precepts and live virtuously; the samādhi level of training mind, so that mind is stable and steady and can function most effectively; and the paññā level of training mind, so that mind has the wisdom to know what it should know as a human being—namely, how to quench dukkha. This is the full meaning of mental cultivation. Other teachers may explain it differently, but we're not responsible for that. It's my responsibility to tell you that psycho-spiritual cultivation must involve training that integrates sīla, samādhi, and paññā.

Development Must Reach the Level of Buddhology

We can map out another set of three levels for our citta-bhāvanā. The first level is the ordinary animal mind, with the same basic knowledge as that available to animals. The untrained mind has the instinctual level of knowledge with which we are born. Mind at this animalistic level (*sattvasāstra*, the kinds of knowledge belonging to sentient beings) knows what animals need to know for survival, which amounts to a rather low level of understanding. The second level is somewhat higher than that of animals and is equivalent to the level of our ancestors living in the forests. These people hadn't comprehended Dhamma very well and believed external forces to be ghosts, spirits, or gods. Although this is a higher mental level than that of animals, we consider it the "superstitious" level (*sayasāstra*, sleepology; the body of knowledge that keeps us asleep in ignorance and confusion). This isn't the highest human level, it's a still-asleep level, so to speak. With superstitious beliefs in ghosts, spirits, gods, and whatever can't be explained, we impose our beliefs and opinions without questioning and critical thinking.[1]

The Buddha wasn't interested in superstition. He discovered truths of nature: the facts concerning dukkha, its origins, its quenching, and the way to its quenching. Hence, he taught a new understanding, which we call "Buddhology" (*buddhasāstra*, the science of awakening).[2] Actually, *Buddhology* isn't quite right, but there's no more appropriate term. Anyway, just remember three things: mind on the animalistic level, which is shared with animals living by instinct and animal learning; mind on the superstitious level—that is, the ignorant, blind, credulous, asleep level, which is somewhat better than the animal level; and mind on the Buddhology level, the final level of a Buddha fully awakened to natural truth, to the quenching of dukkha. *Buddha* (awake) is the opposite of *saya* (asleep).

Our spiritual cultivation must transcend the sattvasāstra and sayasāstra levels to reach the buddhasāstra level. Who is interested in this? Some people claim it is too difficult and bothersome; they don't understand what they'll get from it, and so they give up. Such half-hearted study of Buddha-Dhamma is pointless. Such people don't follow the training to the final objective. The full range of citta-bhāvanā is completed with buddhasāstra.

All Aspects of Cultivation Work Inseparably

The three levels of sīla, samādhi, and paññā cannot be detached from one another. We can't live without attending to sīla, to ethics and virtue, because there would then be crime, trouble, harm, and strife everywhere. Wayward behavior would take over homes, workplaces, and society. The ethical system is necessary in human life, whether we live alone or with others. There also must be mental correctness. When sīla is active, samādhi, mind's healthy correctness, comes about easily. And when mind is correct, wisdom arises all by itself. Mind must follow this natural line of development so that it can rise above the animalistic and superstitious levels to enter Buddhology. To do so, there can't be any shortfall where sīla, samādhi, and paññā are concerned.

The more you understand this cultivation and how the three components go together, the more you will see that mind well established in samādhi (stability, clarity, and unity) experiences sīla as a by-product. The commitment to meditate with and for samādhi includes sīla, without needing to consciously intend having it. Nor is it necessary to undergo a ritual of receiving the five precepts. Just direct your attention to cultivating genuine, balanced samādhi, to gathering together the strength of body and mind, and then the full meaning of sīla will be immediately present.

Upon developing true samādhi, paññā emerges. Because cultivating samādhi improves mind, knowledge concerning things we don't know but need to know naturally occurs. Things that were unrealized gradually come to be realized. In the Buddha's words, "*Samāhito yathābhūtaṃ pajanati*" (one with samādhi mind, unified mind, can see all things as they really are). The desire to know can't be fulfilled when mind lacks samādhi, because distracted mind indulges, gets entangled, and is corrupted. Once mind is clear and spotless, true knowledge simply emerges quietly. "Insight" isn't trumpeted. With clear, balanced mind, many kinds of knowledge can emerge depending on how attention is inclined, whether consciously or subconsciously. Mind that's comfortable is well-suited to knowing. Hence, when we commit to meditation, sīla is present, too; and when mind is samādhi, paññā gradually flows in line with paying attention to what needs knowing, whether that attention is guided intentionally or unintentionally.

Be aware that we all want to know certain things, even if we aren't conscious of it at the time. Perhaps we once consciously wanted to know something, but lost track; still, that desire to know something is stored inside. We go on wanting to know the next thing, and then another, and such wants continue endlessly. We store up all these questions about things we want to know. Once mind is in good shape and fit for knowing, the answers emerge. We are able to ponder and know an unbelievably great number of things because we have cultivated a mind fit for knowing.

I appeal to you to be interested in mind having samādhi (unified stability), as samādhi is the backbone and mainstay of mind. Simply gather together in samādhi, and sīla will be present for the time that mind is established in that samādhi. However, if there are failings of sīla to begin with, you will have to do something about that first, such as cleaning up your behavior and confessing transgressions. Then you can immerse yourself in calm, steady focus (*samādhi*) so that wisdom gradually arises.

Sīla, samādhi, and paññā are balanced and work together quite naturally. In doing any kind of work, the three can't be separated. In carrying out ordinary tasks, let alone Dhamma practices, the work to be done and the body doing it are coordinated physically, mental regulation keeps mind focused appropriately, and the knowledge necessary for doing the job properly oversees it all. Something as simple as splitting firewood requires physical control of the hands, which is sīla; regulation of mind, which is samādhi; and knowledge of how to split wood into kindling, which is paññā. Hence, in any beneficial activity, there can't be any shortage of sīla, samādhi, or paññā. If there is, we won't be able to perform the task properly. Just try cutting firewood without being in physical control of the situation; you will probably split your foot instead. No matter what we do—school studies, household chores, livelihood activities—we must have adequate levels of sīla, samādhi, and paññā operating together.

This is the most important principle in Buddhism: there must be sīla, samādhi, and paññā combining together harmoniously and operating as one. When these three are expanded as the eight factors of the noble path (*magga*, the fourth noble truth), all eight must operate as one in order to carry out the duty of cutting through the kilesas.

It's the same reality, whether expressed as three components or eight or however many: all factors must work together as one.[3]

The Experience of Samādhi

What is it like to have samādhi? Some students may think that being in samādhi means sitting stiff as a board, locked in a trance, but that doesn't fit the facts. Samādhi isn't just about sitting. Mind trained in samādhi has certain qualities whether one is walking, sitting, standing, or lying down. In the ancient Pali texts, many characteristics are used to define samādhi, but the most important three are: *parisuddho*, mind purified of the nīvaraṇas and untroubled by afflictions; *samāhito*, stability and steadiness of mind; and *kammaniyo*, mind agile in its immediate function. For there to be samādhi none of these three can be deficient. First is parisuddho, mental cleanliness. Then there is samāhito, firmness and stability; mind with its energies gathered together so that it's strong and secure. And kammaniyo, which is mental readiness and agility in carrying out the present duty. These three factors can be fully present whether we walk, sit, stand, lie down, think, or act in any other way. This samādhi mind isn't about sitting stiffly in absorption or meditative trance, which requires too much concentration for our needs and may go to extremes in our training. The time spent in such pursuits is time that we don't put to good use. Sitting in absorption (*jhāna*) is also samādhi, but it isn't the kind of mental unification that is useful in the tasks and works we undertake.

When we begin to meditate, there's a little samādhi, which is known as "preliminary concentration." We start off by, for instance, focusing on our breathing so that a little samādhi gathers, which we then increase until "access concentration"—the gateway to the highest form of samādhi. Continuing on from there, "attainment concentration"—that is, jhāna—is attained, which represents the still, silent mind, which can be further refined and deepened to the highest possible level, at which point even breathing will be absent. However, we can't really do much with such samādhi, although it's a lesson in mind's capacities. Instead, after reaching the jhāna level of samādhi, we relax the absorption a bit and return to access samādhi, in which we can walk, sit, or think, and mind will still be in samādhi. Whatever the activity, even when walking or thinking, mind will still retain its purity, its firmness and stability, and its quickness and agility. This will be sufficient samādhi for the task of investigating the quenching of dukkha. Any more samādhi than that, such as in jhāna, can't be used for that purpose. Of course, we might use it for dwelling in bliss or taking a break. We could practice a great amount and reach the highest jhanic levels, but that's not the best way to use our time. While hanging out in jhāna, investigating the truths isn't possible. Even if we attain absorption, dwelling in the more ordinary level of access samādhi is more useful, for it supports reflection and contemplation.

A mind imbued with the factors of samādhi is a necessity even for children. Mind that is pure, stable, and ready to do its duty is necessary for students and undergraduates too. If we want to cultivate mind in a useful way, we should aim to bring about this kind of samādhi and then put it to good use. A mind freed of the kilesas and nīvaraṇas that have disturbed it is clean, undistracted, sensitive, and quick in its duties. This kind of samādhi is practical and useful, neither too much nor too little, and genuinely beneficial.

Let's look further into the factors coming together as the elements of samādhi. There are many types and forms of samādhi cultivation—that is, meditation.[4] The Buddha talked about various forms, and later teachers added more until their number became far more than anyone can hold in memory. The number of temples with their particular styles of meditation and teachers promoting their own forms of meditation is ludicrous. What madness to have all these branded meditation styles! Suan Mokkh doesn't have a style; we don't claim any "Suan Mokkh meditation." Instead, there is the Buddha's form that we've studied, investigated, selected, and implemented. Although we consider it the Buddha's form, it's actually—and no disparagement is intended—nature's form. The Buddha couldn't invent the natural law that causes the arising of samādhi. Rather, it was something he discovered; he didn't create it. He awoke, through discovering the way to the supreme samādhi, and later taught several ways for cultivating it.

Among the several forms that the Buddha revealed, *ānāpānasati-bhāvanā* (cultivation of mindfulness with breathing) is the one I most appreciate. This approach is smooth and gentle, relaxed and quiet, cool and peaceful. It's not disturbing or frightening like death meditations and contemplations of loathsomeness. Meditation based in gathering attention on the breathing is always quiet, peaceful, and cool, or something has gone amiss. We appreciate and favor the full system of *ānāpānasati* (mindfulness with breathing in and out) that the Buddha praised and taught; he recommended it as being the most effective, most peaceful, most quiet, and coolest form of meditation. Most saliently, he dwelt in this cultivation of mindfulness with breathing during his awakening.

We can accumulate as many forms of meditation as we like, but the essentials of cultivating mind with samādhi will be the same. First is suitability and fitness. Our surroundings must be suitable for cultivating samādhi. Our body must be fit enough, without illness and disturbing conditions. The object of samādhi, such as the breathing as followed in ānāpānasati, needs to be suitable too.

Find a Kalyāṇamitta, but Let Practice Be the Teacher

The second basic need is a splendid, noble friend (*kalyāṇamitta*) who will give us assistance. In the past, the teacher of a meditation practice wasn't referred to as *ācariya*, master or teacher, as today. Instead, practitioners spoke of *kalyāṇamitta*. The Buddha is recorded to have said that all beings subject to birth, aging, sickness, and death, should they rely upon the Tathāgata as their kalyāṇamitta, would go beyond birth, aging, sickness, and death. Here, *Tathāgata* refers to the Buddha himself, the supreme kalyāṇamitta. He spoke of relying on kalyāṇamittas, rather than on gurus, teachers, or leaders. In ancient texts such as the *Visuddhimagga*, as well as by custom here in the Chaiya area,[5] meditation teachers are referred to as *kalyāṇamittas*.

This seems to have been the standard term among those who meditated regularly. In other words, we need more than a teacher; we also require noble friendship.

In practicing meditation, we should find someone who can provide appropriate knowledge, advice, and assistance in all necessary ways. A pure-hearted kalyāṇamitta gives the proper advice, but doesn't sit watching over us day and night. Exclusive teachers who collect fees are something else. In the Buddha's time, students received their meditation teachings and themes from the Buddha, then practiced on their own. They struggled, often mightily, through ups and downs, until reaching a dead end. After consulting their kalyāṇamittas about how to resolve their problems, they returned to practicing independently. They weren't encouraged to come every day, and they didn't need to ask about every little thing. Hence, it's not necessary to have a kalyāṇamitta sitting over us and telling us what to do. Meeting together with a virtuous friend and advisor occasionally and as needed is enough.

One of our challenges when we begin meditating is that various unfamiliar, strange, frightening, and amazing things happen. This is just the nature of mind. If someone is frightened and doesn't know whom to ask for help, the situation can get out of hand. If we follow the old school, we know not to be afraid, that such things happen, and there's no need to make much of them. These strange phenomena happen but aren't our purpose. Remember that we aim for calm and clarity, then start afresh and look inward for calm and clarity instead. We needn't have our kalyāṇamitta watching over us in the same room; a good advisor we can meet with from time to time is more than enough.

The third basic need is to take up a suitable meditation object for the beginning stage, which is called "preliminary cultivation." This meditation theme must be within our abilities, and we should have sufficient information and explanations to work with it effectively.

Finally, the only thing left is to do it. You'll fail, so try again. Give it another go and fail again. So we try again, and we fail again. We try, we fail, we try, we fail, and so on. It's much the same as learning to ride a bicycle all by oneself. Nobody can instantly ride a bicycle. Although we see how it is done, have it explained to us, and it looks easy, when we get on and try to ride, we fall off. So we must get back on again, but we fall again, and repeatedly, until finally we succeed in riding the thing after twenty or thirty attempts. Let the work be the teacher. Don't be so foolish as to pick up all kinds of explanations from people. Let the practice itself teach you.

We practice our preliminary stage of cultivation. We practice, practice, and practice some more. Although at first we can hardly do it, and we stumble through many attempts, we improve a little bit with every attempt. It's rather like an infant learning to walk. We hold them up and they plop right down once we let go. At first, babies can only sit or lie down. Then they learn to crawl, then to stand, and finally to walk. Of course, while getting used to walking, they fall down a lot, but infants continue trying to walk and eventually succeed. This is how nature teaches us. Even paddling a boat must be practiced, and practiced many tens of times, before the boat can be kept straight. Nobody can manage it immediately, no matter how much one has watched or read about it. Therefore, let your repeated attempts be the teacher and your efforts will eventually come to fruition, just as in attempting to row a boat, learning to walk, or riding a bicycle. In this preliminary cultivation, we try, try, and try again until we succeed.

To continue, the second level of samādhi develops from the cultivation of access concentration. This is where mind starts to become peaceful. When this happens, mind is in a different condition, no longer the same as it was at the beginning. Develop this further; gather and increase samādhi until it becomes stable and firm. At first, we cultivate as beginners, then we enter the access phase, and finally we attain the level of stable fixity.

These three levels are associated with every form of meditation. In the initial stages, there is usually turbulence and confusion, but there's no need to be afraid. There's nothing to fear from unfamiliar experiences. If it isn't peaceful yet, don't pay attention to the distractions and continue giving attention to calming. Steadily, little by little, we calm down as we approach access samādhi. And then, proceeding onward, there's attainment of jhāna. On entering absorption, mind will be firm and stable, but we'll be unable to do much of anything with that fixity. Mind can't, for instance, do any discursive thinking, neither can we walk nor even stand up. When in jhāna, one needs a stable, balanced sitting posture. Staying in jhāna a long time is referred to as *samāpatti* (accomplishment). There's no need for us to bother too much with this because it isn't for everyone. Nature didn't intend entering and dwelling in samāpatti for all people. The Buddha didn't teach it for everyone. However, anyone can concentrate mind on the level of well-integrated parisuddho, samāhito, and kammaniyo. Everybody can do this through attaining access concentration. If we can reach jhāna, there will be a lot of samādhi. At such times, mind is said to be composed of samādhi, and we can benefit from that samādhi. To do so, we need to exit absorption first. When exiting jhāna, when coming out from samāpatti, we are alert and have enough power of samādhi remaining to do anything we care to take on, and in a much better way than would normally be the case. So the power of samādhi that we, all of us, can develop and use genuinely is the power of access concentration. This is so because we can walk, sit, lie down, think, or do anything within reason—most especially the studying of difficult books—while this kind of samādhi mind persists.

So, the correct conditions must be present: suitable surroundings, a suitable meditation object, and appropriate counsel. Then we can cultivate the levels of preliminary, access, and, if we wish, jhāna.

Samatha Is Looking and Vipassanā Is Seeing Clearly

To complete this overview of samādhi and meditation, we need to consider two words that are frequently confused—*samatha* and *vipassanā*. *Samatha* means "calm, quiet, and still"; and *vipassanā* means "seeing clearly, directly, and experientially." Samatha is the initial stage of meditation (*samādhi-bhāvanā*) in which mind is calmed and quieted. The ensuing stage is vipassanā, in which mind sees directly and clearly. The meanings ought to be clear: samatha brings calm and peace and isn't concerned with thinking or intellection. It cultivates a peaceful mind in samādhi. Knowledge naturally occurs with the rightly collected, quiet, peaceful mind.

Vipassanā means seeing clearly and directly. At present, it's often misunderstood as thinking, pondering, and reasoning. I used to believe that, because that's what we were taught as young monks. In truth, however, vipassanā isn't about thinking and intellectual activity. Put simply, samatha is about "looking," while vipassanā is about "seeing." We must look first, then we see. Looking and refining how we look is samatha, and the naturally resultant "seeing" is vipassanā. We start with looking. For a while, the looking is fitful because mind's eye is too dim, murky, and blurry. So we brighten and clarify it. This involves expunging the five hindrances to samādhi and insight. The five nīvaraṇas are like dust and dirt that distort the surface of the eyeglass lenses, rendering them unable to focus a clear image. After wiping the lenses clean, we can then look at something and see it clearly. Similarly, mind's eye is translucent when unhindered, and looking becomes seeing.

The five hindrances are natural inclinations of mind toward *kāma chanda* (sensual desire), *byāpāda* (ill will, aversion, and crankiness), *thīna-middha* (mental sloth, torpor, desiccation, and sluggishness), *uddhacca-kukkucca* (distraction with excessive energy), and *vicikicchā* (doubt about what is happening). These are the naturally occurring nīvaraṇas that constantly disturb mind. Related phenomena also occur and can be considered variations on the nīvaraṇas. The mental eye must be wiped clear of them, like cleaning our eyeglasses, or like applying eyedrops that make the eyes healthy, bright, and clear.[6] The samatha aspect of meditation is this cultivation of a peaceful mind so that the inner eyes are fit for looking. Then vipassanā sees, which is the insight stage of meditation. Samatha is looking, and vipassanā is seeing. Although we speak of stages, these two aspects of meditation can't be separated. Wiping eyeglasses clean, looking, and seeing clearly are interdependent. Some groups speak of the whole thing as vipassanā, as in "practicing vipassanā," when a specific technique is meant. That distorts the proper meaning of vipassanā or pretends that there can be insight without adequate samatha. Don't confuse or blur them. Samatha amounts to necessary preparation for vipassanā. And don't worry; sīla, the ethical practice, can't be absent. When our practice is already well established in virtue, it's naturally subsumed in the samatha and samādhi phase.

Please be careful to understand the word *vipassanā* properly. It's a matter of looking, not of thinking. If it were about thinking and reasoning, our prior knowledge would lead that thinking and often take a wrong direction. We would think mainly in line with what we've learned through study, we would pursue those ideas, which would obstruct actual vipassanā, which is seeing anew, freshly. Without developing samatha, our clouded and obscured eyeglasses would prevent looking with unbiased freedom and seeing the truth clearly as it appears. Mind's cultivation through samādhi requires these interdependent aspects of samatha and vipassanā.

Once the nīvaraṇas are wiped clean, looking brings seeing. The three universal characteristics of conditioned phenomena appear clearly: *aniccaṃ* (impermanent, unable to stay the same), *dukkhaṃ* (unsatisfactory, inherently stressful), and *anattā* (not-self, lacking independent essence). Seeing these fundamental realities of all conditioned experience is seeing *dhammaṭṭhitatā*, how these characteristics are natural and ordinary, and *dhammaniyāmatā*, the natural lawfulness that all conditioned phenomena have these characteristics. All of these aspects of insight can be gathered together in the phrase "seeing *suññatā*," seeing that phenomena are empty of essential being. Or, to use a quite marvelous word, there is seeing *tathatā*, thusness, everything as simply "just so." This pinnacle of seeing, of insight, realizes that there's nothing worth grasping at or clinging to: nothing worthy of falling in love, of falling into anger and hatred, of fearing, of longing after, of jealousy, of envy, of any reactive ego emotions. Seeing thusness sees that everything is simply thus.[7]

Seeing the Buddha in This Very Life

A wonderful way of describing vipassanā is "seeing the Tathāgata." The mind that sees the Tathāgata is the mind of Tathāgata. Tathāgata means one who has gone to, realized, become thusness (*tathatā*). The Buddha often referred to himself as Tathāgata, pointing to his profound realization of life's fullness. When vipassanā is cultivated, seeing thusness—along with impermanence, unsatisfactoriness, essencelessness, and voidness—is seeing the Buddha. Further, seeing Tathāgata includes seeing all the arahants, all the worthy awakened ones, for they too have realized thusness, the truth of everything being "simply thus." The Buddha is chief of all arahants. They're all tathāgatas and the Buddha is the pinnacle of Tathāgata. Vipassanā is seeing the reality behind the Buddha speaking of himself as Tathāgata, one who has realized tathatā.

Vipassanā isn't a plaything. Nor is it a mechanical ritual or technique. Vipassanā is about seeing all dhammas as they are, which is seeing the reality of Tathāgata. This, then, is real seeing. Looking and then seeing has wonderful benefits; all the benefits that ought to be realized are enjoyed. When ignorance believes there is self, something essential we really and lastingly are, there is also birth, aging, sickness, and death. We stop birthing, aging, falling ill, and dying when we stop believing in and clinging to such self (*attā*).

Even though we live in this world, and must work and sweat, there isn't any dukkha whenever we see Dhamma, whenever we see tathatā. We enjoy work because it is "just like that." Cultivating rice fields, tapping rubber, buying and selling, and any other work we might do is "just how it is." For students, any difficult courses and programs are "just like that" and consequently aren't dukkha. We can work hard and enjoy what we are doing, which is a marvel. People without Dhamma curse themselves while working. They suffer and curse the spirits, ghosts, angels, and gods while they're at it. People with Dhamma see everything as "just so," do what they must, and are content.

I call this the butterfly lifestyle. A butterfly goes about seeking sustenance by drawing nectar from pretty flowers in the beautiful forest. It both earns its living and finds pleasure in its life-sustaining work. It has no dukkha at all. If we humans are able to apply knowledge of tathatā in carrying out our duties, our satisfaction in all our works and actions is happiness. This is like a butterfly's life—and we don't mean the butterfly's fragility and brief life span. The only meaning we need is to work and find happiness in working. Learning is happiness, teaching is happiness. One is able to make any kind of work happiness in itself when mind is "just thus."

Then, communally and socially, people wouldn't be selfish and there wouldn't be any social problems. People would love one another because they weren't selfish. Being kind to one another unselfishly, they wouldn't be able to kill, steal from, sexually abuse, or lie to others. They wouldn't indulge in intoxicants and disgust others. Naturally, social decency would flourish. To summarize the main point: when people have Dhamma minds, there will be social decency, happiness for all, and the end of cycling around in the mass of dukkha.

May we all cultivate mind and fully train it in all three aspects of sīla, samādhi, and paññā. Leave the basest mental levels behind and uplift yourself steadily from the animalistic to the superstitious, for starters, and then leave superstition behind to embark on Buddhology. This is genuine mental cultivation and the heart of meditation.

How will we do it? We're born lacking true knowledge. We're born ignorant and additional foolishness is frequently instilled, until we regularly suffer because of it. Becoming aware of the suffering, we start to realize that we must move in the opposite direction if we are to be free of dukkha. Inspired by suffering, we start to cultivate mind in order to conquer dukkha.

Mental cultivation (*citta-bhāvanā*) is realistic and within our means; it isn't beyond our abilities and talents. It's still possible in this hyperbolic day and age. Citta-bhāvanā can be practiced all the time and isn't limited to any period or epoch, such as the Buddha's era. If people have the wisdom to see the dukkha that arises in life, they must do something in response and realize that citta-bhāvanā is what they must do. Everything is connected with mind. The causes and conditions, the results and effects, and the stream of causes and conditions concocting results and effects all come together in mind. There are no exceptions. So we manage mind, which is mental cultivation and the development of life.

The word *development* (*pattana*) is popular these days, but it runs mostly in the wrong direction. The more there is of such development, the more craziness there is; the more "progress" there is, the more problems there are; and consequently the more dukkha there is. All of that adds up to wrong development, which develops so much of everything that the world is overrun. We can see this in our world today: the more development, the more progress, the more problems, the more violence, the more mental illness, and the more difficulties and distress.

Let us seek the right sort of development, which turns inward toward our own depths. Making mind right comes first, so that we are genuine human beings. Then our life journey won't lead to more suffering. As everything gathers in mind, cultivating mind is essential.

> *Jivitaṃ attabhāvo ca sukhadukkhā ca kevalā*
> Everything, including life, self-image, well-being, and pain,
> *Ekacittasamāyuttā*
> Occurs together with this single mind.
> *Lahuso vattate khaṇo*
> Change proceeds very rapidly.

So, don't be negligent and passive. Practice promptly amid the ceaselessly and rapidly changing moments of time. May you be successful in this precious human birth that has discovered Buddha-Dhamma.

4

THE RESULT OF MENTAL CULTIVATION IS PATH, FRUIT, AND NIBBĀNA

Today, we'll look at the result of mental cultivation, which is path, fruit, and nibbāna.[1] Some of you might shake your heads, thinking that you've heard enough about meditation and psycho-spiritual development and the magga-phala-nibbāna that results. If any of you feel this way, please be patient, focus, and listen especially well because this talk isn't about anything you already know well. There are things you as yet don't know about or know well; profound things that you need to understand. So bear with us and pay attention while we expand the subject of mental cultivation and its result—path, fruit, and nibbāna. We will cover the topic exhaustively, comprehensively, in detail, and in every way one could want. This won't just be repetition of old stuff; if you listen well you will realize that.

Down-to-Earth Levels of Path, Fruit, and Nibbāna

You probably have heard about path and fruit (*magga-phala*), about realization, already, but only as a lofty matter. You might have heard of them as the province, for instance, of those who dwell in seclusion and strive to attain them in order to be arahant. Perhaps you don't realize that these words may refer to quite ordinary affairs. There is realization of path and fruit even in villages and homes. The ordinary meaning is to successfully accomplish something, although not to the extent of becoming arahant.

A similar thing happens with nibbāna, in that people hear the word and immediately think of the nibbāna of the arahants. Or they think of it as a place—the whereabouts of which make no sense. Perhaps people think of some other world where we go when we die. Either way, they won't be aware of the more down-to-earth forms of nibbāna that we must have in our everyday lives. If we didn't recognize this ordinary, domestic level of nibbāna, then as a rule, there's no way that we would be able to understand the fullest version, that of arahant. Unless we have nibbāna with us every day at home and at work, we'll never find the path to the fullest nibbāna. Hence path, fruit, and nibbāna have down-to-earth meanings that we should be aware of.

Regarding path and fruit, anything we do can realize them on the level appropriate to that activity. Hence, we might say that this year's rice cultivation didn't achieve the necessary level of path and fruit because this year's harvest was poor. To fall short in something means that path (the proper means to achieve something) and fruit (the results of path carried out skillfully) haven't been fully realized. As a start, you ought to be interested in this sort of magga-phala.

Nibbāna should be considered in a similar way. *Nibbāna* means "cool," and it manifests within life, making life cool. *Nibbāna* can describe the ordinary household life when it is cool, without trouble and strife, and people are satisfied. Regrettably, we've lost this everyday language meaning of nibbāna; it has become something too rarified for ordinary people to comprehend. In ancient times, the term was commonly used with regard to all kinds of household matters when they involved something cooling down. For instance, putting out a fire was referred to as "making the fire nibbāna." When a goldsmith dowses gold that has been heated till glowing, the gold is "nibbāna-ed." Even in the kitchen, when waiting for rice and curry to become cool enough to eat, the word *nibbāna* applies. The everyday, ordinary meaning of *nibbāna* was "cool," "cooled," or "made cool."

Let's comprehend the meanings of each word in every day, worldly language and in Dhamma language to understand Dhamma in a truly beneficial way. As it is, much of what people learn about Buddhism isn't put into effective practice, no matter how much they claim to understand. Therefore, we must reexamine all these terms to reach a genuinely beneficial understanding. When path and fruit are with you in your daily life, you will do everything as well as possible; and anything done properly with care and attention will result in a peaceful mind and cool heart, which is the meaning of nibbāna. Even cooking food can be a cultivation of path and fruit that results in nibbāna.

Understanding the Dhamma Language Created from Everyday Language

All Dhamma language is borrowed from ordinary, everyday speech. The hundreds of Dhamma-language terms found in the Pali texts are borrowed from languages already in common use. Those who searched for and discovered Dhamma couldn't create a new language to explain their experiences because nobody else would understand. Only by borrowing from languages already in use could people begin to comprehend.

For example, the word *nibbāna* means "cool," as in the everyday meanings already mentioned. Hermits and ascetics who lived in the forests for long periods discovered the Dhamma that cools the heart. On returning to society, they told ordinary people about discovering coolness, which was a new kind of coolness that householders had yet to experience. These ordinary people were interested because the ordinary coolness they experienced wasn't sufficient, fully satisfying, and of the highest degree. Once those forest dwellers discovered something superior, they still used the word *nibbāna*, "coolness," when describing it to village and city dwellers.

One can ascend through the levels of nibbāna, through the "cool," the "cooler," the "cooler still," until the "coolest of the cool" appears—that of the ending of the corruptions. Not having experienced more refined kinds of coolness, one might understand the satisfaction arising from the acquisition of a desired object, which cools the desiring mind, as being nibbāna. However, that isn't sustainable. It's merely a brief coolness and is ultimately deceptive because it doesn't deal with the underlying causes of heat. Still, people didn't understand any better until the meditative discoveries of mental calmness and stability, absorption, and attainment. These were believed to be nibbāna and were enthusiastically pursued. Each deeper level was successively cooler, and the Buddha's last two teachers taught the coolest levels: *ākiñcaññāyatana* (absorption in nothingness) and *nevasaññānāsaññāyatana* (absorption in neither experiencing nor not-experiencing).[2] The Buddha-to-be, however, couldn't accept that these were all there was to coolness and freedom. He continued searching until he realized the ending of self-clinging, kilesas, and karma. When self-clinging ends, the corruptions dry up and disappear along with all karma, both old and new. Karma naturally disappears when self-clinging is wiped out. This is how the Buddha finally discovered true nibbāna, the ultimate coolness, and then informed others using that familiar name.

Other groups had their own versions of nibbāna. The term was used widely but with varying and particular meanings. The lowest level is found in the story of Kīsā Gotamī, when she calmed down after losing her mind over family tragedies. This can still be called *nibbāna.* Then there's the king who saw the Buddha-to-be and said, "Whoever this person is the son of, that mother and father will be cool (*nibbuto*)." The parents won't have any anxiety or worry about their son. This was the ordinary level of nibbāna in general usage back then. Higher levels of nibbāna were discovered subsequently.

When we recognize that there are many levels of nibbāna, which are available according to our circumstances, we discover the sort of nibbāna we need, the kind that we should want, which is the accessible level of nibbāna that we can have all the time. Get to know this form of nibbāna, bring it into life. Even though it's not the highest form—not yet the coolness arising from the complete ending of the kilesas (corruptions) and *āsavas* (effluents)—we all can have a contented, "cooled" life here and now. Don't just go on living with the heat and continual disturbance of the afflictions. Path, fruit, and nibbāna have levels of realization, so live a life accompanied by some level of nibbāna. At least be someone who is contented. Don't worry about putting an end to the corruptions and being arahant. Just live your life, but be smarter and more careful than other people, and dwell with a contented mind, achieving wholesome worldly benefits as you are able. Perhaps genuine nibbāna will be your final destination.

The Coolness of Suññatā

That was, more or less, what the Buddha said to a group of householders, along with their wives and children, who called on him. They asked him to explain the dhamma, the teaching, that would be most useful for people such as them. In response, the Buddha spoke of the core sutta teaching concerning suññatā. That is, he told them that if they lived with understanding of suññatā, voidness of self, in whatever happened there would be no need for agitation and affliction. He said this to ordinary householders, to farmers, with families and homes. Whatever happened, they would suffer no dukkha because of family affairs, possessions, and livelihood. He taught suññatā, this highest teaching of Buddhism, on a par with nibbāna, to ordinary people. Understanding suññatā means that things are just what they are and follow their nature. Fields and crops, cattle and buffalo, work and business, play out according to their natural realities. Whatever happens, there's no need for anxiety. Just deal with it as needed. Don't take such things to be "me" or "mine," then nothing that happens to them will create distress, agitation, or dukkha.

When I say these sorts of things, some claim that I'm lying, and others accuse me of deceiving people. Well, I suppose the people around here are the most deceived anywhere, because they regularly hear about the level of nibbāna that's available to those living ordinary, everyday lives. Everyone can say what they like, but I'll always tell people, no matter what kind of life they lead, to dwell with understanding of suññatā, that anything and everything is naturally void of any meaning of a lasting or essential self. And that when things change, as indeed they must, we needn't like or dislike the results and confuse ourselves. Such a life is cool and calm. Don't do anything with expectation, with foolish desire, with hunger, or with selfishness. Then, for instance, farmers will work their fields properly, in the best possible manner, and will enjoy their work. They will be happy waiting for the seed heads to fill out and ripen, and they will be contented when harvesting the crop. Such wise farmers won't harbor any hopes or expectations that the crop will ripen early or with heavy yields, because it would be foolish to live that way.

Consider the Buddha's story of the hen, how the hen incubates her eggs properly, and the chicks hatch themselves when the time comes. If that hen were to be disturbed by expectations or anxieties concerning the chicks, worrying when they will hatch, she would be a crazy hen. So be careful to not be a crazy hen, a crazy farmer, or a crazy entrepreneur. Rather, be cool from beginning to end, be cool throughout the year, be cool through understanding suññatā enough for *suññatā-paṭisaṃyutta*, for living especially connected with suññatā.[3]

Such knowledge enables us to see that anything and everything is empty of and free from the meanings of "being self" and "belonging to self," which brings mastery. When things are as they are and happen and change as they do, they are seen as just so and suffering over them is pointless. We do the best we can under the circumstances, and things will happen as they ought to. If there's a mistake, let it pass and don't worry. Slipping up once every four or five chances can be disregarded. Learn to let go. Live bearing in mind that whether something comes our way or doesn't come our way, it will be "just like that." Whether we get what we expect or we don't, it will be "just how it is." We won't dwell in hope and expectation. If we must hope for something, we do so with mindfulness and wisdom rather than a hope that is foolish, full of hunger, and mixed up with corruptions. With mindful, wise wishes, we'll want what we ought to want and we'll do what we can without harboring any hope or expectation for a particular result.

Living in such a way doesn't involve taṇhā, ignorant desire. It involves *saṅkappa* (wise want). When monks give blessings, they don't wish that your desires come true. Instead, they wish for your wise aspirations (*saṅkappas*) to come to fruition. If there is expectation, because it comes from foolish desire, there will be dukkha. Whenever our desire is wisely guided, there isn't any foolish expectation. Then if something doesn't happen as aimed, we'll accept it with a smile—that is, without any dukkha. When feelings of disappointment happen, let them go, observe them, and learn. If a wish falls apart, don't let it bite you. After all, that's just how life is.

Life is cool when we live wisely. Cool living is what we've been building up to. Life isn't hot and anxious when we live rightly. There's contentedness and well-being as fits our reality. We live without neuroses or worse, unlike the majority who live the hot, tortured life and have the neuroses and mental imbalances to show for it, if not even more serious problems.

Hence, I encourage you to widen your understanding of path, fruit, and nibbāna until they become part of your everyday life. When raising chickens or pigs, or growing rice, or whatever your livelihood, let it be a matter of path and fruit. Doing our ordinary activities as a matter of path and fruit just means doing them properly, in the most complete and correct manner. This is the kind of life we all need, so I invite you to consider the meaning of path, fruit, and nibbāna, which is the fruition of citta-bhāvanā.

Understanding Citta-Bhāvanā in Every Opportunity

Next, we need to explore the meaning of citta-bhāvanā (mental cultivation) because most of you have only heard of meditation as something practiced by people in forests and caves for developing samādhi and vipassanā. That understanding is too narrow to be of much benefit.

Mental cultivation must mean making mind completely clear and unblemished. Anything that improves mind to some extent is mental cultivation. Even if it's only a little bit better, that still is citta-bhāvanā. We don't have to do it the same way as others, sitting in the usual postures with the approved methods. Even if we follow a method of our own that other people don't accept as valid, if our method is capable of developing mind, it qualifies as citta-bhāvanā. We make today's mind better than yesterday's. Any approach that restrains, clears, or stills today's mind so that it can solve problems better than yesterday's mind is mental cultivation. Providing, that is, the cultivation is the result of our own activities. When mind just develops naturally that isn't considered mental cultivation, because we haven't done anything. If it's better because of our activities, studies, and training, we can call it *citta-bhāvanā*. Let's just say, one is a little smarter day by day.

Any kind of work that one has observed well and done better and smarter than before is mental cultivation too. Hence, an artist working skillfully and thinking creatively is automatically cultivating mind in the process. Everyone who must be mindful and intelligent in their work should recognize the mental cultivation of improving mind. Farmers, businesspeople, doctors, lawyers, or whomever, when acting in ways that improve their minds, becoming sharper and cleverer, fall within the scope of citta-bhāvanā.

We've been looking at the terms *path*, *fruit*, *nibbāna*, and *mental cultivation* to generate a broader understanding of their meanings. Try to see these important terms, which are usually interpreted too narrowly, in a new light that is more correct and profound. Understand their meanings more fully. Mental cultivation isn't about sitting in the forest and muttering to oneself. It's about making mind better no matter where, when, or how it is done.

Anyone who, day and night, always does things in a careful, comprehensive, and well-balanced manner cultivates mind nicely; while anyone who does things carelessly, excitedly, or hurriedly doesn't understand the meaning of citta-bhāvanā. The more formal approach to meditation, to vipassanā and the like, such as finding a peaceful, isolated place to practice, is correct as far as it goes, yet may be too specialized for most people, or may become ritualistic. We need to adjust and improve our approaches so that ordinary people can manage, which will allow them more opportunities to improve mind. Speaking a little vulgarly, we might say that it's possible to cultivate mind while sitting on the toilet. If you don't believe this, go and try it. I guarantee that it can be done, and even may be done more easily or conveniently than at other times because when one sits on the toilet, worries and anxieties disappear. Sometimes the sensations of passing stool become the sole focus of attention and one can contemplate effectively because mind has just one object. So practice mental cultivation at every opportunity and at all times, even when sitting on the toilet. While this seems inappropriate to bring up, if I don't mention it, you might never find out.

This Mind Can Be Trained and Developed

We need to continue talking about mind-related matters, although it's something we've already talked about so much that some people are bored by it now. They shake their heads and don't want to listen. They feel I've been overly repetitive in saying "mind is the sort of nature that can be improved, trained, and cultivated." Regardless of that, there are a great number of ignorant people who claim mind can't be trained, that it isn't possible. They excuse themselves with hackneyed expressions, such as "You can't teach an old dog new tricks." I, however, insist that it can, that habits and traits of mind are things that can be rectified. Don't be delusional, thinking that it can't change. Mind can change when we use the right methods.

Old habits can be rectified and uprooted. Only foolish people would blindly insist otherwise, stubbornly insisting that character can't be changed. If we follow fundamental Dhamma principles, such as the law of conditionality (*idappaccayatā*), the law of nature, there isn't anything that doesn't change. If Buddhism has any meaning, habits and traits of mind can change. Those who cling to the view that such things cannot change will have to die that way. Anyone who thinks such change is possible and follows genuine Dhamma will benefit accordingly.

In fact, habits are just repeating patterns of behavior that, through usage, increase in strength over time. If we don't repeat them, they weaken and diminish naturally. When we're greedy, if we repeat that sort of behavior, little by little we deepen the greed habit through repetition. Some people go crazy with anger because the habit was gradually built up over many repetitions. We can weaken these habit patterns by not indulging the habit when triggered to do so. Every time something tempts us to anger, simply allow it to pass without an angry reaction, and the strength of that habit pattern will decrease. Every time we manage ourselves skillfully, we diminish the habit of anger until it disappears altogether. This would mean that the anusaya, the underlying tendency toward anger, had disappeared.

The anusayas are underlying tendencies or inclinations toward certain behaviors. The underlying tendency toward greed is called *rāgānusaya*, the underlying tendency toward anger is *paṭighānusaya*, and the underlying tendency toward stupidity is *avijjānusaya*. The Buddha spoke of these tendencies as things that can be decreased little by little by not activating them when provoked. So don't mess with them. Whenever something happens that could stimulate greed, expectation, passion, and the like, don't mess with it. The greedy tendency will decrease a little. The next time something similar comes along, don't mess with it either, and the greedy tendency will decrease a little more. We deal with habitual traits such as anger and fear in the same way. Each time we do so, the habit loses strength. When something comes along that normally provokes fear or any form of foolishness, don't be afraid, don't be foolish. If we're mindful each time, fear won't arise. The habit of fear thereby decreases until we're no longer foolishly afraid of anything. This is how to remove such tendencies and habits.

Please understand that mind can be improved until it seems the complete opposite of what it was before. Once prone to greed, to foolish desire—not anymore. Once prone to anger and hatred—not anymore. Once prone to fear, to foolishness, to delusion, to carelessness—not anymore. Mind can be improved until all of them—greed, anger, hatred, and fear—are uprooted and no longer occur in mind. Such exalted results require an advanced way of practice.

On a more ordinary level, even children can improve their minds. So, parents, don't be foolish. Don't raise your children to increase their greed, anger, and hatred, or to fear things they need not fear, which build unhealthy habits of mind in them. Don't deceive children and foster infatuation with pretty and lovely things or fear of things such as spiders and lizards. Parental ignorance is at the bottom of such foolishness. So don't teach children wrong habits that cause them to fall badly into the thicket of loving, hating, and fearing. Too much of that is hard to escape from and makes cultivating mind so much more difficult. If parents raised and taught their children correctly from the start, these problems of excessive greed, anger, and fear wouldn't exist. Wise parents haven't harmed their children by causing problems that are difficult for the children to correct as adults. Unfortunately, when parents make such mistakes, they create difficulties for their children and eventually for us all.

That mind can be improved means that it can be cultivated. With such understanding, citta-bhāvanā occurs naturally. For anyone who disagrees with this and stubbornly insists mind can't change, mental cultivation won't happen. Their obstinacy prevents it. In other words, for anyone to cultivate mind, they must first have this basic understanding.

To sum up, there is this natural fact that mind can be cultivated. It's quite possible to completely remove the undesirable factors. The unfortunate habits of mind that have been developing since early in our lives and that cause us to repeatedly go astray can be effaced. Even patterns carried over from previous lives can be removed. However, I don't want to talk about previous lives now because that sort of thing can't be demonstrated directly. Being coerced into believing what others assert without ourselves personally experiencing the matter goes against Buddhist principles, so we don't talk about things that can't be seen directly and personally. I don't want to make anyone believe anything. Others can do what they please; here, we'll just talk about things that can be experienced. Any habits that have been built up since infancy and childhood can be put right. They can be adjusted, they can be abandoned, until character totally changes and there's no more dukkha.

Mind Learns and Improves of Its Own Accord

Let's now look in detail at the phenomena known as citta. Mind is strange and marvelous. One marvelous quality is that its true nature is to be one of the elements (*dhātus*, fundamental properties of experience), but not those you hear about the most—the earth, water, fire, and wind elements. It is an element of another kind, variously called *mano-dhātu* (sense-experiencing element), *citta-dhātu* (mind element), and *arūpa-dhātu* (formless element), each term highlighting an aspect of mind. This mind element is similar to the usual elements in merely being a natural element, although its properties make it different. The functions of mind element are knowing, feeling, and experiencing. It can experience and know everything if it is properly trained. At present, it only knows certain things and operates in a limited way. However, when trained properly it becomes fully aware.

Babies, after emerging from the womb, begin to learn from experiences. For instance, picking up things that bite, they learn to not grab such things again. Touching fire and feeling the heat, they learn to not touch fire. This is a natural property of the mind element: it knows and learns things for itself. As children grow up, they gradually learn to discriminate, to make choices, to reckon, and to think. Mind knows sense contacts and their results. It feels the pleasant and the unpleasant sense experiences. Feeling pain with a sense experience, such as grasping something hot, mind learns the lesson of that sense contact. The pain teaches it to be afraid to touch it again. Children know this; they don't need their parents to explain it. When told not to touch fire, children don't just believe the adults; they touch the fire and then believe through knowing for themselves. Similarly, children avoid contact with stinging insects once they know from experience what the result will be. At first, they lacked such knowledge. After grabbing insects and getting stung or bitten, they learn their lessons. Mind, then, knows fear and is unwilling to do the same thing again.

I hope you will be interested in how this mind can be aware, experience, and learn from its experiences, and consequentially develop stage by stage. As with children being careful around fire, mind learns to be careful, make adjustments, and improve of its own accord. What's a better way to do something? Small children steadily observe and learn gradually, thus increasing their understanding of many things. Parents and teachers can't teach them these sorts of things and don't get any chances to do so, since children do what's necessary themselves, which amounts to an amazing quality of mind.

Physical control and self-restraint increase as the burgeoning variety of sense experiences teach and chasten children. They learn what's dangerous and are satisfied with good results, steadily learning what's better. This is a truly marvelous quality of mind. With eyes, ears, nose, tongue, and the body surface, and the stimulation of visual forms, sounds, odors, flavors, and touches, mind is brought into play. Through these involvements, mind grows ever more intelligent in such matters. Thus there is increasing development in every way through the influence of mind. When mind inclines in some way, the body will follow its lead. There are many details to this for us to observe. Perhaps you've learned useful perspectives from science that can aid mind's cultivation. Recognize the qualities of mind. Learn to make the most of mind's marvelous qualities. We can derive much benefit from its prodigious capabilities.

For the reasons just mentioned, you have good hopes for mental cultivation. Please take advantage of this and receive the benefits of citta-bhāvanā—either directly in your own case, or indirectly where others are concerned, such as your children. Particularly where it concerns those yet to be born, the future generations, give them opportunities for the sort of psychological and spiritual cultivation that will be useful and healthy. Otherwise, theirs will be aimless, unplanned, and confused development. Their minds will go astray and develop wrong understanding, becoming a danger to themselves and to everyone else.

Understand the difference, then commit to cultivating mind in the right way, so that it will be able to attain all the levels of path, fruit, and nibbāna.

Dhamma Studied Adequately Avoids Developing in the Misguided Way of Materialism

If mental and spiritual cultivation had been correct from the time of our forest-dwelling ancestors up until the present time, the human world would be much better off than it is, a more excellent place. At present, it's full of wickedness and treachery because development, for the most part, has been allowed to follow its naturally ignorant course. As a species, little of our development has been guided by mindfulness and wisdom. And we're still going in the wrong direction, which is sad and disappointing.

When humankind arose into the world, we knew how to find food and survive. As we experienced material progress, we grew infatuated with the material side of life instead of focusing our interest on psycho-spiritual cultivation. Through simple unawareness, humanity developed only materially and quite unconsciously fell into the worship of materialism. The more materialism satisfied us, the more involved we became. Hence, one-sided material development fostered delusion. Although there was some psychological development and those who explored mental cultivation, they couldn't challenge the materialistic developers. Hence, materialism came out on top; it has been more powerful and attractive, enticing people into the materialist path with its many forms of stimulation. Consequently, material progress has been rapid, especially in the last century. It has prospered greatly since the time of the forest dwellers who, to give one example, hadn't domesticated animals for transport, while people today fly in airplanes.

This is the result of lopsided material development. Spiritual cultivation, which lacks the stimulations and enticements, simply can't compete. The pioneers of former times who recognized the gratifications of the materialistic path as deceiving, and who sought to explore psychically and spiritually, couldn't compete. Those hermits and sages (*munis*) found meaningful spiritual contentment but their examples were no competition for materialism. Material progress has been allowed to lead the way right through to the present time. Spiritual cultivation that offers peace and quiet, that doesn't excite and stimulate the nervous system, that doesn't arouse tainted feelings and desires, hasn't been a leading force in human progress. With humanity having gone astray since the start, materialism has prevailed such that there's hardly anyone now who prefers the quiet and peace of spiritual contentment.

I calculate that if humankind had taken the way of mental cultivation from the start, since the original forest-dwelling times, the world would be pervaded with it now and, as a result, would be free of decadence and evil. Ours would be a wonderful, inspiring world. But how can this come to be while the whole human world is in the grip of rampant consumerism?

Take a good look and you will see that we're living in a mess that we humans have created ourselves. Humanity prefers material progress to the extent that the whole human world is intoxicated with it. Interest in Dhamma and spirituality can't compete. The thirst and passion for stimulation is very strong. We worship material things that satisfy our corrupted desires, and consequently we must deal with the karmic results. In this world beset by ignorance and the worship of materialism, there is steadily increasing selfishness. Competition, envy, violence, and oppression have become the norm because this world doesn't know the value of spiritual cultivation. Most of humanity lives in this way, while a small minority of seekers must also live with consequences of others' unskillful behavior.[4]

It's up to us to find a way to avoid being stuck with the majority, to have a method for our minds to slip outside the mainstream. Although everybody else may be insane, we won't be. We'll stay true to living in the right way. This shows us how much Dhamma understanding is needed—enough that we don't go crazy even though everyone else may be crazed with material things. How do we live in a world worshipping and spinning around with material things—technology, consumer conveniences, and physical health? With enough Dhamma, we can remain sane midst the materialism. Dhamma can manage this challenge; otherwise, we'll end up jumping on the consumer bandwagon too.

This is the obstacle confronting mental cultivation. We need to resist it. Followers of the Buddha can't just give up; to be real Buddhists, we need to preserve the Buddha's qualities of knowing, awakening, and fully blossoming. Thus mental cultivation must always be in the mix; if lacking, we won't be Buddhists anymore. Especially now, we need to combat the burgeoning misunderstanding prevalent in the world. Of course it is difficult, but it must be done, because the hardship is better than dying. To fail is to die spiritually, left with mind degenerate and crude. Such spiritual death is more sinister than physical death. Therefore Buddhists are dedicated to keeping alive the qualities of awakening, wisdom, and freshness. Buddhists are triumphant by not sleepwalking through life, understanding how things are and blossoming in well-being and coolness.

A New Life of Sīla, Samādhi, and Paññā

Genuine mental cultivation is the development of fully integrated sīla, samādhi, and paññā in which the three elements support one another fully and work together harmoniously. Like the legs of a tripod, leave out one and the whole thing falls. This is as true of everyday life as of meditation practice. All the physical aspects of ordinary household life must be well ordered, carefully arranged, and correct—behavior and speech, the home, possessions and livelihood, bodily health, and manners. "Right" or "correct" means that we are sufficient without being excessive in what we do and use. We apply ourselves so that we do what is right without being tense or slack about it, so that we are relaxed and balanced in sīla. Merely reciting precepts doesn't cut it; sīla is about how we actually behave regarding all physical aspects of life.

Ordinary folks also require mental balance and naturalness, which is what Buddhism means by "normal." When we're mentally correct, we have the mental steadiness, focus, and strength (*samādhi*) to carry out all our activities and work, large and small. We aren't forgetful and distracted. Then, correct sīla and samādhi work in tandem.

We cultivate wisdom by studying and learning how to live as human beings. Don't follow the wrong understandings that can't tell right from wrong and safe from dangerous, that lead to doing things we shouldn't do and accumulating things we shouldn't acquire. We need the understanding that properly guides life in all activities and all situations in what is truly beneficial. We apply wisdom in our homes, with our families, and in all areas of our lives.

This natural sīla, samādhi, and paññā is the genuine kind, much better than showy recitations. Living them each day is of real benefit to ourselves and others. Don't just talk as a Buddhist, live Buddhism in down-to-earth sīla, samādhi, and paññā. This is how we integrate them as one and they become one with our lives.

We can't force sīla, samādhi, and paññā on anyone, but parents can lovingly train their children in appropriate and integrated sīla, samādhi, and paññā. Similarly, sincere Buddhists happily show others how to have all three legs of practice in everyday activities.

Without genuine, natural, and integrated citta-bhāvanā, we are deficient as human beings, which bankrupts and ruins us. Even animals require the healthy integration of the sīla, samādhi, and paññā, appropriate to their nature. Otherwise they die. When all three are correct, animals thrive. Human beings are on a much different level than other animals, so we need to cultivate sīla, samādhi, and paññā even more so, as fits our human nature. May you be satisfied with our human needs and potentials. Please, make sure that the three components are each sufficient and that they cooperate seamlessly. When properly functioning together, they form the foundation of our life.

This is the life of cultivation. Developing life involves cultivating mind, and cultivating mind means developing life. This life of correct, balanced, and integrated sīla, samādhi, and paññā can be called "new life," because we never knew it before. The prophets of certain religions have offered new life to their followers. Although we have no record of the Buddha using this term, if he had, he would have meant life replete with true and natural sīla, samādhi, and paññā. If it seems new, that's because it's the sort of life we haven't known before.

Try practicing according to these principles and you will discover new life. Formerly, life will have been murky, hot, and trapped. Under the spell of kilesas, life is uncomfortable and heavy. Now you'll get a life that is cool, bright, and free. Before, when the corruptions had power over life, there wasn't genuine freedom. If life is dominated by the afflictions, we react greedily when greed is provoked and angrily when anger is provoked. That kind of life isn't free. Now that we offer you new life, you needn't carry those old conditions anymore. New life is cool, without burdens. In this sort of life, the afflictions and hindrances can't make demands.

Formerly, the kilesas laid claim to life, took it over, and made us do whatever they wanted. Even the hindrances—more ordinary and less powerful than fully formed greed, anger, and delusion—made demands, provoked our minds, and disturbed life. The nīvaraṇa of sensual desire induced mind to keep busy with sexual wishes, demanding acquiescence. The nīvaraṇa of ill will induced aversion and antipathy. The other hindrances induced mental lethargy and dullness, or distraction and scatteredness, or doubt and confusion, such that we didn't know what was going on. Previously, even the minor forms of affliction, the nīvaraṇas, laid claim to life, pushed us this way and that, and led us around. That wasn't freedom.

Now we can dwell above the power of those things. They can't bother us even when there's cause for full-blown corruption. New life, as promised by various prophets, is available through the life of well-integrated sīla, samādhi, and paññā. You can expand these three into the noble eightfold path; still, the three legs are the essence of new life. This is the fruit of citta-bhāvanā.

5

THE NEW LIFE OF PATH, FRUIT, AND NIBBĀNA

In the previous chapter we began looking at the new way of life that comes with proper mental cultivation. Other religious systems make this point too—especially Christianity, wherein Jesus talks about giving people a new life. Although Buddhists have similar teachings, and take them further, nobody is much interested in the new kind of life taught in the Pali texts. Because we hold the Pali terms as sacred and are rigid in how we translate and interpret them, we have trouble translating such teachings in understandable and meaningful ways. For our purposes here, we will maintain that developing life by developing mind results in a new kind of life.

Now, many questions can be asked as to what constitutes this new life, far too many to deal with here. But we can say that, essentially, the new life is trouble-free, free from the kilesas and nīvaraṇas.

Understanding the Corruptions and Hindrances

The normal life of worldly people, what we could call "old life," is just the sort that the kilesas and nīvaraṇas can make demands upon.[1] The kilesas (corruptions, afflictions) are lobha, dosa, and moha (greed, aversion, and delusion). These arise and dominate mind, pull it around, and make it think and react in troubled ways. This is what the early Pali texts meant by "make demands upon." *Rāga* (lust), a close companion of greed, pulls mind into lustful thinking, all the more so in this era when the human world is full of lust-inducing things. The worldwide, ever-increasing production of goods and services that people buy to enjoy serves to encourage rāga and lobha. Hence, lust and greed have many opportunities to lay claim to the minds of people, making them chase after what stimulates them. People are routinely under the power of the corruptions of greed, lust, and passion.

Dosa, also, regularly takes possession of the human mind, as when one feels ill will toward someone else. Displeasure, opposition, malice, and misanthropy are versions of dosa making demands. Aversion, anger, and hatred are regular ways that dosa makes demands on our minds and takes over human life.

Moha—delusion, foolishness, misunderstanding—consistently creates demands because it is full of ignorance and confuses intelligence. With it, we don't know things as they really are. Moha causes uncertainty and doubt, even about knowing what is safe and healthy for own lives. Moha makes us wary and keeps us on edge. In this guise of uncertainty or foolish fear, moha is a regular, taxing occurrence. These three are the basic corruptions on the full-fledged level: lobha and rāga, greed and lust; dosa, aversion and hatred; and moha, delusion and confusion.

The Hindrances Are Weaker and More Common

Then there are the nīvaraṇas (hindrances). The nīvaraṇas have the same lineage as the kilesas but aren't strong enough to be considered full-fledged kilesas. The nīvaraṇas are lighter versions of troubles that arise often, easily, and instinctually. That is, they don't need a strong stimulus or object to concoct them. We should have a clear and sufficient understanding of the nīvaraṇas; otherwise, they will boss mind day and night. As long as we don't know about them and how they pester us, we can't be fully awake.

The first of the nīvaraṇas is kāma-chanda: the inclination toward or desire for sexual stimulation, often aimed at the opposite sex. This is quite troublesome because it's basically instinctual. Nature gave us the sexual organs and the urge to use them. Children are born into the world equipped with their sexual apparatus. When the time arrives for them to fulfill this function, the demand for sexual satisfaction arises. For instance, adolescents have feelings of this kind disturbing and dominating their minds. This hindering may seem to be without immediate cause, because it happens so frequently and easily. How much do they disturb mind? Anyone who has been through adolescence knows how intensely and often the nīvaraṇa of kāma-chanda disturbs mind. In the special life of path, fruit, and nibbāna, however, this sort of thing makes few, if any, demands. When we understand kāma-chanda as basically natural and instinctual, we will see the value of path, fruit, and nibbāna. We will see the value of the psycho-spiritual cultivation that results in a new life in which such demands don't exist, or barely so and well within our power to manage.

The second nīvaraṇa is byāpāda (ill will), which is akin to dosa and kodha (aversion and anger). It isn't as intense as the full-scale kilesa, but still wears us out. This feeling of displeasure, dislike, or irritation is a common mental darkening, the keynote of which is dissatisfaction. People who have a particular problem with this nīvaraṇa are always ready to find fault with something or other. Because of this, they are continually stressed, tense day and night. Their minds are consistently simmering. If, however, such people have more developed minds, the new life that comes with path, fruit, and nibbāna isn't bothered by this feeling. How much better, more comfortable, and cooler would that be?

The third nīvaraṇa is thīna-middha (dullness and drowsiness of mind). It produces a mind lacking energy, that is tired, slow, and sluggish. Sometimes we're weary, bored with life, or so fed up that we don't want to do anything. At times like that, even if we do something, we will do it badly. This sort of thing disturbs mind often. However, that can't happen to the well-cultivated mind.

The next nīvaraṇa moves in the opposite direction and is equally demanding. Uddhacca-kukkucca is wandering and scattering busyness. The distracted and scattered mind is busily disturbing and can't do anything beneficially. It occurs easily, naturally, and instinctually. Consider just how much and how often there has been restless distraction in your life. Then consider how the new life isn't bothered in this way.

The last hindrance is vicikicchā, being uncertain as to "what's what." This mind is disturbed by insufficient knowledge and dull intelligence such that it can't cut through doubt and uncertainty concerning what we need, must do, or is true and correct. Life is full of things to inspire mistrust, suspicion, and doubt—particularly where life itself is concerned. Are we safe? Am I living in the right way? We seek certainty about such matters. However, there is no certainty in life about who we are, what's safe, what will benefit us, or what will make us happy. This nīvaraṇa of doubt keeps us looking for the impossible till our last moments. New life is free of such doubts.

New Life Is Free of Hindrances and Corruptions

The nīvaraṇas are a big deal, but people aren't much interested in them. There is widespread willful ignorance about how they hinder and bother us, because people don't understand how harmful and dangerous they are and how much they disturb the inner life. Consequently, they are seldom abandoned.

If asked whether the kilesas or the nīvaraṇas are more difficult to leave behind, perhaps we might choose the nīvaraṇas. If we compare the two, the kilesas are like the bite of a tiger, something that can be fatal, while the nīvaraṇas are akin to the gnats that swarm around our ears, eyes, and nose. Seldom a danger to life, they are regular pests that create plenty of disturbance and are difficult to tolerate. Perhaps we are more bothered by the everyday annoyance of the gnats than the bite of a tiger, which is less common. At times, the gnats are almost intolerable.

Please think about this: Life without the demands of kilesas and nīvaraṇas, just how much of a new life is that? When such contaminations aren't active, we can do whatever we must without the usual disturbances. Things such as sexual passion don't lead us by the nose. We can relax when such demands don't dominate us. We can sleep soundly at night without them keeping us awake thinking about satisfying our desires or aversions. Even though we don't get up and follow our desires, we are tormented by the demands made by desire. The Pali texts tell the story of a warrior king with great power and wealth who could hardly sleep because his mind was plagued by the nīvaraṇas—especially that of sexual desire. He followed their demands and sought satisfaction, but once he returned to his room, the disturbance would always return and keep him from sleeping. If the kilesas wake up, it's like having a blazing fire in mind. But if it's like a smoldering, tiring kind of disturbance, then it's the nīvaraṇas doing their thing.

New Life of Harmonious Ethics, Focus, and Wisdom

New life is free of being stimulated, cluttered, and consumed by the kilesas and nīvaraṇas. Understanding this is a start to further deepening and clarifying our understanding of what new life is like. In other words, it helps us to understand the results of cultivating mind—namely, path, fruit, and nibbāna. As discussed earlier, this cultivation occurs through the harmonious mix of sīla, samādhi, and paññā. Living correctly by way of ethical actions and speech; gathering mind in samādhi that is pure, strong, fit, and ready to do its work; and understanding wisely, deeply, and truly. These working together as one is the fruit of true psycho-spiritual cultivation. If the body and speech aren't developed, mind can't be developed either. This is because sīla forms the basis on which psychological development depends. Hence, we have proper sīla first, and then there can be proper samādhi and proper paññā. When these three components are correct, the cultivation of life and mind is expressed as path, fruit, and nibbāna. Remember this: developing life, developing mind, results in path, fruit, and nibbāna.

Together, path, fruit, and nibbāna provide another meaning to life—new life, a cool life untroubled by the demands of corruptions and hindrances. And this clarifies the purpose of citta-bhāvanā. Please don't put this in a sacred chest to worship in words but not know in experience. If we know how to practice genuine citta-bhāvanā, we will taste the new life of coolness. It is free, liberated from all those demands.

We Buddhists like to talk about *vimutti* (deliverance, liberation), but we usually aren't clear what we're escaping from, because we haven't understood what is pressuring and binding us. This makes us ignorant Buddhists, ignorant of the kilesas and nīvaraṇas, the very problems we should take as the starting point for serious and progressive study.

The Flowing Benefits of Citta-Bhāvanā

The Buddha spoke of many benefits from citta-bhāvanā. Here, we can look at four benefits surveyed in the *Samādhi Sutta*,[2] although there are many others mentioned throughout the Pali suttas. First, when mind is well cultivated, it experiences happiness here and now, in this life, without having to wait for a heaven after death. While we can't be sure about who will be there to experience something after death, we are fully capable of experiencing this happiness ourselves here and now (*diṭṭhadhamma*). The well-developed mind can experience peaceful happiness whenever it wishes. It can free itself from troubles and suffering whenever it wishes, be at peace and contented right here, whether sitting, walking, standing, or whatever the posture. Such peace and happiness here and now in this life is the first flowing benefit (*ānisaṃsa*).

Without sufficient cultivation, we experience mostly greed, lusty love, anger, hatred, fear, anxiety, longing after the past, jealousy, envy, boredom, depression, and the like. We have no real happiness, no real contentment. If we develop mind, we'll possess the ability to chase those states away and live with a peaceful, healthy, stable, and contented mind. We'll have a mind that, depending on our level of attainment, can enjoy spiritual freedom, joy, equanimity, and real happiness—not the corrupted, deceptive version—and we might have it in this life whenever we wish.

Too often, people seek the troubled and deceptive kinds of happiness. Those who have the money jump in their cars and seek out places of entertainment and sensual stimulation. But is that true happiness? Or is it foolishness and infatuation? And might that border on insanity? On the other hand, with this first benefit, it's a simple matter of adjusting mind whenever there is the need for happiness. Without having to get into a car or spend any money, there is cool, peaceful happiness in line with nibbāna. This is the peacefulness of the kind of samādhi that puts an immediate end to the heat of the torments and corruptions, so there is real happiness right here and now. This is the first flowering of mental development.

The second benefit named by the Buddha concerns supernormal powers. These surpass the abilities of normal humans—that is, miraculous powers such as the "divine ear" and the "divine eye." They appear because mind has been properly developed. I don't want to emphasize these powers because they aren't the direct aim of practice. Nonetheless, they are possible and are mentioned in the Pali texts. It's possible to develop abilities beyond what is ordinary. This, then, is the second flowing benefit, although there's no pressing need for us to talk about it here.

The third benefit is essential: the perfection of *sati-sampajañña* (mindfulness with clear comprehension), both in worldly and Dhammic aspects. Sati-sampajañña is necessary for us to avoid making mistakes that create opportunities for afflictions that cause dukkha. Developing full and complete mindfully clear comprehension guarantees that the kilesas can't cause suffering. This is clearly comprehending mindfulness operating on the Dhamma level. Now, however, there's no such guarantee. We're short on sati-sampajañña, allowing the corruptions the opportunity to arise and bring dukkha.

The worldly level of mindfully clear comprehension allows ordinary people like us to manage our lives decently. Without this basic level of mindful, clear comprehension, our thinking is sloppy and our actions are careless. We hurry and don't take care. Our work suffers, whether farming or in business. Even minor things don't go well and our lives are cluttered with mishaps.

Having cultivated mind with excellent results—path, fruit, and nibbāna—we have full sati-sampajañña to use in both worldly and Dhamma affairs. We don't make mistakes or go astray in the worldly and the higher Dhammic aspects of life. With robust mindfully clear comprehension, we manage our affairs and stand up to the kilesas and quench dukkha. Path, fruit, and nibbāna resulting from mental cultivation bring the flowing benefit of full mindfulness with clear comprehension.

At present, everyone shares the basic daily problem of lacking sati-sampajañña when there is sense experience. With our eyes, ears, nose, tongue, body, and mind, which interact with sights, sounds, smells, tastes, tangibles, and mental objects, there is sense contact (*phassa*). As we don't have full sati-sampajañña, the corruptions arise: liking and disliking, followed by craving, clinging, becoming, and birth. If we have fully mindful and clear comprehension when sense contact occurs, these afflictions, these corruptions, won't happen. *Sati* (mindfulness) is the bringer of knowledge, and *sampajañña* is the appropriate knowledge it brings. Whatever we meet with the senses, sampajañña knows it's really "just like that." Hence, we don't fall into liking or disliking, pleasure or displeasure, and the troubles of corruptions aren't born. With mindfully clear comprehension always at hand, we put an end to the problems. This brings enormous benefit, so please, be interested.

The Highest Benefit Is Freedom from Effluents

The fourth benefit is the ending of the āsavas (effluents, outflows). With spiritual cultivation maturing in path, fruit, and nibbāna, mind is free of āsavas. Because it has been skillfully trained, regulated, maintained, and protected, all of which are aspects of citta-bhāvanā, mind changes completely. Mind that could do wrong now doesn't. It has a fully developed conscience. With sati-sampajañña, the anusayas aren't activated or added to, and the āsavas don't leak out. If the anusayas, the underlying tendencies of mind, are absent, so are the effluents. The āsavas are the "inflows" (into experience) or "outflows" (from the subconscious) of the anusayas, the underlying tendencies toward and familiarity with afflictions and troubled ways that have built up over the years. If they flow, there's a mess and dukkha.

Now we'll know the end of the āsavas, so there's no more outflowing of corruption. Because of mind's cultivation, it isn't polluted with visiting afflictions (*upakkilesas*). This mind is luminous, bright and clear in its original nature. Having been skillfully trained, nothing can trouble it ever again. Ending the effluents, causing the āsavas to dry up completely, is the level of arahant. For ordinary practitioners, for now, it's a good start to lighten and lessen the āsavas. Decreasing the anusayas and other kilesas is part of ending the āsavas. Our custom of wishing for each other that everything is a condition for realizing nibbāna means just this lessening of kilesas, anusayas, and āsavas. When they are finished, cultivation has reached the very highest level.

Human beings who have ended the āsavas are the pinnacle of the species. Ordinary worldlings live with ordinary āsavas and kilesas. Humans at baser levels of existence live with even more āsavas and kilesas. The noble ones have begun to have diminishing kilesas and āsavas because their cultivation is correct and proper. Eventually, the end of the effluents is realized and there's no more chance of the kilesas arising. The anusayas and āsavas are finished. For those who have ended the effluents, there's really no need to mention the nīvaraṇas again. The nīvaraṇas, the pestering gnats of mind, swarm no more, because the roots of those troubling instinctual reactions have been cut off. The tigers have met with the same fate. This life is then free from all things that disturb; there's nothing that can provoke suffering anymore. This is the highest benefit of psycho-spiritual cultivation.

With these four flowing benefits, all problems come to an end. How satisfying and desirable is that? Through harmoniously cultivating sīla, samādhi, and paññā so that they operate as one path, we get both worldly and spiritual results. There will be ordinary happiness here and now and possibly supernormal bliss as well. We might even discover supernatural powers, which still have a worldly character. Sati-sampajañña can be both worldly and above the world. The complete ending of the āsavas is exclusively spiritual and transcendent.

With Right View, Utilize Path, Fruit, and Nibbāna in Everyday Life

Now, don't keep path, fruit, and nibbāna on an altar. Make use of them to free yourself of the things that disturb life, that are dukkha—the nīvaraṇas, kilesas, anusayas, and āsavas. The five nīvaraṇas are common, instinctual, and disturb to a certain degree. Kilesas are stronger, more intense, and blazing with heat. Through the repeated indulgence of kilesas, the underlying tendencies (*anusayas*) toward and familiarity with kilesas accumulate. Once these anusayas build up pressure, they flow out as the āsavas. Now we've cleaned all of that out of mind. We've removed nīvaraṇas, kilesas, anusayas, and āsavas.

Have we Buddhists reached this level? If so, we've survived, we're safe. We can't find fault in ourselves, and neither can any wise being who examines us. We know thoroughly that inside we're good, we're all right. Knowing that we've put an end to our problems, there's nothing to find fault with. This is the best way to know what sort of Buddhists we are.

To most people, *path*, *fruit*, and *nibbāna* are just words, just names. They've become sacred and magical things that we don't know what to do with. So we leave them on an altar gathering dust and becoming moth-eaten. How would it be if we kept locked in closets the tools, utensils, and furnishings that we need every day of our lives? In the same way, path, fruit, and nibbāna are meant for daily use. We should make everyday use of Dhamma, not leave it on an altar, forgetting about it, as most Buddhists do. Yet we may believe that we have Dhamma, which is deluded. Pretend Dhamma doesn't have any real use because it can't show us how to quench dukkha. Path, fruit, and nibbāna have the power to free us when they are integral to our lives. Don't leave them on an altar somewhere or locked away in the holy scriptures.

We shouldn't inflate ourselves, get ahead of ourselves, or pretend to be better than we are, but we must try our best. If we can't yet manage path, fruit, nibbāna correctly 100 percent of the time, we can still manage 5 or 10 percent and go from there. If we aren't arahants, we can follow in their footsteps. The words of a reflection chant are appropriate: "We will follow the footsteps of the arahants today." Just this is enough, is excellent. Although we are not arahants, we follow the path of the arahants, which is citta-bhāvanā, cultivating mind and developing life in line with the footsteps of the arahants.

Path, Fruit, and Nibbāna as Insight Knowledge

I've said enough about matters related to path, fruit, and nibbāna. Now it's time to look at the meaning of path, fruit, and nibbāna in a way that's clearer and easier to grasp. Path, fruit, and nibbāna are difficult to understand when the words in ordinary language mean one thing and something else in the Dhamma language of the noble ones. When ordinary Buddhists use these words, it's the sacred path, fruit, and nibbāna left on the altar. People know the names and designations, but all they can do is talk about them. And that's all they will do. In these cases, no real benefit comes from such path, fruit, and nibbāna. This doesn't stop people from getting excited about having these wonderful things to talk about and feeling special, but that's the most they know how to get from path, fruit, and nibbāna.

How can path, fruit, and nibbāna be in the lives and activities of people generally? If we understand the meaning of these three words properly, we'll know that they must be intertwined with the actions and everyday life of everyone who has some degree of right understanding (*sammādiṭṭhi*). Except for thoroughly foolish worldlings who are still caught in all their old habits, we can open our ears and brighten our eyes to have enough sammādiṭṭhi to progress.

Let's consider each of these three terms in turn. The first, path (*magga*), is intuitive wisdom (*paññā*) cutting off the corruptions as soon as greed, aversion, or delusion start to arise. The appropriate clearly comprehending mindfulness (*sati-sampajañña*) arrives to dispatch them. If any of the five nīvaraṇas show up, sati-sampajañña sweeps them out of mind as with a broom. With spiritual cultivation, even someone who isn't yet arahant and who still refers to themselves as "ordinary" has this kind of insight knowledge and wisdom because they have listened and practiced a great deal. Hence, whenever greed arises, there is mindfulness, clear comprehension, and wisdom present to sweep out the greed. Together, they operate as the path. We can call it *magga*, most simply, or *magga-ñāṇa* (path knowledge), as later texts have it. Wisdom manifesting as a weapon capable of cutting through kilesas is the essence of magga.

Fruit (*phala*) is the wisdom or insight knowledge that knows that the kilesas have been severed. Tradition calls it "fruition knowledge" (*phala-ñāṇa*). The insight knowledge that arises to cut through the kilesas is path knowledge, and the insight knowledge that arises when the kilesas have been cut off is fruition knowledge. When the kilesas have been cut, knowing the experience of coolness is nibbāna knowledge (*nibbāna-ñāṇa*). The cool peacefulness of mind that arises because the kilesas and nīvaraṇas are gone is nibbāna, which is known with penetrating insight.

These *ñāṇas* are demonstrated in the final four steps of mindfulness with breathing.[3] Here, the contemplation of Dhamma, of natural realities, begins with contemplating impermanence, where clear, direct insight into impermanence in all conditioned things occurs. Contemplation of Dhamma deepens with contemplating the fading away of habits of foolish desire and clinging. Such wisdom, the realization of impermanence, amounts to path knowledge. Then the quenching of clinging to conditioned things and the quenching of the kilesas is contemplated. This contemplating of quenching is equivalent to fruition knowledge. Finally, the realization that these things have been quenched completely and will never be a problem again is contemplation of returning to nature, which is an aspect of nibbāna knowledge. In addition, the review that confirms what has come about, reviewing knowledge, is also a nibbāna-ñāṇa, insight knowledge concerning nibbāna. In the practice of ānāpānasati, sixteen steps are grouped in four tetrads, and the final tetrad contemplates Dhamma truth and reality by means of contemplating impermanence, contemplating the fading away of clinging tendencies, contemplating quenching of dukkha, and contemplating returning to nature (Dhamma). Anyone who really grasps the significance of these four contemplations will realize that insight knowledge of path, fruit, and nibbāna are contained therein.

On a more mundane level, whether at work or at home, the knowledge that allows us to do things well—knowledge that eliminates foolishness, that destroys the sort of ignorance that limits our abilities—is path (*magga*). How things go once foolishness and incompetence are removed is fruit (*phala*). Then the benefit, the satisfaction and well-being, is peaceful coolness, nibbāna. Hence, even ordinary housework and labor come under the umbrella of path, fruit, and nibbāna. Usually people can't, for instance, farm in the way of path, fruit, and nibbāna, so they don't get the highest benefits. However, removing ignorance from the work is path. Then there is rice to harvest, which is fruit. Finally, the peace experienced is nibbāna. In this way, the essential meanings of path, fruit, and nibbāna are found in any and all kinds of activities.

This is the basic Dhamma truth that I wish everyone could see: to do anything successfully and beneficially, it needs to be done with foolishness removed—that is, done as path, fruit, and nibbāna. Is there anything that this principle and approach can't be applied to? Please consider this truth diligently to make the most of path, fruit, and nibbāna. Whether we are children or adults; farmers, market gardeners, merchants, government officials, or teachers; householders or monastics—bring path, fruit, and nibbāna to each and every experience. Be someone who, whenever there is anything to do, uses the approach of path, fruit, and nibbāna.

Transform something that is usually just fancy words—realizing path, fruit, and nibbāna—into something we actually use in our daily lives on any genuine and significant level. Then develop this approach on higher levels until we're able to put an end to the kilesas and be arahant. To be arahant, we need the insight that cuts through the corruptions, then we apply the insight in the effective cutting. From that, we recognize what has been removed and released. Finally, we know the full flowering of arahant. Such is path, fruit, and nibbāna on the arahant level. For now, we are ordinary Buddhists, still worldly people, but dwelling on a decent level, not too foolish, not too inflated. We are people endeavoring to uphold the proper meaning of path, fruit, and nibbāna. We seek genuine knowledge of the path that wisely bears fruit in the elimination of afflictions and realizes the cool peacefulness of nibbāna.

Cultivating Mind for Genuine Refuge

There is one more matter to consider: going for refuge. When going for refuge is mentioned, most Buddhists assume refuge is a simple business, the simplest of all things to acquire. But be careful; don't let refuge be like the good grass next to the cattle pen that the cows rush by to get out into bigger fields. Those who think they can genuinely take refuge without proper mental cultivation are like foolish cows in a hurry. Merely parroting the traditional phrases can't hope to achieve genuine refuge from the problems of life. We can recite "*Buddhaṃ saraṇaṃ gacchāmi, dhammaṃ saraṇaṃ gacchāmi, saṅghaṃ saraṇaṃ gacchāmi*" (To the Buddha for refuge I go, to the Dhamma for refuge I go, to the Sangha for refuge I go) many thousands of times and never know the Buddha, nor Dhamma, nor Sangha. Until there is the wisdom that sees the Buddha and Dhamma and joins the Sangha of right practice, we are just working our lips and throats, at most showing sincere interest but not yet finding true refuge.

When the skillfully cultivated mind sees the kilesas, knows how to cut the kilesas, and realizes the end of the kilesas, it then knows the true Buddha, Dhamma, and Sangha. The undeveloped mind, however, can only see and parrot formulas. It's one thing to teach these traditions to children, to prepare them for later understanding. Adults, however, ought to cultivate a higher level. How many thousands of repetitions does it take to reach the true Buddha, Dhamma, and Sangha?

Intermediate between the refuge of received tradition and true refuge is the refuge of superstitious belief. This involves repeating mantras in order to be protected, to earn merit, and to avoid dukkha without understanding how any of that works. Those who don't know how to actually escape dukkha will just follow what others tell them, which is to take refuge in credulous belief—that is, superstitious refuge. This might be fine, when the advice is good. It might be better than not doing anything. If the belief leads to cultivating mind, it's moving in the right direction. Although still under the umbrella of superstitious belief, people can begin to develop mind in the way of sīla, samādhi, and paññā, if they are told to do that, even if they don't understand why or how.

The third level of refuge goes beyond mere words and traditions. It no longer relies on someone else's words. At this level, we practice developing mind until we understand the kilesas and nīvaraṇas. We practice until we have seen how they can be severed and removed, then do it. Mind, thus clear of obstruction, realizes that this is what the Buddha is about. The Dhamma and Sangha are just like this. The genuine Buddha, Dhamma, and Sangha appear; they're no longer just words. Then when someone takes refuge *in the Buddha*, they mean the true Buddha, one with such a mind. When they take refuge *in the Dhamma*, they mean the true Dhamma, which has the property of destroying kilesas. And when they take refuge *in the Sangha*, they mean the true Sangha, those people with Buddha-like minds. This third level is genuine Buddhist refuge, which follows tasting the true path, fruit, and nibbāna. Although this knowledge may not yet be complete, it is enough to understand the proper meaning of path, fruit, and nibbāna and thus finds genuine refuge.

Let's consider the three levels of refuge with clear distinction. The lowest is that based on custom and tradition, which children and people with childlike understanding first meet. Then comes the superstitious level, which involves dependence on something outside of us, which is treated as supreme, a most sacred thing. This will help us, if we surrender to it. This superstitious refuge is based more or less in credulous faith, at least at first. If we believe sufficiently, we will practice accordingly and eventually arrive at the true refuge. The final level is reached when mind is cultivated enough to see the true Buddha, Dhamma, and Sangha directly. There is actual experience and knowledge of the end of the kilesas, nīvaraṇas, and āsavas. Refuge develops through these three stages.

We must discern for ourselves which level of refuge we have found. It isn't about judging each other, which only makes trouble. I don't want to judge anyone else, yet I do want to clarify the three levels available to us. People can decide for themselves. There is the refuge that is just words; the refuge that is a product of faith, of credulous belief that hasn't acquired wisdom but can lead to practice; and the refuge of clearly seeing the realities of Buddha, Dhamma, and Sangha.

Now you may find yourself asking, "Have I reached the third level yet?" Perhaps you've heard about this subject dozens of times and are curious, "Have I discovered real knowledge of the Buddha, Dhamma, and Sangha yet?" Once you have, you are saved. One is at least stream enterer (*sotāpanna*). Knowing the genuine Buddha, Dhamma, and Sangha, you know the true and genuine refuge without any remaining doubts and trembles.

If less developed, you have the refuge of customs and beliefs that is fairly superstitious. It's this way in all religions, no matter what their basis. People can't immediately realize the pinnacle of their religion. They all must make their way gradually, usually depending on others for a while. To reach the highest understanding of their particular system, they have to gradually come to it in this stepwise manner.

As for we Buddhists, after wrestling with this for dozens of years, to what level have we uplifted ourselves? We ought to have some idea of how much we've developed. Inevitably, our level is the fruit of our mental cultivation. It reflects our degree of dedication to the psycho-spiritual cultivation that is the heart of developing life. So, what level has our development of life reached? Do we know the meaning of path, fruit, and nibbāna yet? And how deeply and fully do we know? Do we know the real meaning of the words *Buddha*, *Dhamma*, and *Sangha* yet? If we do, if we've arrived at this level of understanding, we've saved ourselves for sure. Even though our understanding isn't yet at the highest level, still, when we see the Buddha, Dhamma, and Sangha clearly enough so that there's no more uncertainty and confusion, that gives us a true refuge. This, at least, is the level of stream entry (*sotāpatti*). If our refuge remains with customs and tradition, or in superstitious beliefs, we can't count on safety. That's the level of ordinary worldlings who can't yet break away from worldly habits to become noble members of our religion.

We have described the result of citta-bhāvanā. Successful cultivation of mind realizes path, fruit, and nibbāna, which are knowledges seen with clear insight. Otherwise, we are stuck and haven't fully entered the path. The cultivation process is blocked because clear understanding is lacking. Mind doesn't prosper and thrive in the Dhamma way. We need to have clear understanding of path, fruit, and nibbāna so that mind can flourish. Hence, we come to study and reflect, to spend time developing a clear understanding of these things, however tiring it may be, so that their proper understanding leads to fruitful citta-bhāvanā. Our up-and-down efforts gradually become steadfast and true.

✳

My aim has been to make bright and clear that which was dark and indistinct, so that our treasured Buddhist words become real in our lives, so that sacred things stashed away on altars are now brought down, dusted off, and put to good use. The opportunity of being Buddhist, of having been born human and having met with the Buddha's teaching, won't then have been wasted.

6

HOW SUPERSTITION INFLUENCES MENTAL CULTIVATION

Dhamma is a matter of the psychological more than the physical, of mind more than body. It's a matter of inner truth. Consequently, mental cultivation consists of training mind to the highest level, where the most profound truths are realized. To do so properly, we follow the principles of the Pali texts, which is Buddhology, the science of awakening. Nevertheless, there is always the possibility of going astray into superstition, sleepology, the science of lying down on the job, which is governed by confused views and misguided thinking. With superstition, understanding of mind and of path, fruit, and nibbāna is insufficient and incorrect. This is sayasāstra, Buddhism confused by superstition, as opposed to buddhasāstra or true Buddhology.[1] Cultivation dictated by superstitious wrong view (*micchādiṭṭhi*) creates misguided, unnatural development. The many and various forms of wrong view emanate from a faulty understanding of mind and lack of skillful cultivation. When citta-bhāvanā is correct and natural, it is Buddhology. When foolishness obscures the nature of mind, citta-bhāvanā is tainted by sayasāstra—the science of lying down on the job, sleepology.

Foolish understanding of things is the reason why superstitious belief outweighs genuine Buddhism. It's why human development, both personal and collective, goes astray. Consider superstitious fears of the unseen and unknown. How much are people afraid of mysterious and supernatural things? Comparatively, how much fear is there of tangible things, such as harmful wrongdoing? Isn't it foolish to fear things we can't see while having little fear of doing obviously bad things and generating bad karma that causes trouble?

When sleepology dominates, we don't progress in Dhamma life. This problem has befallen many Buddhists, denying them adequate space for confidence, observation, contemplation, and insight. In that condition, our understanding remains crude and uneven, and we are Buddhist in name only. An example of superstitious Buddhists are those who believe in bad omens. There are Thai Buddhists who become anxious when hearing the greeting of a *jingjok* (small house lizard), which they interpret as an evil portent. On a day they encounter a jingjok, they won't do anything because they believe something bad is going to happen to them. They fear they will encounter misfortune or even die. Sometimes things fall unexpectedly, and they take it as an omen that something bad is on the way. Do any of us harbor such beliefs in bad omens?

There was a senior Royal Thai Government lawyer with an important case against the French concerning Khao Phra Viharn on the Cambodian border. On the day the verdict was to be heard, as he was about to leave to go to the court, a picture fell from the wall and broke into pieces, with the frame and glass shattering. He was terrified. He took it as a sign that he would lose the case and would be disgraced. Sure enough, he lost and the land was given to the French colonialists. For the rest of his life he believed that the fallen picture caused the loss of the case. He never considered that it was a coincidence or that the judges had decided even before he woke up that day.

Thinking in such ways keeps us from being thoroughgoing Buddhists, yet it is common. We ought to do something to clear this up so that our Buddhism is reasonable and based in actual conditions and their consequences.

Sleepology is powerful because it comes from a deeply ingrained and habitual ignorance passed along through our ancestry. Intelligence, mindfulness, and wisdom haven't received the same degree of attention, nor been passed on through generations to the same extent. Further, we must admit that some superstition is a necessary springboard for people to begin to practice as they ought to. They aren't ready to believe the true wisdom teachings, so they need to be inspired with presentations that fit the belief systems acquired from their ancestors.

If something isn't couched in superstitious and fearful terms, it won't catch the attention of most people. For instance, if we warn children about trying to catch water coming out of the gutter pipe because lightning will strike there, they will probably believe what we say and act accordingly. Whereas if we simply explain that the bowl is easily broken that way, they won't think it important or scary. As long as foolishness pervades humanity, many things will need to be couched in fear-inducing, superstitious terms. Mysterious, awe-inspiring explanations, charismatic presenters, and sacred terminology typically have a better chance of encouraging more useful and beneficial forms of behavior. Direct explanations of what is most beneficial won't convince people still influenced by sleepology.

Ignorance and Fear Keep Superstition Alive

We all harbor fears, particularly fear of death. If someone promised to save us from death, many of us would happily jump on that without much consideration. This fear makes it easy for us to accept sayasāstra. Sleepology accumulates around worldly people who let foolish beliefs and fears run the show. These two together—foolishness and fear—give birth to superstition. The forests of southern Thailand provide an interesting example of sayasāstra as not always a bad thing. The high-quality timber trees, such as ironwood, were believed to house spirits. Not wanting to risk death by offending a spirit, people were afraid to cut down those trees. We used to have lots of ironwood trees around here, but they've disappeared since people stopped believing the old superstitions. This example makes it hard to say whether sleepology is good or bad. If applied wisely, it can be good. Since we can't yet live without superstitions, we need to improve them for the good and to pave the way for the ultimate good.

Sleepology can be used to lead people to the right path by identifying a sleepological belief that can be connected to something important for their development. This may be necessary for them to get started; afterward, they can continue more wisely. In the case of psycho-spiritual training, a superstitious belief, such as in magic powers, can be used to get people to train their minds. Such beliefs, when the believer is convinced something is real, can inspire weak-minded people with the mental strength and confidence to practice. Also, observe how children who have fallen down can be charmed by a magic formula to stop crying; it provides emotional strength, and they forget their hurt. In short, sayasāstra is still needed for those not yet ready for buddhasāstra, such as children and those lacking in Dhamma understanding.

Sleepology is comparable to pain-relieving medicine: when we have a headache or toothache that is hard to bear, we take medicine to manage the symptoms; however, such medicine doesn't cure the disease. To do that, we must go to the source of the pain. After taking a pain reliever, we can deal with the underlying disease itself. Unfortunately, some people get stuck on the medicine of superstition and quick fixes, and they stay stuck throughout their lives, so they never discover the real truth of Dhamma. Once we are truly ready for buddhasāstra, we won't need the sayasāstra anymore.

Buddhology and Superstition

Because Buddhology and sleepology are intertwined, we need to study them together to grasp them properly. The Pali word *saya* can mean "better than." From this angle, superstitious knowledge can be considered "better than" knowing nothing at all. Think back to our forest-dwelling ancestors, some of whom had knowledge of matters that ordinary people didn't. Hence, they became the leaders and guides for the rest to learn the same things. As this satisfied the recipients, such knowledge was accepted as better than knowing nothing at all. Superstition, in this sense, has the meaning of "better knowledge than knowing nothing," even if such knowledge isn't complete.

Saya can also mean "asleep," contrasted with *buddha*, meaning "awake." Asleep, in this instance, refers to the sort of knowledge that, while good enough for solving trivial problems, isn't awakened to deeper truths needed to solve spiritual problems. As with taking medicine to get rid of pain, having enough knowledge to take the medicine is "better than" not having any knowledge. Yet if that's as far as one goes, that sort of knowledge won't be enough to remedy the causes of disease that caused the pain to begin with. Sleepy knowledge can be useful until one knows what's what and how things work, which is to be awake.

Awakening from the sleep of ignorance is referred to as "Buddhology." This involves waking up to the basic law of nature, especially idappaccayatā, the law of conditionality that governs inner and outer natures, both physical and mental. Seeing the relationships among causes and effects in line with idappaccayatā, we can solve our problems. Thus awakening science replaces the sleeping science. People realize Buddhology personally through sufficient training and practice.

At present, however, from childhood onward, people are taught to be superstitiously inclined. Since emerging from the womb, children are taught various superstitions and are needlessly afraid of things. For instance, children are told that if they don't stop crying, a gecko will come and eat their liver! Or the boogeyman will get them! Such things are akin to the ABCs of superstitious belief. Children acquire sleepology in abundance, and it stays with them through their teens and into adulthood. They are taught to believe without reasoning regarding things in which causes and consequences can be seen. Hence, foolish belief expands in ever-widening circles. When a superstition corresponds with something one desires, such as washing one's face with sacral water to be beautiful, it's eagerly seized upon. Charms, love potions, and sacred mantras are much in evidence among people who haven't received a proper Dhamma education. Even people living in developed cities and countries will be dominated by superstitions if they don't have the opportunity to study and practice Dhamma properly. In Bangkok, where there's so little opportunity to study Dhamma properly, superstition dominates. There is more sleepology than Buddhology in the developed city. An obvious example is those guardian spirit houses that were once hard to find even in the countryside. They are all over Bangkok now, so much so that they're overflowing back into the countryside.[2]

Please don't think there's no superstition in modern cities. In such places, people will, if anything, be more superstitiously inclined. This is because development for them consists in getting more and more. They have desires, more desires, and extreme desires. When someone tells them that acting in such and such a way will fulfill their desires, they seize on that with alacrity. Such people tend to fall easily into sleepology. Those who don't want excessively won't be nearly as superstitious. Those who never want anything more than is necessary, such as arahants, aren't superstitious at all.

Superstition Blocks Spiritual Nobility

If superstitious belief isn't abandoned, there's no way to reach spiritual nobility. The first level of nobility requires leaving superstitious beliefs behind. Dhamma students know that personality view (*sakkāyadiṭṭhi*), doubts (*vicikicchā*), and caressing of precepts and rituals (*sīlabbataparāmāsa*) are given up for stream entry (*sotāpatti*).[3] Believing one is a coherent, independent personality is the basis of all superstitions. Being in doubt is an inherent component of beliefs that haven't been carefully examined. Foolish misuse of precepts, rituals, and duties can turn any practice into superstitious behavior. Superstition is even further left behind by the higher levels of spiritual nobility.

Sakkāyadiṭṭhi is the initial ignorance that "this body is me." This is the crudest level of attā, self. It has stuck to us since childhood and takes up a lot of space. The belief that "this body is me" is the first superstition to be abandoned. Vicikicchā, doubt—not knowing how to respond when faced with an experience and confused thinking about it—is superstitious too. Then there's sīlabbataparāmāsa, superstitious understanding of precepts, vows, and spiritual duties, which manifests when people practice religious observances without understanding the true reasons for them. Rituals are superstitious when not in line with, or even opposed to, their original purpose. A common example is keeping precepts for the sake of worldly profit or benefit rather than their purpose of overcoming the corruptions. Perhaps you've heard of purifying yourself, washing away your sins, by going to the temple or a holy place. Nobody knows how this actually works, but many believe in it. Though rather odd, it's still somewhat of a good thing. Even though one might go to such places for superstitious reasons, not really understanding what the temple is for, at least one would go, which is better than not going at all. In going many, many times, people can slowly begin to understand the purpose of the temple and what one is meant to do there. This can be a start to understanding Dhamma. What started as a superstitious ritual gradually found the proper path.[4]

Be aware that almost everything in the lives of ordinary worldly people will be interfered with in some way by the superstitious beliefs buried deep in their minds. The standard acts of Buddhism—doing good, making donations, helping, living simply—mostly fall under the umbrella of superstitious belief, because it's easier to involve people in such activities through superstition than straightforward explanations.

Our ancient ancestors, going back to when they still lived in the forests, ordered their lives in thousands of superstitious ways. Taboos were created that instilled fear, such that nobody dared break them. Explanations weren't needed, just fear. With such taboos, questioning wasn't encouraged. Belief is all that was required. Our ancestors organized their communities with such powerful methods, and many of these superstitions are still with us to this day.

However, we Buddhists should ask ourselves whether such methods are appropriate for those who honor and take refuge in the Buddha, Dhamma, and Sangha. How can we put our faith in karma and the law of idappaccayatā if we're still superstitiously inclined? Please recognize this as an important issue, one we need to think about clearly if we're to have a cleaner, purer, more genuine Buddhist community.

Comparing Awake and Sleeping

What does this have to do with citta-bhāvanā? Misguided mental cultivation tends to promote superstition. Displaying psychic powers and miracles has a powerful attraction and can easily lead away from the path. Put bluntly, if such powers produced actual results, there would be no need for those possessing them to earn a living. Simply by performing one of their miracles, they would have food to eat every day without lifting a finger. With miraculous abilities, a monk would be able to conjure up halls, shrines, and temples without having to solicit contributions from householders. Clearly such powers aren't real. The Buddha sometimes had to eat horse feed; he didn't satisfy his hunger by using supernatural powers.

Through Buddhology, the noble ones (*ariyas*) are without even a speck of superstitious belief. Worldly people are ignorant and have ignorant desires. These two—*avijjā* (ignorance) and *taṇhā* (craving)—are what tether us to the stake of superstitious belief. The problem with superstition is that it creates foolish belief everywhere. It cannot elevate mind, which only happens following the arising of Buddhology.

Buddha means "the one who knows, is awakened, and has fully blossomed." This is the best and most correct interpretation of *buddha*. Contemplate these three characteristics: being one who truly knows, being awakened from the sleep of ignorance, and having blossomed into the highest freedom. You won't find even the slightest trace of superstitious belief there. This is how Buddhists should be, not a superstitious crowd. Although the world is full of superstitious belief, we aren't narcotized by sleepology. When sayasāstra slowly fades out and buddhasāstra takes its place, one gradually wakes up and opens one's eyes to a wakeful world, which represents the advancement of the human mind. Otherwise, mind stays asleep, without any advancement at all.

Buddhology differs from sleepology in that it depends on wisdom. Starting with the first bits of real knowledge, Buddhology makes use of Dhamma knowledge and develops into wisdom. It doesn't depend on untested belief like superstition does. Buddhology questions and examines; its belief, when it comes, depends on direct spiritual experience. Such belief is backed by knowledge of causes and conditions, which constitutes right understanding (*sammādiṭṭhi*). It leaves the foolish beliefs and wrong understanding (*micchādiṭṭhi*) of superstition behind.

Why Do People Accept Superstition So Easily?

Both Buddhology and sleepology involve faith. The faith of budchasāstra is consonant with wisdom, while the faith of sayasāstra believes foolishly and blindly. Now let's consider the question of why humans fall for superstition so easily. There are deep, hidden causes and conditions we need to consider in suitable detail to understand.

The first condition to consider is that superstition easily cooperates with unknowing instinctual responses. It fits well with congenital ignorance, in that at birth one can have no knowledge of liberation from mind's problems. Hence, at the start of its life, any child will be primed for the fall into superstitious belief.

The second condition is that superstition fits easily with our instinctual inclination to let others do things for us. Children have someone to help them at all times, and with instincts still guided by ignorance, they lack the knowledge to help themselves. They only understand how to rely on others, which suits the growth of superstition very well. It's superstition that always turns us to other people, sacred things, or mysterious forces for help. Of course, it's natural and ordinary that we're born needing help, and this makes us ripe for superstition. This is as it must be and shouldn't be taken as harmful. Once we're born, we meet things that suit us, including superstitions.

Hence, we continuously gather superstitious knowledge, beliefs, and clinging. The people close to us surround us with such superstition, especially the words and language meant to awe children into doing this and not doing that.

The third condition is that a superstition requires less of an investment; a superstition is a less tiring and much simpler proposition than finding out something for oneself. Superstitious rituals require little input or effort. The offerings at shrines usually cost much less than what people want in return. Participating in superstition is less wearisome because it's so easy to do. Chanting an incantation of just a few lines is a tiny investment, yet vast riches or flocks of sexual partners are expected. Children thus pick up many prayers and formulas easily, rather than putting in the time and effort required for real learning.[5]

The fourth condition is that superstition is appropriate for people of weak intelligence, who don't know things as they really are. This kind of weak intelligence isn't a birth or brain defect. Most people are weak in wisdom because they don't understand things properly and don't strive to do so. Whether from East or West, whatever the nationality, most people exercise intelligence weakly, which makes them susceptible to superstition. Buddhology, given its profundity, requires great application just to get through the front door. Many people tend toward taking the easy way, and so they seize upon superstition greedily with their already weak understanding.

The fifth condition is that superstition enjoys the great advantage of questioning being forbidden. When something is raised up to a sacred status, questioning or critiquing it isn't allowed. For example, I know an instance of a child who asked how a wooden image of a god can help us when it can't move its arms, and the child was spanked for his impertinence. Buddhology lacks this advantage because it allows questioning based in mindfulness and clear understanding. With superstition, there is an unquestioning acceptance that if something is sacrosanct, then it is properly a mystery for ordinary worldly people. With questions and criticism not allowed, superstitions become more mysterious and sacred, and something that can't be understood at all becomes the most sacred or holy. Superstition always has this advantage.

The sixth condition is the adaptable, chameleonlike quality of superstition. In Thailand, the statues of gods are blessed in various ways. The same kind of blessings are also applied to taxis, trucks, and even warships. For the statue to be efficacious, someone must bless it. Where does this power come from? These practices are always changing, impossible to pin down, and endlessly adaptable to the needs of foolishness. Wrapped in blind belief, people flip back and forth between one illusion and the other without recognizing what they are doing. Because of this slipperiness, sleepology becomes ever more firmly entrenched.

Sleepology Is Thoroughly Mixed In with Religion

In discussing sayasāstra like this, my purpose is to clarify human understanding. Merely criticizing or acting superior gets us nowhere. Rather, we aim to elucidate a strong tendency that obstructs genuine practice of Buddhism. This is especially true of the seventh condition for sleepology's robustness: it is extremely sticky and able to take over a lot of space in human minds, such that there is a mingling together of superstition and genuine religion, rather like two rivers coming together with the larger channel dominating. Mixed up in the minds of the masses, sleepology dominates and problems ensue, which creates opportunities for scoundrels and criminals. Their exploitation of superstition gives them the advantage. Their unprincipled superstitious practices give them courage to promote evil, even the cruelest, activities. That Buddhism is mixed up with superstition is an uncomfortable truth.

The seeds of sleepology are planted in a child's mind soon after birth. Sayasāstra develops into a thriving plant, and later on, if and when Buddhology is encountered, it inevitably gets mixed up with that superstition. Hence, Buddhology doesn't weaken superstition immediately. Rather, there occurs a mixing together of the two. In the two rivers analogy, one river is clean and pure, one is cloudy and murky. On meeting together, they mix in such a way that the clean and pure is sullied. In the same way, the human mind is comfortable mixing up Buddhology and sleepology.

If we look at the history of religions coming to Thailand, superstition came first, arriving from India in the forms of the Brahmanic creed. Buddhism came afterward, and so the roots of the Buddha's teaching aren't so deeply planted as those of sleepology. Around the ancient town of Chaiya where I've lived all my life, a little investigation reveals that Brahmanic shrines were in front of all the old Buddhist temples. If they hadn't been pulled down, we would see them all over. Ancient temples over a thousand years ago had in front of them Brahmanic shrines where Narayana, Shiva, or other deities were worshipped. This indicates that people then followed both Buddhism and Brahmanism at the same time. The authorities of a place wouldn't say anything against this; they allowed such beliefs and practices because they gave people psychological support and promoted communal harmony and cooperation. Sometimes the Brahmanic shrine is found within the main Buddhist shrine. When the big central *jedi* (stupa) at our local Wat Kaew was excavated, they found a representation of Shiva and an image of Ganesha in the main chamber among the Buddha images.[6] They were all worshipped together. Today, we are still accustomed to worshipping a mixture of Buddhism and Brahmanism. People prostrate to images of both the Buddha and Brahmanic gods. This shows how Buddhists follow a form of their religion mixed up with Brahmanism.[7]

The word *sacred* has many meanings and perspectives.[8] The sacredness of Dhamma is one kind. The sacredness of God is another. This theistic sacredness is easier for children to understand; they can't understand the sacredness of Dhamma. They can recite the Pali words for honoring the Buddha a thousand times without understanding what the Buddha is. However, the sacredness of Lords Indra and Brahma is immediately believed and accepted into their hearts.

This reveals the injustice of sacredness: it's so flexible that anyone can make of it what they like. Consequently, we have many versions of "the sacred." The kinds that children can understand have an advantage, and all the beliefs easily understood by children are sayasāstra. Consequently, they deeply pervade our religion and understanding of "the sacred."

Further, all human beings have ways of thinking and imagining that create personal ideologies according to their tastes. All of us can observe in ourselves how we want our own personal system that is unique. I call these "personal creeds." Not carefully or wisely worked out, they are naturally mixed bags. We collect this, that, and the other according to what we wish to believe and what pleases us. Unless properly guided by Dhamma, our choices are hit or miss. We follow our foolish preferences and accumulate hodgepodges that we are likely to cling to until we die. Unless there's realization of nobility through path, fruit, and nibbāna, our personal creeds inject sleepology into whatever mixed-bag Buddhism we profess. These easily end up as confused jumbles of ideologies lacking self-awareness.

Thus we end up with a false, adulterated creed. Call it "a thousand ways," like we do with the food we eat. We eat Thai, Chinese, Vietnamese, Indian, Middle Eastern, Italian, French, and more. Many kitchens and homes are a cultural smorgasbord. This is what people like: lots of variety to entertain their preferences. Psycho-spiritual creeds are pretty much the same. We pick up all sorts of interesting and pleasing bits and pieces from all over the world. This creates a false, adulterated creed of "a thousand ways" because it doesn't grow with genuine wisdom.

Viewed from this perspective, it is disappointing, even depressing, that most Buddhists still hold beliefs so mixed up that we don't know what's what. For example, we accept the gods of other religions and mix them up with the Buddha, Dhamma, and Sangha. Think of how our traditional water-pouring ritual for sharing merit arose and how it has become mixed up.[9] Today's ceremony didn't exist at the time of the Buddha. Although it probably didn't happen immediately, as time went on, the rituals and ceremonies were adulterated. Non-Buddhist elements were included. Reciting the virtues of the Buddha, for instance, became a superstitious petitioning.

To sum up, we follow an adulterated, polluted religion so that—as the saying goes—we don't know what is gold, what is copper, or what is brass. We mix many things together and take it as ours. Consequently, we don't get the true benefits from the best thing of all. To continue with the analogy, when we mix gold with copper, brass, and tin, we devalue the gold, and we can't make the most of it. So it is with the very best of things, with Dhamma. Attempting to separate the gold from the base metals so that what remains is good, true, and genuine would bring us much more benefit.

When the general situation involves all these admixtures, we can follow the principle of avoiding mixtures whenever that is best. At times, we will have to accept some of the mixtures when that turns out to be necessary. We will follow what is most beneficial. We find admixtures in all our Buddhist temples and shrines, including rituals that aren't really Buddhist. Even the Buddha images turn out to be mixtures when we examine them carefully. For example, people go to great lengths to dress the images with fine cloth. Is this necessary for images made of metal or stone? If people think the Buddha will be cold, that is superstitious logic. People make offerings to Buddha images just like they make to spirits they want to appease. Others believe the images are alive with a spirit. Some ask for fertility from them, which is quite a stretch given that the Buddha was celibate. I once met someone who believed her child was fathered by the image. With such things happening with Buddha images, how can anyone say that there is no adulteration?

So let's look around carefully and learn to distinguish what is Buddhology, leading to awakening, and what is sleepology, keeping us sleepwalking. Let us establish ceremonies that wake us up. Rather than attacking the superstitions, all we have to do is leave the incoherent sleepology alone and it will fade away. We need only keep what is correct and genuine. So don't sloppily go along with whatever is easiest or just follow your friends. Use discrimination.

There's a Way to Separate Ourselves from Superstition

Knowing that sleepology remains powerful and widespread, how do we keep it from dominating? How do we go about separating ourselves from sayasāstra, so as to be more correctly Buddhist? How do we combat superstition? An excellent example is that of venerables Sona and Uttara sent by King Asoka[10] to promulgate the Buddhist system in "the golden land" where we live. They had to do battle with the incumbent hosts of demons and evil spirits, and it was only when these had been defeated that Buddhism could take root here. The strong belief in the old sayasāstra made it impossible for people to accept the new Buddhist religion. They resisted vigorously. The two monks had to be very skillful to overcome the host of ghosts and demons, and get the people of this country to accept and respect the Buddhist way. Of great interest is how the record of that time says they used the *Brahmajāla Sutta*[11] as the means to achieve their mission.

Many people don't know what the *Brahmajāla Sutta* is. The *Brahmajāla* sets out the list of sixty-two wrong views people held around the time the Buddha taught. The monks used the sutta's "magic" to overcome belief in powerful demons and spirits. This means that they taught people to see where their beliefs were misguided and confused, so that they could change and come to respect the religion of awakening. Hence, they used one of the deepest, most difficult-to-study texts in the Buddhist canon, the *Brahmajāla Sutta*, as their means of driving out the hosts of sleepology from the land and establishing Buddhism successfully.

We can see, however, that superstition wasn't utterly defeated. It still exists and flourishes in various corners. Even though the superstitions aren't as powerful, and we consider ourselves a Buddhist nation, we basically follow a mixture of Buddhology and sleepology. We need to know how to remove the superstitious part, just as venerables Sona and Uttara used the *Brahmajāla Sutta* to destroy ogres and demons.

Understanding Idappaccayatā Correctly Eliminates Sayasāstra

Properly understood Buddhology will eliminate superstitious belief. The basis of this genuine Buddhism is the Dhamma that enlightened the Buddha-to-be and which afterward he revered. The core of Buddhology is the law of *idappaccayatā-paṭiccasamuppāda*. This law of dependent co-arising (*paṭiccasamuppāda*) reveals how dukkha arises and how dukkha quenches, which is the true heart of the Buddhist system. Idappaccayatā is the universal law of all nature: everything that happens, changes, or passes away does so in relation to causes and conditions. The Buddha awakened to dependent co-arising and honored conditionality as supreme. This is the Dhamma that will eliminate superstition. With understanding of idappaccayatā, there's no way that superstition can persist. The mind filled with knowledge of universal conditionality leaves no room for sleepology to enter. Study and explore the Dhamma of idappaccayatā until it is clear, obvious, and brilliant in mind. Then Buddhology will function perfectly, and sleepology will disappear. Don't trouble yourself to get rid of sayasāstra directly. Simply bring the natural reality of idappaccayatā to mind and there won't be any need to get rid of superstition. It will diminish of its own accord.

Hence, we invite you to study idappaccayatā, to let knowledge of it become clearer as each year goes by. As the Buddha stated in many discourses, "Due to having this as condition, this arises." Thus we ought to know that with ignorance as a primary condition, superstitions arise. Due to ignorance and craving in mind, superstition enters and grows. Come to know this, then there is right understanding and incorrect understanding disappears. The Buddha also said, "Due to not having this as condition, this doesn't arise."[12]

The highest Dhamma, like the highest god, is the law of idappaccayatā. Take it in thoroughly and the ghosts, ghouls, and demons are finished. Of all the blessings and incantations in ancient languages, we ought to be reciting idappaccayatā as the most powerful of all. Through it we know that living life is a stream of conditionality, without an abiding self or any personal assets involved. Such knowing ends the belief in an abiding self, so that superstition has nothing to stand on. The same results from seeing all experience as impermanent (*aniccaṃ*), unsatisfactory (*dukkhaṃ*), and not-self (*anattā*). Such insight replaces sayasāstra.

Realizing idappaccayatā, we understand the reality that there's no separate being or truly individual person, nor is there karma and its fruits. Without anybody living life, there's nobody to create karma—that is, karma is transcended. People say that life happens according to one's karma, but this is still partly a superstitious belief, connected to the idea of an individual self. Teachings from outside Buddhism explain karma as if there's an abiding self that cycles around being born and dying, over and over, according to past actions (karma). But this isn't actually part of the Buddhist system. A proper Buddhist understanding doesn't involve attā. There is just mind, responding either ignorantly or intelligently, dwelling along with the body. There's no need to drag in a separate self. Karma is intentional activities of body, speech, and mind that are guided by ignorance, which is governed by idappaccayatā. Seeing this, karma is transcended. Superstition, too, is transcended.

With real knowledge of idappaccayatā, we dwell above karma. "Dwelling above karma" refers to the way of life that puts an end to karma. Not assuming self, old karma becomes sterile. Previous karmic activities can no longer bear any fruit. Further, no new karma is being created because there isn't a "somebody" to create it. When there is true knowledge of idappaccayatā, superstition gets torn out by the roots, leaving nothing behind. Then there are no more corruptions and afflictions because we know how to manage the stream of conditions. With the supreme god of idappaccayatā in mind, we uproot ignorance, which prevents the stream of dependent co-arising from concocting the afflictions of greed, aversion, and delusion. Superstition then has nothing to base itself upon.

Proper Education Is Needed

It's time to consider a closely related matter—incomplete education. An incomplete, inadequate form of education is the kind designed solely for earning a living. Worldly education, which is mostly for vocations and jobs, is necessary but far from sufficient. Such education doesn't bother with knowledge of how mind works, how afflictions are concocted, the cycles of ego birth and death (*saṃsāra*), or nibbāna. Lacking such crucial dimensions of human life, it is incomplete, which leaves the door open for superstition to enter and take over. Hence, we need to arrange matters so that education is complete, and if the government won't do that for us, we'll have to do it ourselves. We believe that the students who come to Suan Mokkh suffer from deficient education and are seeking the understanding they lack—that is, how to be complete human beings. With well-rounded and profound education, there won't be any room for superstition. This leads to steady growth in our humanity until we are ennobled in the Buddhist sense.

Eventually, we'll need to be courageous. At present, we're still timid, afraid of ghosts and goblins, afraid of anything we don't understand, so we don't dare challenge superstition. There's a story, somewhat coarse, that illustrates the courage I'm talking about. When the main highway was being constructed between the cities Phatthalung and Trang, the official in charge drafted a great many local people for labor. They made good progress until they came to an especially large termite mound. There, all worked stopped. They feared dying should they upset the spirit of the mound, and there was no way around it in those coastal mountains. The government official was a real big shot. He told them, "I'll climb up there myself and piss all over it; you all dig. Once I've pissed all over, that spirit won't have any more power. You just dig." This illustrates how someone with courage can undermine superstition.[13] Also, notice how some children have more courage to question sayasāstra than most adults have.

It's the same today. If we have a little courage and put our faith in the true Buddhist system, superstitious beliefs will end. With cowardice, we are afraid to abstain from harmful things that the wise avoid and we equivocate in what genuinely needs doing. When you go down the stairs and a jingjok makes its characteristic sound, then so what! Don't be afraid of a little harmless lizard, because if you are, you won't have the backbone to do anything worthwhile. Don't let little fears and doubts hold you back. With proper Buddhist study, we have the wisdom to transform sleepology into Buddhology.

Courage and faith based in proper education allow us to uphold idappaccayatā as god above everything. Then we cultivate mind and free our lives of superstition. We invite the god of idappaccayatā to chase away all the demons and ogres so that only Dhamma remains, the heart of Buddhism rather than the superficialities. We honor the Dhamma just as all Buddhas do, present, past, and future. True Dhamma takes the place of the protective charms and rituals we once relied on. We need not pray for special help; we just live wisely with idappaccayatā in our hearts.

Align the Instincts with Buddhology to Leave Behind Sleepology

It's important to understand how our instinctual desires encourage superstition. Have you ever thought about what we human beings along with other animals want most of all? In the first place, living beings want to feel safe. They instinctually seek safety from danger and death, so when a superstitious protection is proposed—buy this amulet, mouth this incantation, receive this blessing, and you will be safe and prosperous—people are quick to accept it. They do so without questioning or reflecting. This is more convenient for sleepology than for the Buddhist approach, which teaches people to find safety and security through behaving properly in physical activities, speech, thought, and imagination.

Second, people need the four requisites of life to sustain themselves comfortably. We require food, clothing, shelter, and medicine to live reasonably. Everybody wants to eat. When someone tells farmers to simply chant a prayer or perform a ritual to avoid problems with the rice crop and ensure an abundant harvest, then, given ignorance, the various superstitious practices concerned with rice growing are quickly and easily accepted. Be aware, however, that merely chanting special verses or performing rituals aren't enough to achieve the required result; just try it and see. Farmers need to understand how to prevent damage to the rice crop and to manage its growth. This requires diligence, not the lazy way of sleepology. Still, a beneficial superstition would strengthen the farmer's heart enough to do what's needed.

It's the same with clothing and other basic needs. Magical thinking won't provide them. When we're afraid, we fall under the power of superstitious belief. Medicine is full of this because we don't know how to take care of ourselves and to make use of the scientific knowledge available.[14] Because we're too afraid and in too much of a hurry, we seek the easy way out and give in to superstitions. Hence, there is still an abundance of superstitious treatment of disease. We can decrease dependence on superstition in the pursuit of the four requisites of life when we are inclined to follow the correct way, the way of Buddhology.

Sayasāstra will always be needed by the weak-minded. As long as there are great numbers of people who lack the strength of mind to face things they consider frightening, sleepology will have a ready foundation—fear and ignorance.

The third instinctual area is that everybody wants to have some power over others, to be better than others in some way. This instinctual feeling is seen in dogs, cats, crows, chickens, and other creatures. I have raised many, many chickens, dogs, and cats here, and have seen this kind of behavior very clearly. Wanting to be better than the others, each one promotes itself and suppresses others. This competitiveness is basically instinctual. People display the same sort of desire. Consequently, when someone comes along and tells us that reciting a certain mantra will lift us above others, then, given ignorance, we're inclined to believe it. People exert themselves in meditation and austerities to gain power and authority over others. Sayasāstra promotes that sort of thing.

The fourth instinct is basically the opposite of the previous one: everybody wants to be loved. Don't expect sleepology to be consistent. This is particularly the case with those we ourselves love. We want them to love us too, of course. So when someone gives us a magic verse, a charm, or a love potion to get what we want, we are predisposed to believe it straightaway.

When I was a child, some of my classmates had notebooks full of *gāthās*, and I went for them too. These magic verses were to make girls fall in love with us, to become rich, to be talented, to protect against ghosts, and those sorts of desires. I copied them all proudly, but when I took them home to show off to my mother, she chased me out of the house: "Don't bring that garbage into our home!" I was just a child and was impressed with the gāthās. The books told how wonderful the verses were: just recite them a few times and they will bring what you seek. For a small investment, great benefits were to occur. My classmates and I were infatuated with these verses and thoroughly believed in them. Practicing Dhamma won't make someone fall in love with you, so it can't compete with reciting a gāthā a few times.

We can't avoid observing the fact that superstition has the advantage because it goes well with our ignorant, instinctual desires: for security and safety, for plenty of the four necessities of life, for power over others, and to be loved. When we merely follow these desires, there's no understanding of idappaccayatā, no trace of Buddhology associated with any of those instincts.

When we take refuge in superstition, we turn the Buddha into a sacred wonder worker and the Sangha into people who take care of us. There's no self-help in that, no practicing of Dhamma to help ourselves. Such refuge is deviant, a superstitious refuge. Even if our Buddhism amounts to more than that, if we're still inclined to believe what has always been taught, then our refuge is imitative and we are like parrots. It will stay that way until such time as we come to really know Dhamma. Only when we truly understand Dhamma, and especially idappaccayatā, will we have a true, genuine Buddhist refuge.

Buddhology is at a disadvantage to superstition simply because it doesn't square with our original instincts—that is, with our original ignorance. If we don't transform original ignorance into true knowledge, we'll just go on worshipping superstitions. If any progress we make—whether personally, organizationally, nationally, or globally—is through sleepology, there will be serious problems. Whereas progress based in Buddhology won't have those problems. Hence, we should put our trust in Buddhology so that the problems will decrease.

Conclusion

To sum up, citta-bhāvanā can occur in Buddhist forms and in superstitious forms. Either approach can foster mental fortitude, courage, and progress. Which form our Buddhism takes depends on our choices and actions. It's up to us to cultivate mind—to train it, guide it, improve it, and make it thrive in the right way. The more we know about proper Buddhist mental cultivation, the more we will be able to do the job properly. Hence, sincere Buddhists need to take responsibility in this. Don't be indifferent or follow the crowd. We, collectively, need to make adjustments, to improve ourselves, our homes, and our Buddhism to be the real thing. Don't fall for superstition and waste the opportunity of a human birth that has encountered the Buddha's teachings. Don't confuse superstitious beliefs with Dhamma truths. Let's be properly Buddhist so the story of suffering can end.

7

A SYSTEMATIC OVERVIEW OF LIFE'S DEVELOPMENT

In previous chapters, we have explored mental cultivation and the development of life. This chapter provides an overview and general outline of such citta-bhāvanā. We need to see the whole process clearly and systematically to engage with it properly, just like any other field of important work. Every kind of work has its techniques, progressive structure, and the rightness of each step.[1] We uphold a fundamental principle that all significant actions and work can demonstrate an appropriateness that is profound, progressive, and interconnected, and that can be viewed in outline form to reveal its extensive structure and hidden subtleties.

Commonplace endeavors such as growing rice follow this principle. Every step of the process must be correct. The right plot of land must be chosen, as well as the right time of year. The equipment and draft animals must be fitting. The right seed varieties are needed. All the methods of cultivation must be appropriate up through the harvest, threshing, and storage of the grain. All of these steps must be correct and in right relationship with one another. Because this knowledge has been passed down through traditions and customs, it isn't studied much. Because it's familiar, it isn't considered difficult or technical. Still, all aspects of growing rice must be correct if the results are to be satisfying. Cultivating mind and life is the same.

Development must mean growth and progress that are correct and proper. At first, it may seem silly to say so, but there are the sorts of progress that are wrong, that are insane, yet are still called "development" nowadays. Misusing the word *development* is itself improper. Any true development has to involve the sort of progress that is right and not in any way dangerous or harmful. This is especially true of mental and spiritual development. Having said that, the most easily acquired development is the wrong sort, and the more of that there is, the more disorder there is, until meditation becomes crazy-making.

In this chapter, we'll distinguish two levels of development: one of which can be expressed in worldly language, and the other in the language of Dhamma. When using worldly language, we describe the development of life, of an individual, on the external, more obvious level. When using Dhamma language, we describe the less obvious, internal process of mental cultivation. It's really all one evolution, but we're going to discuss it in two aspects and observe development as it takes place on both levels.

Growing Naturally with External Situations

On the more obvious level, the individual develops automatically, our interactions with nature and our surroundings obliging us to acquire knowledge, as a result of which we gradually come to know more and more. For instance, when we're small children, without being taught or discussing with anyone in particular, we gradually learn from our contacts with surrounding nature. When very young, from our own experiences and observations we come to know things such as hot and cold, soft and hard, and painful and pleasant. Through experience, we learn to struggle and survive; we know to avoid certain things and to be more careful next time we meet with them.

Animals, likewise, learn through experience that something is, for instance, dangerous, recognizing that there are snares and traps made especially to catch them and that they are dangerous tools of humans. There are nonhuman predators too. Animals learn through being observant, which is a natural form of education, so that they aren't caught in the same way again. Even puppy dogs and kittens, if they are in a cold place, learn to move to a warmer spot.

Real learning is learning from experience. Through personal experience we learn how to protect ourselves and put things right by ourselves. This sort of education is much better and more effective than the sort that is acquired from others. Although there are countless instances of living beings acquiring knowledge naturally, with their surroundings teaching them, most of us don't give such learning enough attention. We take it for granted and are none the wiser. Without anything forcing us to be more interested, we can't develop this natural learning into something more profound. Being observant encourages further development, so let's be thorough in our observance. Let's be the sort of people who are careful and subtle.

As for the sort of education received from others, well, since birth and all through the growing-up stage of life, traditional knowledge is transmitted through customs and ways of life. Children learn from their parents, from the people who raise them, and from friends, depending on circumstances. They learn from what interests them, and they may also be compelled to learn, such as in school. Whatever the form of education, the learning will occur, because curiosity and the desire to understand are strong in humans. When children see anything that is outside of their experience, they will ask about it. They will experience wonder and want to know what it is. They will exert themselves to acquire the satisfaction of knowing, and in such a way they will gradually increase their stock of knowledge.

In our Thai Buddhist culture, a traditional method of acquiring knowledge is temporary ordination. Most young men ordain as monks as a matter of custom, each intending only a few months' training as a monk. This traditional form of education is imposed more often than not. Men who don't ordain aren't accepted by society; people won't trust them. They will be crudely labeled unripe and immature. If someone is properly ordained for a long enough time, however, they will be recognized as trustworthy and worth associating with, even if they don't formally study the teachings. Ordination as a monk or novice isn't the only way to follow traditions and conventions to learn what members of a community are expected to learn. These traditions have social and personal benefits, so are encouraged in various ways. They bring about a general, basic knowledge of that which should be known in a community, and provide a good foundation from which to progress and develop further.

Developing in Response to External Challenges

The problems that occur in life are important occasions for learning. There are things—how to get out of difficulties or save themselves from harm—that even children must solve for themselves. Circumstances and situations can force us to learn, often on our own. Difficulties, hardships, pain, trouble, and strife happen, causing everyone to struggle with the particulars. Such difficulties force us to acquire knowledge and wisdom. Those who have the strength to solve their own problems are quick and clever in life; they know how to deal with tricky situations. People who live long experience many such situations and consequently have a lot of knowledge. For this reason, they ought to make good guides and leaders. It's natural that everyone experiences a greater variety of situations as they age and so come to have a broader and deeper store of knowledge than youth. Hence, many societies teach children to respect elders. Problems increase our understanding of life, and as we age, we gain the wisdom to understand the deepest and most difficult dilemmas.

Each and every person differs externally and internally. We have minds, habits, afflictions, abilities, and so on, but we don't know who provided them or from where they came. In reality, there will be various causes and conditions underlying the individual differences. Following tradition, we attribute the differences to merit and karma.[2] Desirable things are credited to merit, and undesirable things to karma. That isn't quite right, however; we should attribute the difference to causes and conditions. If we're true Buddhists, we'll hold that everything is a matter of causes and conditions, of idappaccayatā. Merit and karma can't exert a fixed and rigid control over results, because we have the means to make adjustments, modifications, and improvements in line with idappaccayatā. If we have good parents and teachers, we'll have a good chance of meeting with this sort of knowledge. The great virtue of good parents and teachers is that they enable foolish children to confront, adjust, and improve the various conditions of their lives, eventually becoming the sort of people able to skillfully solve the problems of life.

Parents and teachers should take an interest in the law of conditionality, so that they can help children deal with their problems. Children should be interested in hearing the advice of parents and teachers concerning how to correct their deficiencies. Such interest and acceptance is in line with the Buddha saying that among all the many kinds of children, those who honor and obey their parents are most excellent. He spoke of parents as being our first teachers. Through respect and obedience to parents, children receive the benefit of being helped from the beginning of their lives.[3]

Four Categories of People

We now come to consider the different mental qualities of people as set out in certain texts. Although the texts in question are commentaries (rather than the original discourses), they contain useful information and can help us with our studies and development.

The commentarial tradition distinguishes people into four basic categories. The first category is clever and incisive people; when hearing something, they understand it completely, even understanding more than was explained to them. These types of people clearly and immediately understands without explanations being necessary. There are even some children who when told something, can understand without the need for further explanation and perhaps understand even better than their teacher does. We ought to reflect whether we have ever been such incisive learners and what we can do to be more like this.

The second category includes those who require detailed explanations and perhaps further help. While there are children, employees, and students who fall within the first category, there are many others who will need more than a few words of explanation. They will do only what they have been expressly told to do but won't be able to make the necessary connections, think ahead, and do all of what is needed. Consequently, damage occurs. This is the case with many people today, including monks, novices, and college graduates. Everything must be explained extensively, and sometimes further help is needed for them to carry out work assignments and their studies.

The third category is that of those who can be led but only when dragged along. Their intelligence and comprehension are sluggish. While they are dense and slow-witted, they can be guided and led, although with difficulty. If these people don't have parents and teachers with great patience, they won't get anywhere. Many of our children who are considered worthless and good for nothing, and who can't take care of themselves, are like this because they haven't met with clever, patient parents and teachers. For this category of people, the parents are very important. We've seen people who, when faced with a little difficulty or trouble in parenting, just leave their children to their fates, let them do as they please, and then give up on them. Such children are ruined.

The genuine teacher can help such children to develop, but such a teacher is hard to find in this world. The most important qualities of a teacher are understanding and kindness. If we open the chest of a true teacher, we'll find within them wisdom and love side by side. The teacher with only knowledge and understanding but without loving-kindness (*mettā*) cannot really be a teacher. It's difficult to train foolish children and turn them into something better. As the saying goes, "It's better to fight with a tiger." Hence, a teacher with mettā, who sacrifices their own happiness for the good of their pupils, is hard to find; a teacher with intelligence and wisdom is also hard to come by. This world of ours is short of true, genuine teachers. Consequently, we have a lot of people who haven't properly developed, which is a dangerous thing for society.

The fourth and final category contains those beyond anybody's ability to guide, at least at this particular time. Such people represent an extreme case of being mentally slow. We must specify "at this time" because they are beyond help currently, being too ignorant and stubborn to be helped. But don't think that such people can't ever be helped, because according to the highest Dhamma principle, all things proceed according to causes and conditions. Unteachable people require helpful causes and conditions, such as meeting someone patient and self-sacrificing enough to help them improve, far more than anyone. Yet it is difficult for them to come by such opportunities.

There are lots of untrainable, stubborn people. We find them everywhere, careless and proud. They may be clever enough to work and so can be helped in that area; however, as far as Dhamma is concerned, they can't be guided. Notwithstanding that, don't believe that they are absolutely beyond help, because there isn't any conditioned thing that doesn't undergo change. Nothing is fixed, eternal, or absolute. All that is needed is the right causes and conditions intervening in their lives. If we have enough love and sympathy, we will seek out the appropriate causes and conditions with which to surround stubborn people, although it will be hard work. This is called "polishing a brick into a mirror."

So there are four categories of people: the first category requires just a single word, the second needs things explained to some extent, the third needs to be dragged along with a lot of instruction, while the fourth category cannot, at this time, be shown the way. Nature produces people in these four categories, and all four are subject to the law of causes and conditions determining effects and results. Hence, development is possible, as is deterioration. Lack of development is a condition for deterioration, while development is a condition for improvement. Both will be the result of a certain set of conditions predominating.

Please don't consider development to be a trivial matter. If you do, you'll just leave the strugglers alone. If you don't care, or if you just worry, nothing good will result. If you don't surrender, if you strive to help people to improve matters, progress will be possible.

Even though your efforts seem like grinding down an anvil until it becomes a needle or polishing a brick until it becomes a mirror, the results will still be better than doing nothing.

This development of life, of people, is the external and more obvious level. We have viewed it broadly. Get to know these categories and stages so that development actually occurs, whether through our own efforts or the efforts of parents, teachers, and compassionate, loving people. Such development is a duty human beings must undertake.

Now we'll consider the second phase, psychological and spiritual cultivation, which is the heart of practice because it deals with the most important elements of developing life.

Developing Internally through Mental and Spiritual Cultivation

Mental cultivation is delicate, subtle, and difficult. Nevertheless, it is necessary because true accomplishment in life depends on it. Psycho-spiritual development is the truest accomplishment in the successful conduct of life. Observe particularly how mind undergoes change quite naturally, as in the case of children, who, once born, know more and more as they increasingly experience their world. There are external signs that a child is growing more knowledgeable; however, on a deeper level, the child's mind is what's actually developing. Citta, mind, is at the center of it all.

In the natural changes that occur during growth, the physical and mental forms are interconnected. Anything impacting the body will cause mind to feel, respond, and change accordingly. Thus mind develops and gets smarter with each new experience. Even though it meets with some form of dukkha, of trouble and strife, it will be sharper and smarter having had to deal with that.

In truth, troublesome forms of experience are more useful for mental cultivation. Fun, delicious, and pleasurable experiences hardly cause any useful thinking or learning at all, what with mind busily indulging. They tend to foster more ignorance than intelligence. Still, we mostly prefer the beautiful, fun, delicious, and pleasurable even though they only increase our foolishness, while we hardly credit the pains, difficulties, and problems that really make us smarter. Most people label them difficulties and see them as bad luck. I think we're made smarter by these difficulties and obstructions. We make them out to be *bad* only because we look at them simplistically, rather than intelligently, and are unable to solve our problems. If we can see the good in them and make them our partners in the struggle, they make us smarter and help us develop. Hence, a person happy to meet the problems of life is one with the good fortune to be able to make lessons out of life's troubles and progress accordingly.

So be content to meet with life's downsides, even with dukkha. See dukkha as the friend of development, as the ancients taught. Consider experience as being the very thing that teaches us. For instance, when we step on something hot, that teaches us how fire is. When a sharp knife cuts our hand, or a thorn pierces our skin, or we fall down, these experiences teach us the way things are. So don't bother complaining.

It's beyond doubt that we develop, come to know more, and become smarter every time mind is impacted. Unfortunately, some people appear unable to make use of these experiences; only the clever seem able to take in and use experience to become cleverer still. This is the starting point, the root of mental cultivation.

Accumulate Experiential Learning Rather Than Recreate Suffering

Now, what else is there that will cause greater, faster psychological development? Continue the process from life to life. Here, I'm taking advantage of the widespread belief in "rebirth" to point out "the development that connects births." Most people who have heard something about "births" will assume it means this present birth, or life, and the next. They usually understand it to mean the sort of birth that comes from the womb and ends up in a coffin. In their understanding, the development achieved in this life carries over into the next, and from that to a third, a fourth, and so on. Those who think like this must do their best in the present life for progress to occur; they can't just wait for the next one.[4]

Here, however, I'm not in favor of that explanation, although I won't say that it's wrong. The word *birth* (*jāti*), as far as we're concerned, refers to psychological birth. In Dhamma language, *jāti* refers to any occasion of clinging to the feeling of "me" and "mine," which is a matter of mind, not of body. Each occurrence of such clinging is considered a birth, a psychological birth. *Birth* in this second sense means an instance of clinging to being the "me" who gets something, loses something, is something, or becomes something. *Lifetime* also has this meaning in Dhamma language. During the course of one day there can arise many births and lives. In just one day, there can be many dozens of lives, depending on how many times the sense of "me" and "mine" arises. Further, we hold that a child newly born, who doesn't yet know the "me" and "mine" sort of thinking, is really still to be born. The child hasn't undergone birth in the sense we're concerned with here, although the child is alive in the conventional sense—that is, biologically. When born but not identifying as "me," how, then, can the child be the "me" who is alive? Hence, the child born from the womb won't have been born in the truest sense until it grows enough to experience the feeling of being "me" for the first time, of being the "me" who is like this or like that. Many days or months of physical life must pass before this happens.

Please consider which of these two understandings of birth is the serious problem. Which kind of birth or lifetime is dukkha every time? You'll find that birth from the womb doesn't bring dukkha with it, but birth from upādāna, clinging to being "me" and "mine," is dukkha immediately and every time. In the moment the eyes see a provocative form with desire and affection arising, there also arises the sense of "me" and "mine." Once the ears hear a sweet sound, the nose smells a fragrance, or the tongue tastes something delicious, the assumption that it's "me" who has got something good, delicious, beautiful, sweet-sounding, or whatever the case may be arises. The clinging involved is what represents birth here, and this birth bites every time it manifests. Hence, every time there is birth of this kind, there is a life compromised by dukkha.

Let's observe the connection between this kind of ignorant suffering and what follows in the next moment. One either can be foolish and suffer repeatedly, or one can learn to not suffer. Seeing these connections, let the first mistake be beneficial so that a second mistake doesn't happen. Or if slipping again, learning from the second mistake will prevent a third or fourth mistake. In this way, we make mind smarter with every passing lifetime, with every passing experience. Take dukkha as the basis. Let the dukkha that follows our mistakes be our teacher when the next meaningful experience arrives. Let every event, every experience, connect together during the course of life. Let each experience, whether big or small, be of benefit to the next. As these experiences connect, wisdom develops. Simply put, if something hurts, remember it. If we forget something painful that happens, there has been no connection between births. Whereas, if it is remembered, we become smarter and we know how to protect ourselves should it arise again.

This is the sort of development that continues from birth to birth—direct psychological development between lives. Whether it's rebirth in the ordinary meaning or here-and-now birth in the Dhamma meaning, let there be development from life to life. This requires living with care, circumspection, and intelligent observation. Unfortunately, this isn't common. For the most part, we're careless, overconfident, and forgetful. Consequently, life-to-life development is rare.

The Supreme Life of Cultivating the Parāmīs

Our outline of life development continues with cultivating the perfections (*parāmīs*) over a series of births. The parāmīs are accumulated virtues that enable one to cross over to the "other shore" of freedom from afflictions and troubles. In the old understanding, these perfections or supreme virtues are fulfilled while passing through many physical existences or rebirths. You may be familiar with the Jataka tales that recount the 550 lives of the bodhisattva who became the Buddha Gotama after perfecting pāramīs over the course of all those lives. There's no harm in that belief because its intention is beneficial. Accomplishing the pāramīs requires devotion to doing one's best over many rebirths, as generally understood. However, the direct and immediate benefit occurs for this birth or lifetime in the Dhamma-language sense, which holds that a life is one burst of thinking concerned with one particular event or experience. Believing that one is cultivating these supreme virtues through many physical rebirths won't hurt. However, don't cling to the idea of there being an abiding self (*attā*) involved, that it's the same self all along, because that goes against the basic principle that such a lasting self cannot be found. Let it be just about mind, mind becoming increasingly wise with every passing event, with every birth that occurs, whichever kind of birth that might be.

Cultivating pāramīs and growing in intelligence as portrayed in the Jataka tales is a natural evolution. None of it should be mistaken as happening to a lasting self or the same continuing person. Still, the beings born one after the other are smarter each time. Both the people and the animals born later are smarter than the earlier generations because of steadily accumulating knowledge, intelligence, needs, and wants. Even plants evolve and progress. Nowadays we have trees and flowers that are more beautiful, unusual, and marvelous than before. People have bred new varieties, both plants and animals, beyond counting.

These examples illustrate the passing along of qualities between births. Such development can be material, and it can be psycho-spiritual. We must accept that infants today are more developed than infants in the distant past. These are the fruits of psycho-spiritual cultivation occurring between births and connecting lifetimes.

Please understand this and make the most use of it. Use every mistake to increase intelligence. This is directly possible with every Dhamma-language birth. The rebirth of ordinary language, if it really happens, ought to foster greater intelligence too. If used for getting smarter each time, conventional rebirth will benefit the birth of

Dhamma language. Even if there isn't any such conventional thing, still there will be results for the birth of Dhamma language, the many births that occur in a single day.

Even so, that the growth of intelligence should be a long, drawn-out affair involving many lifetimes isn't satisfactory, so we'll consider developing here and now the system known as *brahmacariya*, the supreme way of living. The Buddha explained this practice, improving on what the sages of former times taught. The brahmacariya is a system designed to bring about psycho-spiritual cultivation in this life, here and now, where the fruits are seen directly and personally. Then there's no need to guess how many rebirths and lifetimes it will take. Such calculations have no use here and now. We can see in our direct experience what the results of our development are. Let us cultivate our minds and hearts right here, today, each day.

The Buddha Adapted Existing Systems of Cultivation to Serve Awakening

Systems for developing mind existed before the Buddha's time; ways of cultivating samādhi (well-grounded unification) were already happening. Although they weren't the best, most useful forms of the genre, they provided a base from which the best developed. Raising mind's samādhi to the level of the four *rūpa-jhānas* (meditative absorptions based in form) and four *arūpa-jhānas* (formless meditative absorptions) already had been achieved, as plainly set out in the Buddhist records. The Buddha-to-be found and studied with those able to teach him the seventh and eighth levels of meditative absorption. However, seeing that these jhānas only suppressed dukkha temporarily and couldn't quench it completely, he wasn't fully satisfied.

He continued his search until he discovered the most complete system of practice in which all essential components are gathered together. Samādhi alone is insufficient; it requires sīla and paññā to reach its full power. As the Buddha related it, this full form of practice consists in these three trainings: sīla, samādhi, and paññā—that is, virtue and ethics, stable unification of mind, and experiential wisdom. Accomplish this path and mind will be developed in this life. Hence, there's no need for the trouble and strife involved in passing between rebirths. Practice here and now and the result is here and now; we can develop mind fully in this life without having to wait for the fruits.

Elements from various beneficial systems taught before the Buddha have been retained in the Buddhist system. The Buddha wasn't the originator of the jhānas; they were already known and taught. He learned them, was able to describe how to practice them, and then showed how to use them for ending the āsavas, the outflows of affliction and corruption. Therefore, train samādhi through the four rūpa-jhānas and then give rise to knowledge of the cessation of the effluents, or accomplish both the rūpa- and arūpa-jhānas and use them to realize the cessation of the effluents. Further, the rūpa- and arūpa-jhānas are the basis for *saññāvedayita-nirodha* (the cessation of perception and feeling). Sometimes the cessation of perception and feeling doesn't end the āsavas because that samādhi merely suppresses perception and feeling for a time without quenching craving and clinging completely. When accompanied by sufficient insight and wisdom, the cessation of perception and feeling becomes a vehicle for ending the āsavas once and for all.[5]

True Cultivation Requires a Complete System of Practice

The complete system of sīla, samādhi, and paññā is the heart of mental cultivation. Sīla enables the easier acquisition of samādhi (calm, untroubled stability), while paññā is the sort of knowledge that allows all things to be right and proper, so that any activity can be carried out under the umbrella of samādhi. When the three are integrated, sīla is present in the commitment to practice samādhi, and when samādhi develops successfully, paññā resolves any doubt and confusion.

What really needs to be done is to stabilize, focus, and unify mind because genuine psycho-spiritual development lies in its cultivation. In the eightfold path, the Buddha brings forward right samādhi as being the decisive factor: right understanding and right intention lead the way; right speech, right action, right livelihood, and right effort are supporters; right mindfulness keeps an eye on it all; while samādhi is the boss, the governor, and the core component. That which ends our problems is *sammā-samādhi* (right unification) with the other seven factors acting as its supports. Mind can be cultivated using many techniques, but all must involve samādhi, and the best of them end suffering.

Mental training is the ultimate endeavor because the highly trained mind can go anywhere; it can visit any of the realms of experience. The realms of mind are described comprehensively in four groups: the *kāmāvacara-bhūmis*, the realms of savoring sensuality; the *rūpāvacara-bhūmis*, the realms of savoring pure form where gross sensuality is absent; the *arūpāvacara-bhūmis*, the realms of savoring formlessness; and the *lokuttara-bhūmi*, the realm which is above and beyond all the others. Each of these four main realms of experience has several subsidiary levels. The human mind is special, and once trained, it can visit all of the realms and levels.

Now, we'll need to really see for ourselves how it's possible to train our minds to wallow in sensuality. By surrounding mind with sensuality, by pursuing and enjoying various levels and flavors of sensuality, it becomes engrossed in the kāmāvacara-bhūmis (realms of sensual wandering). Or perhaps we've trained mind so that it loses interest in gross sensual matters and is able to dwell in nonsensual samādhi, such as the several levels of jhāna, where it becomes engrossed in the rūpāvacara-bhūmis (realms of wandering in pure, refined form). Or perhaps we've gone above and beyond even those refined experiences to dwell in the arūpāvacara-bhūmis (realms of wandering in formlessness). Once trained, we can easily establish mind in any of the various realms as and when we please.

Don't treat this as an insignificant matter. If we're able to direct mind according to our wishes, we can solve all of our problems. Whenever we encounter something difficult or painful, the well-trained mind won't experience the event as dukkha. Hence, we practice until we can see all things as being "just like that," just what they are. When mind sees and experiences "thusness," there isn't any dukkha, any liking and disliking. Attractive things won't please, and unattractive things won't displease. Seeing them as "just like that," "only thus," we experience things as they really are. Such is the well-trained mind. Hence, we practice as much and as well as we can, and although our practice might not be complete, what we do will bring benefit.

So know that mind can be trained, and that there are various methods available for us to use. We can choose whichever method we need now that we've discovered mind's secret: it can be trained as needed.

Let's recapitulate: Mind, once trained, can go anywhere. It can travel to or come into existence in any of the four kinds of realms: sensual, purified form, formless, and even transcendent. Now, people hardly know anything about these realms, especially the fourth, which is the most important. The lokuttara-bhūmi is essentially the element or reality in which all else is quenched. Liberated from belief in being a separate self, mind doesn't take root in existence (*bhava*) because it's not dependent on those conditions that support existence (such as described in paṭiccasamuppāda). Although this supreme *bhūmi* (realm) isn't a kind of existence, it is still referred to as a bhūmi. Hence, there is a lokuttara-bhūmi that doesn't involve bhava (existence), a transcendent realm without a "me."[6]

The Thirty-One Realms of Worldly Existence

Later books set out thirty-one bhūmis, or realms, that are worldly in nature. You might enjoy having them enumerated. First, there are those realms understood as being places of deprivation. These are fourfold: hell realm, beastly realm, hungry ghost realm, and demon realm. These are usually understood as being places actually existing somewhere in time and space, where we might go after death. They are believed to be inhabited by beings, beasts, spirits, and demons. I have a different perspective. If a certain kind of concocting happens in someone's mind, it has a corresponding result. If, for instance, there's the sort of thinking that causes mind to become hot, like it's on fire, one has landed in hell (*naraka*). This will be the sense-experience hell mentioned by the Buddha, which is more of a reality than any hell under the ground, the whereabouts or actual existence of which nobody knows for certain. The hell that is real, that is personally experienceable here and now, that manifests whenever mind is boiling with the heat of hatred or anger, is largely ignored, but there is plenty of interest in the other kind. How ignorant is that?

The hungry ghosts (*petas*) are representations of insatiable hunger, the most ignorant and insane hunger. The hunger of taṇhā, craving, makes one a peta, which is to exist in excessive, unending hunger. The ignorant mind is often like that, and whenever it is, one has become a hungry ghost.

The beasts of the animal (*tiracchāna*) realms are unknowing. They don't know the things that should be known, or if they do know anything, their knowledge is misguided and easily confused. Whenever one suffers the same kind of ignorance or confusion, that's animal existence. Have you noticed when mind is like that?

In the demon (*asura*) realm, the trend is toward cowardice, the sort of cowardice that is unseemly, detestable, and shameful. Whenever one is in that condition mentally, at that time there is demonic existence. These four—hell, hungry ghost, animal, and demon realms—are described as deprived and woeful (*apāya*).

Now we progress to the ordinary human (*manussa*) realm. This is like the middle ground, the base from which the human mind can become anything—that is, it can move around and through the other realms. It's the nature of human beings to struggle and strive, which we'll do either wrongly or rightly, and as a result we can be, mentally, anything. This isn't considered to be hellish, hungry-ghostly, beastly, or demonic. It's considered human, with the problems and sufferings of human beings.

Next are the *devatās*, the beings of the six sensual paradises. These devatās enjoy sensual pleasures to the full. They can't be compared with humans, because humans, for instance, still bathe themselves in sweat on occasion, while these devatās don't. In fact, if they should happen to sweat, they would drop dead instantly, hence they draw the line at sweating. They experience sensual happiness but without having to sweat for it, something humans can't emulate. The sensual realm of devatās is thus different from humans. There are six levels, or classes, of them. Adding these six to the four deprived realms and the one human realm gives a total of eleven realms thus far. They make up the realms of sensual wandering and spinning.

Continuing upward, we find the gods of pure-form realms known as *rūpa-brahmas*. The rūpa-brahmas dwell in realms of purified form that arise through the power of the four rūpa-jhānas. There are sixteen classes of gods within the realms of wandering and spinning in purified form. Sixteen plus eleven makes for twenty-seven realms thus far.

Then there is the final group, the gods of the formless realms, the *arūpa-brahmas*, which are of four classes: those of the spheres of endless space, of endless consciousness, of nothingness and of neither perception nor nonperception. These are the subdivisions of wandering and spinning in formlessness. Add these four to the others and the total is finally thirty-one. Some people like to memorize the thirty-one realms; students of Abhidhamma can often recite the thirty-one bhūmis with some facility. They are like a map of the ways mind can wander, act, and dwell.

The worst evil and torment occur within the deprived realms. Humans experience both happiness and distress. The beings of the sensual realms experience pleasure based in sensuality. The rūpa-brahmas and arūpa-brahmas experience happiness based in their personal, though still selfish, purity. They are quite proud of this purity that gives them great happiness. However, all of them are crazy! When I say this, people revile me, but I'm not worried. All of these realms are capable of provoking infatuated clinging, which is a kind of madness that makes us incapable of knowing the liberation of lokuttara-bhūmi. All of the thirty-one realms are *lokiya* (worldly). They aren't *lokuttara* (beyond the world). Only when there's no clinging to any existence and realm is there lokuttara-bhūmi.

The mind that is cultivated to the utmost concludes with the lokuttara-bhūmi. Here, mind has begun to or has already reached the ultimate. The aforementioned thirty-one realms are lokiya and of a nature to concoct and to be concocted (*saṅkhata*)—to change and transform continually—according to their particular type. The transcendent realm is unconcocted and unconditioned (*asaṅkhata*); in it, mind cannot be concocted by conditions.[7]

Entering Realms of Existence through Perception

Examining these levels of mind more closely, we may observe that all the aforementioned experiences involve perception and recognition (*saññā*).[8] Saññā recognizes, regards, and apprehends experiences as this or that. "Regarding" and "apprehending" mean that things are assumed to truly be as they are perceived. All beings in the woeful, human, and divinely sensual realms recognize, regard, and apprehend sensuality (*kāma*) in one way or another. Experiencing through the lens of sensuality, they wander in the sensual realms (*kāmāvacara-bhūmis*). They all are caught in sensual perception (*kāma-saññā*), regarding and assuming the sensuous aspect of life. Next, minds among the four levels of rūpa-brahmas recognize, regard, and apprehend refined forms (*rūpa-saññā*). They perceive and assume through the lens of pure form, experiencing without grosser sensuality. Finally, minds among the four levels of arūpa-brahmas recognize, regard, and apprehend formlessness (*arūpa-saññā*) in their various ways. They perceive and assume through the lens of formlessness, which they understand as being without form, more refined, subtler, and without dukkha. They regard and believe this as formless.

Saññā is what determines the level, or realm, that people dwell in. In their subjective regarding, there is the recognition of the satisfying flavor of a particular realm or kind of existence. Those of the kāma-saññā realms regard sensuality as possessing a pleasing flavor. They delight in sensuality. Those of the rūpa-saññā realms regard pure form as satisfying and pleasing. So delighted, they aren't concerned with grossly sensual experience. Those of the arūpa-saññā realms find satisfaction and delight in regarding formless things.

In other words, each realm is marked by different kinds of clinging.

With clinging to kāma, there is kāma-saññā. In clinging to pure forms, there is rūpa-saññā. In clinging to formlessness, there is arūpa-saññā. Ordinarily, beings adhere to sensuality, either in the style of the devatās, or of humans, or even of those in the deprived realms. They all place their hopes in and cling to the sensual quality of experience.

Progressive Quenching through the Jhānas

The mind that raises itself above sensuality arrives in pure-form experience—that is, the rūpa-jhānas. If mind trains in samādhi to the level of the first jhāna (absorption) with noting and experiencing the meditation object, it lets go of perceiving and regarding sensuality. The first jhāna includes the happiness born of solitude, of seclusion from sensuality. It experiences the factors of jhāna: noting and experiencing the meditation object with satisfaction and well-being, and singularity; thus it notes and regards pure form. One who acquires samādhi on the rūpa-jhāna level knows the happiness arising from the mind freed from and uncrowded by sensuality. This is like someone experiencing cleanliness for the first time, who feels satisfaction with it and doesn't want anything more to do with dirtiness. In a similar way, one now sees sensuality as unclean, and one appreciates solitude and freedom from sensual involvement and the refined happiness that is its fruit. The happiness arising from that solitude represents the comfort and pleasure of one who dwells in the first jhāna. There is rūpa-saññā—more refined recognition and regarding—of the object of concentration in jhāna, in that happiness born of freedom from sensuality.

Now, ascending from the first to the second jhāna, one experiences the happiness born of samādhi (unification). Here, there is a graduation from the satisfaction and joy dependent on solitude, which is replaced by interest in samādhi. With samādhi there is even more refined happiness and well-being. The happiness born of samādhi is now the basis of perceiving and regarding. However, this is still the purified form level of saññā.

On arriving in the third jhāna, one's collection of mental factors is further purified. Here, the happiness resulting from purified mind, in which nothing disturbs it, is experienced and savored. The pleasure experienced here forms the comfort and happiness of that sort of mind. Rūpa-saññā recognizes and regards this happiness.

Arriving at the fourth and final rūpa-jhāna, one experiences neither pain nor pleasure. There is just the purity born from equanimity and mindfulness. Mindfulness purified by equanimity forms the happiness that is the basis of rūpa-saññā here. This purified well-being is recognized and regarded in the fourth absorption.

In moving progressively through the jhānas, the refinement and quality of one's happiness increases. In this cultivation, mind gradually develops through these deepening levels of samādhi. This developing refinement moves through four kinds of rūpa-saññā (perceiving pure form) and then four kinds of arūpa-saññā (perceiving formlessness).

If this development proceeds further, one enters the formless experiences. All perceiving and regarding of form (*rūpa-saññā*) within the four form absorptions are now seen as coarse and distasteful. No longer preferred, they are dropped. In their place, the focus becomes arūpa-saññā, recognizing and regarding formlessness.

The first formless level takes space—lacking form, shape, and appearance—as its focus. This formless experience is easeful and peaceful. One enters into regarding and experiencing various formless states: unbounded space, unbounded awareness, nothingness, and the dimension of neither experiencing nor not experiencing. With these arūpa-saññās, perceiving and regarding are increasingly subtle until there's barely any perceiving at all.

The final category is saññāvedayita-nirodha, the quenching of regarding and feeling, which is subtlest. This subtlest experience doesn't adhere to regarding because regarding (*saññā*) and feeling tones (*vedanās*) are quenched, and there's no feeling tone to cling to in the perceptual process, no vedanā to conceive of and recognize. This is the quenching of saññā. However, if there isn't enough wisdom involved, the effluents (*āsavas*) won't dry up. When ordinary experience returns, perceptions and feeling tones will still be influenced by corruption. If wisdom is sufficient, the effluents will end within this saññāvedayita-nirodha. Thus kilesas and dukkha will have ended.

Accessing these nonsensual realms involves a progressive quenching process known as *nirodha.* Kāma-saññā is quenched and replaced by rūpa-saññā; the fourfold sequential quenching of kāma-saññā by rūpa-saññā is nirodha. Further, rūpa-saññā is quenched and replaced by arūpa-saññā; the sequential quenching of rūpa-saññā by four kinds of arūpa-saññā is also nirodha. Finally, saññāvedayita-nirodha quenches the previous eight saññās of the pure-form and formless realms. This step-by-step quenching is known as *anupubba-nirodha*, quenching one after the other. Altogether there are nine stages of this: four rūpa-jhānas, four arūpa-jhānas, and one saññāvedayita-nirodha.

Because these meditative abodes (*vihāras*) occur one after the other (*anupubba*), mind entering and dwelling in this progressive quenching process is known as *anupubba-vihāra.* This is akin to experiencing lesser levels of nibbāna—partial or preliminary nibbāna. Tasting joy and well-being in these nine meditative dwellings is called *anupubba-samāpatti*: *samāpatti* meaning imbibing or tasting the sublime flavors of those abodes. Entering the four rūpa-jhānas, the four arūpa-jhānas, and saññāvedayita-nirodha is a step-by-step accomplishing of happiness and well-being through these sublime abodes; hence, anupubba-samāpatti. Mind's cultivation naturally goes through these stages of perceiving, abiding, imbibing, and quenching.

There also are obstacles to development that arise step by step along the way, and which should be understood. Just as there is progressive success, the obstacles to success arise sequentially too. This is what happens when people who have had a liking for one kind of thing and then, when changing to something else, find that their previous preference comes back to bother them. For instance, those fond of sensuality, when they become interested in samādhi, which is neither sensual nor sexual, find that their previous preference will obstruct their practice of meditation. This is called *ābādha* (illness, oppression). Therefore, interest in the rūpa-jhānas, then liking and clinging to them, will be ābādha relative to the arūpa-jhānas. In other words, the satisfaction felt with the first jhāna will hinder the attainment of the second, and so on. A simple comparison comes from householders who enter the monastery and find that their previous indulgence in sensuality disturbs them. Such indulgences aren't part of monastic life, yet the habit follows them and becomes an obstacle. It gets in the way of their finding satisfaction in the sensually arid monkhood, until they have to disrobe. Simply put, anything one has been accustomed to finding delight in can become a hindrance when one wants to progress higher. Happiness with the first absorption will interfere when we try to move into the second, and when we achieve the second absorption, the satisfaction we feel in it will act as a hindrance when moving on to the third. It will be like this, step by step by step, right up through the ninth level.

Such are the subtleties of mind. Mind cannot advance when sunk in feelings of satisfaction toward things previously experienced. Though aiming to move on to something better, it still doesn't really want to do so. Consider this fact in the cruder, lesser states of the sensual wandering. In the woeful realms and deprived states, there is pleasure in lowly, base experiences. A great many people can't relinquish self-destructive habits because they derive satisfaction and pleasure from those very habits. For example, when invited to give up drink, dedicated drinkers can't stop imbibing alcohol, which prevents them from learning how to appreciate drinking clean water instead. The delight and satisfaction they are used to getting from drinking spirits pull them back. This is considered oppression or illness too. There are nine kinds of *anupubba-ābādha*,[9] in which previously sought abidings and accomplishments become illnesses and obstacles for further progress.

Mind thus has nine progressive quenchings, nine progressive abidings, nine progressive accomplishments, and nine progressive illnesses. This is the story of mind and the techniques for cultivating it. These matters need to be understood fully and contemplated comprehensively so that we can walk the path correctly and deeply.

Understanding the Stages of Cultivation So They May Unfold

If we understand this development well, we are in good stead. We will be able to comprehend truths of the well-developed mind and its conditions and states. Further cultivation is impossible when practice is at odds with these facts. If we're to develop mind here and now, we need to know these ins and outs of practice. If we're not interested, we'll have to let things carry on as they will, according to circumstances, karma, likes and dislikes, and so on. However, if we wish for mind's development to be within the practitioner's power, we need to manage things in the right way and train mind in accord with this system of practice that was discovered and taught by the Buddha.

At present, Buddhism is the repository of this system preserved in its entirety. Means of cultivating mind have been gathered, tested, and included in the system of the Buddha's teachings as recorded in the Tipiṭaka. Nothing essential is missing or deficient. So study it, and use it to develop mind here and now. If practiced properly and truly, we may realize path, fruit, and nibbāna fully and completely in this life. To whatever extent we're willing to practice, we'll get the commensurate results. Our efforts won't be wasted. If we're willing to practice properly, we'll get the proper results—that is, a fully developed mind here and now in this life.

*

This overview is a summary of what is necessary for cultivating mind, for making an ordinary person into one of the highest level, of nobility, even an arahant. May this overview be of great benefit for each of us in developing our minds.

8

ALL-ROUND OBSERVATION OF LIFE

The aim of this book is a comprehensive understanding of Dhamma in one volume. The previous chapters looked at Dhamma from all angles and perspectives: above, below, behind, in front, at the center. I have coined a word for this—*paridassana*, "all-round seeing, seeing from all sides." Previously, I stated that Dhamma and life are the same thing. When we distinguish them, it's only to examine particular features more closely. When we see everything as Dhamma and nature, we realize that it's all one reality. In this chapter, we'll continue viewing both Dhamma and life as one, from many many angles and perspectives.

All-round seeing means to look at something in a comprehensive and thorough way. However, looking into something really deeply can't be done with just the physical eyes; we need to use the eyes of wisdom too. Then we'll be able to see the interconnectedness of all things, such as with the world we inhabit. If we see it correctly, it is one thoroughly-interrelated, interdependent system.

Such seeing is difficult because we don't know where to stand to have the best, most comprehensive view. If, for instance, we wanted to get the best view of the surrounding countryside, we would climb to the top of a hill and then we could see everything for miles around. Or if we wanted to see to the bottom of the sea, we would need water that is tranquil and clear. What will be our method for seeing life all around?

As we're concerned with Dhamma here, especially the Dhamma of emptiness, of thusness, which can't be seen with the physical eyes, we must use Dhamma eyes—that is, wisdom eyes. Wisdom eyes are needed to see life ultimately being the same as Dhamma. With Dhamma eyes doing the seeing, we'll understand ourselves and all things in life much better than we do now.

Our inability to see all things properly means we don't know any of them properly, which leads to misunderstanding them. Consequently, we divide and separate, falling in love with some and hating others, liking some and disliking others, afraid of some and bold with others. All such reactions are equally foolish. Infatuation, anger, hatred, fear, anxiety, longing, envy, and cruelty are all aspects of the ignorance that comes from not seeing things as they truly are. When we see according to reality, we see everything as being tathatā. Seeing the "just like that" quality of things is at the heart of Buddhism. People who cling too much to the written word don't know where the heart of Buddhism lies. For all those without knowledge of Dhamma, we want to say that it lies in seeing all things as they really are, in seeing everything as being "just so."

Looking but Not Seeing

But what is "looking and seeing," and what is "looking without seeing"? The answer is simple: seeing things as lovable, as annoying, as hateful, as fearful, and so on is grounded in ignorance and amounts to not seeing, really. Such seeing is stuck in the world of duality. When we see the natural thusness of things, liking and disliking, aversion and fear, and the like don't happen. That's looking and seeing. We ourselves can be aware of whether we are really seeing or not.

When we look without seeing, we live in the shadow of one ignorance or another. This inability to see reveals itself in the bouts of liking and disliking we experience, which leads to the arising of kilesas, until we always seem to live with some level of corruption. Such life is fraught with the mental disturbance and unease of not knowing and misunderstanding. It's tormented further by doubts and confusion, being in the dark regarding things around us. Inevitably, the stronger corruptions of greed, hatred, and delusion eventually appear.

All of the kilesas and their torments arise from not seeing life as it truly is. The ignorant desire to grab and clutch is a manifestation of lobha, greed. The ignorant desire to get away from or to destroy is dosa, hatred. Confused, uncertain desiring is the province of moha, delusion. Take a good look: our problems and difficulties are due to lobha, dosa and moha. Such life is disturbed, troubled, and unsatisfying. Taking such a good look at the situation is what we mean by all-round seeing. This is a crucial step out from the ignorance that fosters greed, hatred, and delusion—to begin seeing these reactions as they truly are.

When we ask foreign students of Buddhism how they aim to benefit from their studies, their responses are seldom in line with reality. They can't give a clear answer because they don't recognize the problem of being continually disturbed and distressed by lobha, dosa, and moha. Unaware of what agitates and worries them, they are confused about the Dhamma, which is for the sole purpose of resolving their dilemma. Unaware of their problem, they come to practice meditation and study Buddhism without really knowing why. Perhaps they are following a fad or looking for something interesting during their travel around the world. They seem to miss the true purpose.

We Thais, although we're Buddhist, have a similar problem. We don't know what Dhamma is for, beyond vague notions of making merit. We assume that Dhamma is good, even that it's special and sacred, but that's based on what others have told us. In the end, however, we largely fail to apply Dhamma for its true purpose and benefit, which unfortunately wastes time and encourages foolish beliefs.

Instead, we ought to contemplate our fundamental dilemma thoroughly so that we come to know the truth and recognize the "'just like that" quality of all life and of Dhamma. If we look on the obvious level, a satisfying life must have Dhamma. When we apply Dhamma to our lives correctly, there is peace and contentment. If we go deeper than that, we'll discover the truth that Dhamma is life and life is Dhamma. When we get right down to it, there is really only Dhamma. Dhamma is both life itself and the necessary condition for life.

At this time, however, we won't talk about Dhamma itself so much as about the problem that gets in between Dhamma and life: the assumption that there is a "me," a separate self, interferes with the relationship between Dhamma and life. We cling to the ego, which causes unnecessary friction and tension in life. This life wasn't hot or tense originally, and need not be so, but we agitate it with our clinging to self. This is what we ought to address.

The Beautiful Garden of Dhamma

To address this problem, we need to see life comprehensively until we understand how it connects to Dhamma. Then we learn how to manage it so that it becomes something beautiful. *Beautiful* may sound like a word that poets would use, but the Buddha used it too. He used it in reference to Dhamma itself—beautiful and splendid in its study, beautiful and splendid in practice, beautiful and splendid in its fruition. I'm not saying this to sound modern or fashionable; rather, there isn't any better word to describe Dhamma than *beautiful*.

This is a good place to consider something the Buddha once said, "When this world is full of ignorant people, who will be able to pick the beautiful flowers from the beautiful garden?" The Buddha's garden, here, is Dhamma. In this Dhamma garden there are many dhammas—virtues, teachings, practices, insights—that are like a vast variety of flowers in a garden where blooms of every kind thrive. We find flowers that are beautiful and not so beautiful, large and small, fragrant and foul, every conceivable kind. Who, then, can pick the right flower, the appropriate dhamma, that ought to be picked and practiced for the most benefit?[1]

Foolish people will be unable to make the right choices; only intelligent people can choose wisely. People who have realized Dhamma sufficiently, beginning with stream enterers, will know how to pick the flowers from the beautiful garden, the dhammas that quench the immediate dukkha. Stream enterers are the first level of people who can truly quench dukkha. They know how to pick and apply the teachings and practices that quench dukkha in reality, thus solving the problems of everyday life. We, still lacking such insight, don't know how to pick the right flower from the Buddha's garden, the particular dhamma that will quench this dukkha. We don't know what to choose, even though we're Buddhists, disciples of the Buddha, who ought to get the most benefit from the Dhamma garden.

Flowers are beautiful, fragrant, and refreshing. They symbolize the dhammas, the medicines, that can solve our problems, that can quench dukkha. Ordinary, foolish, suffering people are like people with chronic fevers: infatuation, anger, hatred, fear, anxiety, longing, jealousy, envy, and all the other spiritual diseases you can name. Who will be able to choose the beautiful flowers that can heal these diseases and torments?

Why must *beautiful* be used here? Because beautiful Dhamma leads to well-being, happiness, and ease. In the garden of Dhamma, there is more than merely ameliorating pain; well-being and happiness are found. And what sort of people are we to find such beauty? We should be the sort who are able to make the right choices and benefit from an everyday existence that is fresh, cheerful, clear, and bright—a life without any kind of torment. At first glance, looking superficially, there seems to be too many flowers in the garden to choose just the right one. Yet if we have genuine knowledge, it's quite possible to pick and use just the flower, just the dhamma, that will let us defend against and resolve the infatuation, hatred, anger, fear, envy, yearning, or whatever unhealthy reaction threatens in that moment.

Whatever the details, our practice always comes down to the simple expedient that is punctual and specific to the moment. With mindfulness, the afflictions and the concocting of dukkha are caught before they can develop, at every occasion of sense contact that might otherwise give rise to problems. Here I want to emphasize the matter of punctuality, of catching the moment, of being able to bring just the right dhamma at just the right time to solve the dukkha problem, whatever the occasion. This is a personal matter, to successfully choose the right flower from the grandest natural park. Or perhaps we should speak of an herbal garden, the most wonderful medicinal garden that anyone could plant.

In seeing wisely, all things are nature, occuring naturally, like flowers in a park. All these aspects of nature are connected with us, with our inner life, always. Problems happen here, too, in the life of mind. This is why the Buddha said that suffering is understood in this body accompanied by mind. Further, the quenching of dukkha must happen right here, too, right where the dukkha is. This is what I call *paridassana*: seeing life in an all-round, all-encompassing manner, from every angle, and well enough that we end our problems.

As has been said, Dhamma and life are interconnected. If we look more deeply, we must say that Dhamma and life are one and the same. For now, however, we can focus on how they are interconnected, which will inspire us to take a good look at both life and Dhamma together. What, then, is Dhamma? Dhamma has four basic meanings: nature, the law of nature, duty according to the law, and the results of how the duty is done. Each of these are Dhamma, and we need to see them together for a well-rounded perspective on Dhamma.

Now, that which is commonly understood to be life is nature. Body and mind are nature, and the law of nature rules them. Body and mind have duties to perform; they need to operate properly so that dukkha doesn't happen. Their duty or function is their Dhamma. If they function wrongly, then, in accord with the law of nature, there will be fever, disease, even death. Many forms of life have gone extinct because of not performing their duties in line with the law of nature. The forms that remain, perhaps coincidentally, have been able to function in line with the law of nature—that is, they adapted along with other changes in nature. Of some species we only have fossils, while a relative few, such as *Homo sapiens*, have survived. The law of nature requires that life does its duties and functions properly to survive and avoid torment.

This isn't very profound or difficult to understand. Just try going against the law of nature and you'll get sick, maybe even die. You'll suffer. This world is many millions of years old, and a human life has around a hundred years, yet people still can't manage to live properly. There is so much ignorance that we don't make the right sorts of adjustments as we go. Is it worth being born and living for a hundred years or so if we can't live happily? In the nearly one hundred years from birth until death, in all of this life, we ought to learn what we need to dwell without dukkha.

People suffer more problems than animals, in line with our ability to think more broadly, quickly, and deeply. Our thinking takes us far and causes many more problems than animals experience. They don't have the same mental distress as we thinking humans. In this particular aspect, people are worse off than animals. Although we can invent beautiful and stimulating things, we still can't quench dukkha, which makes the amazing things we invent foolish and without real benefit. We could live without them, but we don't, because we aren't paying attention to how we suffer from possessing such problematic cleverness.

There are people who think I'm crazy for dwelling on this issue, just like I think they're crazy for all the investments they make in competitions, conferences, inventions, and marketing without any real progress to end suffering. When I read about such things in the newspaper, there's nothing about quenching dukkha. Often, suffering is worsened.

When the problem of dukkha isn't understood as being a problem, our lives don't receive the result commensurate with having been born human. We should have the greatest happiness, but instead we have almost none. We can't compete with cats for happiness, and even dogs and chickens have less dukkha than we do. It's often assumed that animals dwell in ignorance and that humans are so much smarter, so why then aren't we happier than them? This is a problem that I think should be comprehensively observed, especially by middle-aged people and older, those closer to death, because if such people die in their present condition, they will do so without any satisfaction. They will die still shamed by cats.

If we make the most of our remaining years to manage our lives properly, we can dwell above our self-made problems and without dukkha. This will be more in keeping with our true human potential—to be fully human beyond dukkha. This is why I invite people to take an interest in these things, which in reality boil down to just two: Dhamma and life. Only those two. Investigate them thoroughly, contemplate them comprehensively, until knowing them as "just like that." Then act in line with their thusness and no dukkha will occur. Instead, life will flow smoothly, coolly, and peacefully. In other words, we won't have wasted this human birth and the opportunity of discovering the Buddha's teaching.

Spinning in Circles of Dukkha

How might we go further in investigating life comprehensively? I would like to consider all aspects of life as *vaṭṭasaṃsāra*, which means "spinning in circles, repeating the same old rounds of saṃsāra over and over." Let's explore the cyclical, revolving, repeating aspect of life comprehensively.[2]

Life has meanings both in the language of the world and of Dhamma. In worldly language, life is about animate creatures—plants, trees, and so on that aren't dead yet. In Dhamma language, life has the rather deeper meaning of being fresh, cool, and peaceful. This goes beyond the materialist view of protoplasm being alive, which has nothing to do with happiness and suffering. For us, to be alive is to live without having to suffer. Living with dukkha, in Dhamma language, is a kind of death. When we're distressed by birth, aging, sickness, death, or any other issue, that is a kind of living death. Hence, to be truly alive is the freshness, vibrancy, and clarity of living without dukkha. The life of Dhamma language has this more profound meaning.

If we analyze further, we'll see that one kind of life—conventional life without the benefit of Dhamma—is endlessly concocted by the power of causes and conditions, making it prone to change and transformation because of those causes and conditions. Another kind, living with Dhamma, isn't concocted by causes and conditions, doesn't change because of them, and thus isn't afflicted by dukkha. This is difficult for ordinary people to understand; they take the change of concocting for granted. They can't conceive of nonconcocting as life.

I'd like you to see both kinds of life. There is life fabricated by causes and conditions, and there is life unconcocted by causes and conditions—in other words, the kind of mind that can't be fabricated by causes and conditions—because life is permeated with profound understanding. The latter sort of life has realized *visaṅkhāra* (nonconcocting). After his awakening, the Buddha laughed away craving because, having penetrated visaṅkhāra, nothing could stir it up again. We ought to consider a life lived above any concocting as the most satisfying.

Life that is still ignorant, that lacks understanding of the Dhamma, is full of the problems that cause dukkha. Not knowing how to select the right flowers from the Buddha's beautiful garden, people suffer lives of constant fabricating and spinning in circles. In general, people don't know about the possibility of the nonfabricated life, and so they experience lives afflicted by problems. To understand this, we need to look at vaṭṭasaṃsāra. We contemplate it in order to see what we have been missing or ignoring. Saṃsāra is spinning around in birth and death, while *vaṭṭas* are the habitual patterns or cycles in which saṃsāra spins. Vaṭṭasaṃsāra is the whole worldly universe through which we spin and cycle. Understanding the spinning around and concocting illuminates this life of suffering as well as Dhammic life.

We'll start with the basics of vaṭṭasaṃsāra, the cycle of birth and death. There is birth, then there is death. From birth, life spins toward death. This spinning around in birth and death is the vaṭṭasaṃsāra of those who are still sleeping, who have yet to awaken into full understanding and blossoming. Such lives know only birth then death, birth then death, birth then death. They die to be born and are born to die without ever expanding their knowledge to include how to realize deathlessness. From death, how is it possible to cycle into the deathless? It all depends on causes and conditions. From birth to death, life through all its changes is under the power of causes and conditions. Leaving behind all that death and reaching the deathless requires that the necessary causes and conditions be present too.

Realizing that which doesn't die requires proper human behavior and practice.

Next, we can look with more refinement and consider the natural mind. For example, in the womb, before there is any sort of development, mind is empty, free from dukkha. Infants grow to the point where they experience sense impacts via the eyes, ears, nose, tongue, body, and mind. Only then can there be feelings of pleasure and pain, along with desire and clinging influenced by such feelings, and then dukkha. At the beginning, mind is empty and free, there's no dukkha. Then it starts spinning, and there's dukkha. Please observe that we start out empty-free, without concocting and suffering.[3] With development and growth, the child learns to fabricate, learns to cling, and thus learns to suffer. Dukkha comes and goes with repeatedly thinking about and concocting "me" and "mine," such as the "me" who is reading and thinking about this. Revolving from empty of dukkha to experiencing dukkha goes on throughout the course of each day. Notice that there are times when mind isn't fabricated, when there isn't any dukkha. Although such times may be short in duration, they happen repeatedly, until something stirs up mind into dukkha again. When that something loses its power, the fabricating stops.

Now there is dukkha, now there isn't, now there is, now there isn't. It's empty-free for the sake of not being empty-free, and then it's not empty-free for the sake of being empty-free. All of this alternates quite naturally depending on contacts with our surrounding environment and with responses we're unable to control. We as yet haven't expanded the experience of dukkha fully enough to reach its end, to let dukkha finish once and for all. Although it's dependent on causes and conditions, we can't control it; we don't know dukkha properly, so we continue to cycle through it. We go in circles alternating between dukkha and emptiness, between suffering and freedom, under the power of causes and conditions. Suffering then empty, empty then suffering. This is the vaṭṭasaṃsāra in the minds of common people. There's nothing vast or huge about it, although it may seem so when minds are tiny.

The spinning around between suffering and emptiness is

represented by one of the pictures in Suan Mokkh's Theater of Spiritual Entertainments.[4] At first, there's just an empty circle. Then it separates into a black half and a white half. Empty of black and white, which is free of dukkha, is the natural mind. However, it isn't beyond the influence of surrounding causes and conditions that turn it black and white, happy and sad, good and evil. Concocted by causes and conditions, it falls into the world of duality. We spin around like this—now free, now in the world of black and white, now free, now not free. Externally, we behave like Jekyll and Hyde, which we see in others but not in ourselves. We think others are imbalanced and going crazy, but we don't recognize how profoundly our minds are out of balance. We don't talk about this. Still, the minds of ordinary "normal" people flip and flop between empty and crowded—sometimes free, sometimes black, sometimes white, and sometimes free again. Vaṭṭasaṃsāra is a deplorable, frightening condition to be in.

Through training and cultivation, mind stops reacting to causes and conditions as black and white. When we practice the path of spiritual cultivation correctly, mind won't so easily fall into black and white, nor so often. Although originally and naturally empty-free, this emptiness can change and become busy. Even if it doesn't remain always empty and free, with practice it's less and less busy with black and white. As we practice observing this spinning and its slowing down, we gain insight into radical nonspinning.

When knowledge ripens fully, the busy turmoil becomes empty-free with the emptiness that doesn't change. With sufficient wisdom, with enough Dhamma, we discover the most special flower in the Buddha's garden. Then the emptiness doesn't flip back to the tumultuous spinning between concocted and unconcocted and back. Mind realizes the nature that can't be fabricated by causes and conditions, which we usually name *nibbāna*. This fully realized mind is visaṅkhāra, beyond concocting. There's no more spinning between unfabricated and fabricated by black and white. It remains splendidly luminous whatever the causes and conditions, whatever impacts the eyes, ears, nose, tongue, body, and mind.

Recognize the Conditions for Dukkha in Order to Search Out Its Quenching

This, in some detail, is vaṭṭasaṃsāra as it occurs in our minds for as long as the ultimate visaṅkhāra isn't realized. This state of affairs persists until we know the dhamma to which the Buddha awakened: idappaccayatā-paṭiccasamuppāda, knowledge of the conditioned process through which dukkha arises and the reverse cycle that thoroughly quenches that process. The longest version of dependent co-arising (*paṭiccasamuppāda*) describes twenty-four interlinked conditions. The first twelve dependently co-arisen conditions, beginning with ignorance, culminate in dukkha. Then, the birth of dukkha supports a second cycle that advances via the arising of faith that there is a way to quench dukkha, followed by seeking out that way and then practicing until dukkha is quenched.

If you're still with me, you have seen the dukkha in your life and are smart enough to recognize it as suffering. You are no longer so foolish as to be oblivious to your own suffering, ignoring it and uninterested in doing anything to quench it and its conditions. Nor do you react to suffering with any of the superstitious beliefs and distractions that many people follow. We take to heart the Buddha's teaching that there is dukkha, and we see it. We see further that suffering and distress can be quenched because we see the dukkha of depending on causes and conditions. Thus arises the certain belief—*saddhā*, faith—that dukkha can be quenched. There is knowledge of dukkha, there is faith that it can be quenched, and there is awareness that noble ones live who have quenched dukkha. So we seek out someone who has this Dhamma knowledge and the methods that lead to its gradual quenching. In other words, we seek a way out of vaṭṭasaṃsāra.

If we can't follow this path, we'll just go on repeatedly spinning around in dukkha. Every time the "me" idea arises, there is suffering, over and over again. We'll stay like this until, in whatever way it arises, there's real knowledge that dukkha can be quenched. Then there's faith that something is truly capable of quenching dukkha.

Even though we haven't directly experienced it, we have reasons to trust in it. Once come this far, we're in the first stage of the noble path that leads to quenching, which is called "stream entry." Stream enterers have firm faith in the reality of nibbāna; their minds incline steadily toward dukkha's end. Hence, the faith of stream enterers is the real thing, and not the same as that of worldly people. Advancing in the wake of faith, seek and find the quenching of dukkha.

Here is the modus operandi by which ordinary people such as ourselves can quench dukkha: See the dukkha and recognize the spinning around in it through all the ways discussed above. See the various causes and conditions supporting it. See clearly that dukkha can be quenched, because it only exists when dependent on certain causes and conditions. Study and research this supreme matter with genuine faith that suffering can be quenched. Seek out and practice the method of quenching dukkha, step by step, until culminating in escape from vaṭṭasaṃsāra.

This sequence of events is also referred to as "escaping from saṅkhata" (the put-together, the concocted) and "realizing asaṅkhata" (the unconcocted). Leave behind the saṅkhata phenomena that you've been caught in due to clinging and discover the asaṅkhata, the reality that can't be clung to. Before, life was full of clinging. Now it's found the end of all clinging, the asaṅkhata reality that nobody can cling to. This finishes it. The well-cultivated mind ends right here.

I beg you to study these most practical aspects of how study and cultivation are related. We observe the interactions that make up cultivation more than we focus on the teachings. We talk about the teachings more than enough. Now we must observe the actual problems that create the need for Dhamma. These will reveal the Dhamma we need, which we view from all around so that we can put it into action.

We can briefly summarize this section by saying that falling into the cycles of vaṭṭasaṃsāra is like being drawn into a whirlpool and not being able to get out. A boat, once drawn into a whirlpool at sea, usually can't escape. This mind, when mixed up with ignorance, is in the same predicament. Escaping our ignorant spinning is difficult.

We have no choice, then, but to understand the predicament of being caught in vaṭṭasaṃsāra. It's absolutely necessary that we know all about this particular problem in our personal experience. Don't let it be just talk, merely repeating the words and ideas intellectually. Examine vaṭṭasaṃsāra thoroughly in yourself.

The Rotating, Circular Nature of Things

Vaṭṭasaṃsāra, spinning around in circles, is everywhere and constitutes our normal, everyday experience. Cyclical patterns are common to everything around us, whether we notice them or not. To more easily see this, let's consider images that we can see directly or through the work of scientists. These material metaphors for vaṭṭasaṃsāra, benefiting from the intelligence of scientists, can help open Dhamma eyes. If we are intelligent in our comparisons, modern scientific metaphors won't contradict Buddhist principles.

Take the atom, the smallest divisible part of all elements. In an atom, there is the vaṭṭasaṃsāra of one part spinning around another. Atomic theory explains that electrons circle around the protons and neutrons of the nucleus. We need not worry about all the details to benefit from the scientific example of circling around constantly. Vaṭṭasaṃsāra, in a material sense, can be found in every atom. Atoms form the basis of all material things: combining in molecules, as organs and body parts in us and other animals, and as worlds. Everything is made of atoms, which maintain themselves with circling around. In this material example we can recognize vaṭṭasaṃsāra in atoms.

Now consider something mental. According to established Buddhist principles, a mental moment involves arising, persisting, and ceasing. The *bhavaṅga-citta*, the inactive mind without any thought, arises as individual moments of mind that persist for the briefest time before ceasing. These are like atoms of mind. These are moments of natural mind, before something happens—a flashing into existence, momentary persistence, and ceasing. Each cycle happens so quickly that it can't be timed. We speak of this as "mind," or a moment of what we consider mind to be, which is the foundation of life. It isn't yet the sort of mind that becomes this or that. It's just the basic mind spinning along: arising, persisting, and ceasing. Consider that even before any experience comes in to affect it, mind spins in cycles of arising, persisting, and ceasing.

The fundamental mind, mind before anything concocts it, revolves in its natural vaṭṭasaṃsāra, without doing or creating anything. There's nothing concocting and fabricating. Perhaps there is some inscrutable cause in nature that forces this continual arising, persisting, and ceasing. Just this is what we call "mind," the natural element of consciousness that manifests in order to combine with the body. Mind itself is a circle, a cycle of arising, persisting, and ceasing. No self-existing attā can be found.

Upon close inspection we find vaṭṭasaṃsāra, both physical and mental, revolving in circles. All the constituents that make up the body and all the constituents that make up mind seem to have the same source—turning in circles. Spinning around in cycles, vaṭṭasaṃsāra, is the origin of all things physical and mental.

This is as subtle as we can get, so subtle we can't see the spinning with our physical eyes. We must see with *vijjā* eyes, the wisdom eyes of penetrating knowledge. Nuclear physicists investigate with great subtlety using their powerful physical tools and mathematics to see the fundamental spinning in all matter. In a complementary way, Buddhists and others who study the subtleties of mind reach the same conclusion: citta, mind, is something that maintains itself through a process of arising, persisting, and ceasing. So the subtlest truth of mind is that it spins in circles.

Revolving in Circles Sustains All Things

Body and mind, the basis of everything, are vaṭṭasaṃsāra. Their nature is to revolve in circles. All the things born of them will be the same. Thus we can see this revolving, cyclical nature in the myriad things of the world, especially in their births and deaths. For instance, trees sprout, grow, and then die, leaving seeds behind for more sprouting, growing, and dying. In sum, it's all sprouting, growing, and dying. Things are able to exist through this revolving and cycling. Without this spinning, nothing could happen.

Turning in circles has a special power that sustains things, dhammas, according to their nature. All the planets of the solar system are sustained by revolving on their axes and circling around the sun. All the stars in the universe maintain themselves by rotating and circling. Spinning is necessary; without it, nothing exists.

The life cycle of birth, aging, sickness, and death is necessary for life as we know it. Ordinary life revolves through these powerful forces of birth, aging, sickness, and death. Life is impossible without these cycles.

Further, life is supported by other cycles, by physical cycles, such as the water cycle so essential to human life. Water evaporates, the vapor floats up into the sky to form clouds, the clouds condense, and rain falls to the earth, which in time evaporates, rises up as vapor to form rain clouds once more, and so on. If this didn't happen, the water would be gone. Because of the water cycle, we have water to use, and how we use the water involves further cycles. This is one more example of how cycling is necessary for all systems to sustain themselves.

Even the things humanity creates operate in a cyclical manner, as with the cycle of profit and loss in business. Enterprises lose money, make a profit, or break even. The capital circulates between profit, loss, and breaking even. This is how trade sustains itself. It can't happen in just one way, such as profit all the time or loss all the time. Capital and resources must move and cycle. Gambling is the same. Gambling necessarily involves winning and losing, and perhaps breaking even. That's what sustains gambling circles. No-loss situations are impossible; if there were any, it wouldn't be gambling.

Returning to a more natural example, a buffalo is born and eats grass. When the buffalo dies, the grass will devour the buffalo. The buffalo eats the grass, the grass eats the buffalo—it's all a cycle. The ancients used to say that when the water level rises, the fish will eat the ants; when the water level drops, the ants will eat the fish. It seems that on the material side of things, nature forces cyclical patterns to enable things to exist.

Observing the Cycles of Mind

Let's come back to observing mental phenomena. In the traditional literature, the mental cycles of vaṭṭasaṃsāra are divided into three parts: kilesas, karmas, and vipākas. When afflictions occur, because we're unable to manage causes and conditions, karmas happen—that is, actions performed under the power of afflictions. When there are actions, there will be vipākas, the consequences of the actions, which in turn encourage and strengthen afflictions. Hence the kilesas arise again, and then there are more karmas, more vipākas, and more strengthening of the kilesas, and so on and so forth. Kilesas, afflictions; karmas, deliberated actions done in ignorance; and vipākas, the results of those actions—these three cycle around in mind, keeping us in motion, unable to stop. This is the dukkha within the cycle. There is the suffering inherent in kilesas; there is the suffering inherent in volitional actions; and there is the suffering of the results of those actions too. All of this happens because, lacking proper knowledge, there's clinging to "me" and "mine." Corruptions are "me" and "mine," the actions are "me" and "mine," and the results are "mine" too. Mind, caught in individuality, thus can't escape the power of the kilesas, karmas, and vipākas.

Vaṭṭasaṃsāra is right here, not in the Himalayan clouds or wherever some people imagine it to be. However vast and huge, the cycles of spinning are right here in the living, conscious body of each person. Please observe how marvelous and strange these cycles are. They happen in everything that moves and revolves. Without revolving, people, beings, and things can't exist. They would disintegrate and disperse who knows where if not for repeating themselves through their particular cycles.

Another circle, subtle and fascinating, occurs between viññāṇa (consciousness) and nāmarūpa (active body-with-mind organism). Viññāṇa gives birth to nāmarūpa, and then nāmarūpa, once arisen, gives birth to further viññāṇa. Consciousness and body-with-mind support each other in this cyclical way.[5] This subtlety of the Buddha's teaching is often overlooked; that viññāṇa is the condition for nāmarūpa while nāmarūpa is the condition for viññāṇa is seldom mentioned. In their explanations of dependent co-arising, scholars mostly repeat the standard formula about ignorance conditioning concoctings (*saṅkhāras*), concoctings conditioning viññāṇa, this consciousness conditioning nāmarūpa, body-with-mind conditioning the sense media, which condition sense contact, feeling tones, and so on, so that dukkha fully emerges. However, some suttas specify that consciousness is the condition for body-with-mind, and then body-with-mind is the condition for the arising of consciousness. Take care to not confuse nāma and viññāṇa. While they both have to do with mind, *nāma* refers to active mental functions interacting with bodily functions, while consciousness that has yet to be activated is called *viññāṇa* here. When consciousness is active with rūpa (body), their interactive functioning is called *nāmarūpa*.

Observe, then, that body-with-mind is the condition for consciousness, while consciousness is also the condition for body-with-mind. The two circle around each other, over and over, without end. We must know how to observe this. See how they function from each perspective: see how body-with-mind makes consciousness possible and see how consciousness makes body-with-mind possible. Without consciousness, body-with-mind can't function, while inactive body-with-mind leaves no opportunity for consciousness to function. In short, viññāṇa and nāmarūpa form yet another circle, spinning around in support of each other.

This means that life is in essence heartbreakingly cyclical. It's a struggle to manage and difficult to quench the dukkha involved when life is naturally cyclical. Atoms, mind moments, animals, people, solar systems, galaxies, the entire cosmos—all are naturally cyclical. There's no escaping the gravitational pull of the cycles. We dwell under their power.

That life must be cyclical is the challenge of our lives. When will we see this? When will we dare to look? This is why I espouse the comprehensive observation and investigation called "all-round seeing," so that we'll see with increasing clarity and truly know that everything we experience is really "just like that." When everything is understood to be "just so," we stop liking and disliking the things we experience, stop being pleased or displeased with them, and stop becoming happy or sad over them. Here's where mind is lifted beyond being concocted by things; this is visaṅkhāra, and there is no more dukkha. This sort of looking is fundamental; examine using this basic principle. Start to see in this way and it becomes increasingly clear, until we're able to cut out infatuation and delusion. By dropping clinging, the liberated mind emerges from everything binding and trapping. It's released from foolishness, released from the ignorant spinning in vaṭṭasaṃsāra.

The Liberation of Seeing Clearly

The liberation of mind is right here. There's nowhere else to go; just this is the ending of dukkha. All around, just like before, are things ready to concoct mind, the causes and conditions that have had the power to fabricate. Now, though, mind doesn't fabricate; it's unconcoctable. This is mind without dukkha, which is released from the world and is lokuttara—dwelling above and beyond the spinning power of worldly things. Although the body still dwells in the world conventionally, it's different than before. Before, mind was under the power of the world, but now it dwells above all the many and various worldly things. This is freedom from the world. This is the fruit of looking and then seeing, seeing and knowing, so that life changes radically. The story has ended. Dukkha isn't reborn.

Now, please ask yourself whether it is really necessary to see such things in an all-around, comprehensive manner. Is it really beneficial? Is it worthy of your life energy? If you think not, then don't bother. However, if you see it as truly worthwhile, as more beneficial than anything, then it deserves your full attention. Using the approach I've described, endeavor to look, until you see. We can't make anyone see, but we can point things out for people to look for themselves. We can only advise. Dhamma must be personally experienced. If you believe it's to your genuine advantage, then look and see for yourself.

For as long as you don't see, you won't know the illusory self that is life's basic problem. You won't know the foolish self of ignorance. You won't know how life isn't really "me," thus you grasp at it as really "me," as "self." Your life will be full of "me," "ego," and "mine." Once you see how it really is, such suppositions and feelings won't happen. You can still use the words of society and convention—"me" and "mine"—but mind won't take them seriously and won't identify with them due to seeing the "just like that" quality of everything.

Not knowing life's basic problem is like being in the dark. It's like being blindfolded and left to grope one's way through life. Not seeing these things as they actually are, we wander astray. The blindfold grows thicker and tighter; we are left to struggle alone, fight for survival alone, and grab what we can get. That approach is more wrong than right, and it's full of problems, full of dukkha. When we finally see, these problems disappear. It's like we've opened our eyes and regained perfect vision. One kind of life acts without seeing; this kind of life acts much differently. Seeing clearly, it manages its problems and frees itself to live in the reality without dukkha, which we know as nibbāna, as the end of the dukkha.

Can't See Because Things Are Obstructing

Right now there is something that doesn't let us see clearly. It gets in the way and obscures, or keeps us from looking, and even makes us not want to look or see. Our biggest problem is that we live in this world with ignorance (*avijjā*). It obstructs us, it engulfs us, and it dominates us. The blocking agent that keeps us stuck and prevents light from shining is ignorance, our lack of true knowledge (*vijjā*) that understands all things as they really are. To be without vijjā is to be without wisdom, and without wisdom, there's no proper mindfulness. Mindfulness (*sati*) is the vehicle that delivers wisdom to any event or experience that occurs. When we lack wisdom, mindfulness can't do its job. Sati won't have any wisdom to bring. This causes all our problems with afflictions and torments. There isn't anything to manage the experience properly.

Mindfulness is crucial in that it recalls and brings to mind the intelligence and wisdom that are needed. The knowledge and wisdom previously cultivated are brought to bear by sati. Important realities are contemplated until understanding them is natural and normal. Whenever a situation occurs, there is enough mindfulness to convey the needed wisdom to resolve that situation. Sati and paññā perform their different duties while working together. The root of *sati* is "to sail," like an arrow flies. When recall is fast enough, wisdom appears and is applied to the situation immediately. Consider such events as seeing a form with the eyes, hearing a sound with the ears, smelling an odor with the nose, tasting a flavor with the tongue, feeling a sensation with the body, or whatever happens, such that there is sense contact and a meaningful impression is made. If sati doesn't deliver paññā to that contact in time, then ignorance will be in charge and mind won't know what to do. The nature of ignorance is that is runs the show wrongly, concocting warped views and misunderstanding, followed by afflictions such as greed, hatred, and delusion. That's only possible when paññā doesn't arrive to oversee the event or situation. This lack of wisdom, clarity, insight, and illumination is avijjā. When avijjā has power over a situation, things proceed ignorantly and result in undesirable fabrications such as greed, aversion, and delusion. In other words, we suffer dukkha.

A miscellany of consequences follows from avijjā. When ignorance functions, it may show up specifically as *mada*, *pamāda*, *moha*, *micchādiṭṭhi*, and other members of avijjā's lineage. Ignorance itself is hard to see, so distinguishing its manifestations may help us observe more comprehensively.

Mada is "intoxication" with the charming or attractive quality of something. Ignorance becomes intoxicated with the charming quality of things capable of arousing delight. Intoxication prevents seeing things as they actually are, which leads mind astray and into dukkha.

Pamāda means "fully intoxicated," that is, stupefied into totally forgetting oneself. Without any awareness, one is grossly careless and negligent. Again, seeing clearly and truly is impossible, with the same results as avijjā.

Moha is delusion, seeing things the opposite of what they are. Delusion mistakes the good as bad, and the bad as good. It's like mistaking a razor-edged discus for a lotus flower.[6] Moha worships things that cause dukkha, believing that they improve or replace suffering. We're almost all like this, understanding things in this upside-down way. We stash away genuine refuges rather than benefiting from them, while taking refuge in things that aren't at all safe and trustworthy. Led astray by the world and its charms, people follow the religion of money, believing money to be a truer refuge than Dhamma.

Micchādiṭṭhi is wrong understanding, false beliefs, and half-baked theories. Because of mistaken learning, misunderstandings, misperceptions, and wrong beliefs, people can't see straight. These confused views, these wrong ways of looking at life, are avijjā, ignorance. We don't see things as we should, so we can't overcome vaṭṭasaṃsāra. We sink into the spinning cycles and suffer their distress and torment, as has been discussed.

Please take a full and complete look at life, seeing it from all sides. View all aspects of vaṭṭasaṃsāra comprehensively and understand it completely. See the causes and conditions that combine together to maintain it. See the cluster of avijjā and its spawn that permeate it. Recognize the power of vaṭṭasaṃsāra to cover and rule the whole human world and the whole universe, because cycles of rotation operate in every atom that combines to form the universe. Although some might disagree, there's a vaṭṭasaṃsāra in every mind moment. Anyone who wants to disagree is welcome to do so. I ask only that they take a good look and genuinely inquire into the truth until gradually coming to recognize it. This is what it takes. We start with the foundations of creating correct knowledge, belief, and understanding.

This grows with practice until equal to the task of seeing truly and comprehensively, thus ending the dukkha story.

*

To sum up, we have two kinds of what we call "life": life that is concoctable and suffers, and life that can't be concocted and can't suffer. Life prone to concocting is saṅkhata, and unconcoctable life is asaṅkhata.[7] Understand both kinds of life all at once, because they are connected. See the whole interrelated reality in all aspects. This is what I call *paridassana*—looking at something in a comprehensive manner. May we have increasing paridassana as we go. If you have never seen comprehensively, please begin. If you've had some experience of all-round seeing already, may it expand and deepen.

Spiritual practice, meditation, and psycho-spiritual cultivation are for the sake of paridassana. This is the ability to see thoroughly and comprehensively in accord with the truth, to know all things as they are, so that there's no more clinging to anything as "self," the kilesas don't arise, and there isn't any dukkha. This, then, is the route by which we are released from the fearsome, pitiful cycle of dukkha, the cycle we know as vaṭṭasaṃsāra.

The repeating cycles of spinning are everywhere, within us and without, throughout the world and throughout the universe, inviting us to repetitively spin around in the mass of dukkha. Through seeing all things truly, as they really are, we can escape the rounds. In a manner of speaking, we break up the vaṭṭasaṃsāra, we destroy the circles. When enough of an oxcart's wheel is broken, it can't spin, it's no longer a circle. The knowledge that ends the circle is the knowledge that can end dukkha.

The Buddha laid out how to join the awakened ones who have destroyed the cycles of vaṭṭasaṃsāra, or those who have diminished it, or at least those who have begun to take it apart. Not many people, not even many Buddhists, have been much interested in breaking the cycles. I hope that there will be more interest than before, that our understanding will be commensurate with the benefits, and that we will follow the path more energetically. May you grow in the spiritual life of Buddhism as befits the effort expended, the sacrifices made, and the studying undergone. We gather, listen, reflect, and consult for the sake of better understanding the principles of Buddhism and how to apply them in life.

This chapter has presented an all-around look at Dhamma and at life, which, in truth, are one and the same. Life must have Dhamma; then the problem of dukkha can be conquered. So please take a comprehensive look at all aspects of both Dhamma and life, and then you will be able to deal with your problems. Join those who haven't wasted the human opportunity. Make good use of your remaining time in life to realize the highest thing a human life can realize.

We hope that all of you will accept responsibility for the value of your life and act so as to not waste the beautiful opportunity of having met with the Buddha's teaching.

9

THE TREES OF THE COMPLETE DHAMMA LIFE

Dhamma is everything, excepting nothing. Dhamma is life, the development of life, and that which develops life too. We will continue to examine it in detail.

The study of Dhamma tends to be unsystematic. This may be hard to understand for those who are used to the usual ways. Traditionally, Dhamma is learned without any system. Teachers often speak spontaneously, responding to circumstances, sometimes brilliantly, without any well-defined beginning or end in view, as pleases them. Some teachers compete to say the most profound things, which nobody understands. Listeners struggle to get the point, picking up odds and ends of information, much of which will be forgotten. That is not a systematic approach.

A system is a connected set of parts, or steps, each of which performs their individual functions and participates in the greater whole so that desired benefits are obtained. Perhaps an example from nature will make this easier to grasp and will save time. We'll take the example of trees and today will discuss the trees of life.

Treelike Systems of Dhamma

How is each tree a system? Well, it has to have a foundation, the roots that penetrate the ground. Of course, there must be the ground itself and the earth. Upward from the roots, there is the trunk, branches, branchlets, leaf stems, leaves, flowers, and fruits. This is a sketch of the system we call a tree. For this system to work, the parts must perform their individual functions and work together successfully. The roots go down into the earth for the purpose of drawing up moisture and minerals. These are sent up through the trunk to the leaves for photosynthesis by sunlight so that the various elements that sustain the tree itself can be fabricated. These nutrients then return by way of the bark, thus building up the bark itself as well as the sapwood and the heartwood. All this requires the right sort of water, sunlight, and mineral elements in the soil to concoct the many and various components that come together as a tree. When they work together without error, the tree is a complete and perfect system.

At present, we don't study Dhamma systematically, as something having roots, branches, stems, leaves, and flowers. Carelessly, both in teaching and learning, for the most part, we don't approach Dhamma as a system. We lack clarity and cohesion. Teachers speak what suits them, and students are left confused and dizzy. So let's take the tree, with its easily discernable system, as the model and metaphor for our study and contemplation of Dhamma.

Trees are living things we plant, cultivate, and care for. Most Thai people are familiar with caring for trees. Children are taught to plant trees around the home, even in Bangkok, and enjoy the results, such as pretty flowers to show off to their friends. Teenagers are capable of planting bigger trees, as befits their increased knowledge and abilities. Then, as adults, they plant and cultivate mango trees, coconut palms, and the like. Knowing how to manage these well, they receive the fruits of their labors. Once they reach old age and have more elevated minds, they can plant trees with more elevated meanings, such as pipal trees (bodhi trees), banyans, and other large shade trees.

We're used to planting trees, successfully cultivating and nurturing the different kinds as we grow older. Each stage of life has trees appropriate to it, and each tree has its particular knowledge requirements and techniques that bring fully beneficial results.

Developing the metaphor further, let's consider the trees of life. We need to understand each human life as having aspects akin to roots, a trunk, branches large and small, leaf stems, leaves, flowers, and fruits. What fulfills each of these roles in our lives? Further, how much water and sunlight does our life tree need? What kind of soil and minerals are suited to it? We ought to understand life as if it were the most precious tree requiring great knowledge and care.

If we understand the systems of ordinary trees, we can apply the same perspective with the trees of our own lives. Of course, the details won't be quite the same. We need water, but we don't draw it from the soil as trees do, nor do we have leaves with chlorophyll. Still, our lives need Dhamma too; they require proper knowledge, behaviors, and practices appropriate to each one of us, if we are to flourish.

We can divide the tree of life into four subsystems or areas of investigation, each of which is itself a tree. The first of these is physical: the body tree. The second is the mental system: the mind tree. The third is the wisdom system: the bodhi tree. Thus one tree has become three: the physical, the mental, and the bodhi trees. These, if correctly nurtured, will be very beneficial for each individual. Expanding beyond the individual, there is another tree to consider, which connects us with society at large. The fourth tree is the kindness and compassion system: the mettā tree.

Mettā is friendliness, while *metteyya* promotes friendliness and friendship, helping them to flourish. This system is for interacting with others and the outside world, beyond the individual. Individually and internally we require three systems: the physical, mental, and wisdom trees. The external system is necessary too. The mettā and metteyya system connects us with others, governs how we relate with others, and prevents dangers and threats to life. It should be easy to see that living well internally—the body, mind, and wisdom are right—isn't enough while the external world is full of trouble and foes looking to harm or oppress us. The full benefits of life depend on both inner and outer systems being correct. Then life is fulfilled and perfected, and everything is as it should be.

Just as the system of every ordinary tree in nature must be complete in itself, the trees of life have their complete systems too. In the former, the roots, trunk, sapwood, heartwood, bark, branches, leaves, and fruits all work together for survival. In the latter, the body, mind, and wisdom subsystems must also work together, each doing its work properly. We need to understand them, their cooperation, and how to bring them fully to life.

The Body Tree

The physical system must operate correctly in line with Dhamma principles. Traditional Dhamma views the body as made up of the earth, water, fire, and air elements. All these physical properties must be in proper balance and proportion. Traditional Thai medicine is greatly interested in the elements, and it produces medicines to strengthen, balance, and harmonize them in order to treat disease and foster health. Nowadays, although medical knowledge has advanced—it is more detailed, more precise, and better at certain things—it must not abandon the original principle that everything making up the body must be right and proper. The more genuine knowledge there is, the more good it can do. For example, there's been good progress in curing physical diseases. Medical advances make it possible, for instance, to correct development in the womb, even managing fertility and conception by improving the ability of prospective parents to conceive. Once children are born, they are nurtured and cared for physically so that they have healthier bodies that are better equipped to survive and grow into healthy adulthood. Don't forget that all forms of correctness are about Dhamma. Avoiding Dhamma is impossible because rightness is integral to its meaning. Every stage of the process has its necessary correctness.

Consider how much rightness we have. Although things are correct enough to survive, there's more than a little that isn't right. Because our education progresses in wrong directions, we don't raise children and teenagers well. We let too many mistakes occur. They learn too much of what they shouldn't and not enough of what they must. There is too much pandering to nonnecessities and a huge increase in junk food. These conditions lead, for example, to disruptions and deficiencies in the nervous system by which the body communicates with mind. Nerves are like lines of communication relating body and mind. This system must be right too. If not, the body will be out of balance.

Please understand that Dhamma includes practicing rightly with regard to one's body and all physically based systems too. Don't listen to the fools who claim that Dhamma is only for the temples and churches; that we must pray, chant, and meditate for it to be Dhamma. We must make all the relevant physical systems correct, deal with the body and all the things connected with it properly, wherever we are. Eat proper food, dwell in appropriate places, and wisely manage the household furniture and utensils. Neither disdain the material necessities nor be excessive with money, possessions, and wealth. Everything connected with the body system, including other people, must be correct. This is especially true of the nervous system that connects body with mind, so that mind has a healthy basis. Make all of them correct together. Study these things, become familiar with their functions, and oversee their rightness so that the body is a proper foundation for the nervous system and mind. That's Dhamma as it applies to physical processes.

I wonder who is interested in Dhamma like this. I believe that it's necessary for us to restart how we study Dhamma so that our approach is systematic, complete in all essentials, and right in all aspects, including the physical side of life. At present, even how people eat is confused because they don't know the difference between what the body needs and what the kilesas want. Such people are asleep, clueless about the body's needs and about what the afflictions are up to. Delighting in food may be right for the kilesas but it is wrong for human life and for Dhamma. We ought to choose our food, our methods of eating, and everything concerned with food keeping Dhamma in mind, not the corruptions.

In the technical language of the Dhamma teachings, body is called *rūpa* (form, matter) and *rūpadhammas* (material phenomena). Rightness regarding rūpadhammas and physical things is the concern of the sīla system. Training in sīla—ethical and behavioral rightness—goes beyond merely not killing, stealing, or lying. Get to know all aspects of the sīla system: its requirements, its balance, its relationships. Go beneath the surface level of precepts for real understanding that leads to upholding them faithfully and properly. Develop a deep understanding of sīla concerning the body system and the things connected with it: material things outside us, and the various parts on or inside the body, such as hair, nails, teeth, skin, and the rest of the thirty-two body parts we hear about. Our meditation on them must be real. We must rightly maintain them, the house we live in, the utensils we use, our finances, and the rest of our physical life. Correctness of the body system is *sīla-sikkhā*, training rightness in body and speech, as well as related matters.

We talk about sīla often, but seldom systematically and comprehensively. We tend to study it in bits and pieces. Please expand your study and train systematically, building upon the precepts until ethics and virtue are complete. See clearly and understand insightfully the full system involved here, considering how this tree has roots, base, trunk, branches, twigs, flowers, heartwood, sapwood, and bark, and how they all interact.

Only some aspects of the body tree can be seen with the eyes. Concerning the inner physical subsystems, we must rely upon knowledge and intelligence as our eyes, and then behave properly regarding the body tree. Just as when we were children planting ornamental shrubs that turned out beautifully, and later planted bigger and more difficult trees that turned out fruitfully, we employ similar intelligence, learning, and skill in caring for our bodies. If everything is managed properly, the body tree will be fine, well developed, and correct. It will be able to withstand diseases and fevers. It will be suitable as the seat of mind. If the body is in proper shape, it will support rightness in the other systems that rely on it: the psychological system, the wisdom system, and the spiritual system. This is what correct sīla-sikkhā fosters.

Finally, please notice that this is a down-to-earth affair. It's scientifically based and has nothing to do with superstition. It's about being naturally right. This, then, is the first system, the body tree of life.

The Mind Tree

The second component of life, or subsystem, is the mind tree. In the language of the Dhamma teachings, mind is referred to as *citta*, as *nāma*, and as *viññāṇa*. Sometimes these terms can be distinguished clearly, yet they are often confused. In the last chapter, we mentioned *nāma* as mental function interacting with rūpa. *Viññāṇa* usually refers to sense consciousness or sense cognition of an object through the six sense doors. Here, we will use *citta* as the broad umbrella term encompassing the others.

Anyone who truthfully can claim that their mental system is correct won't have many problems. At present, at least in most cases, the mind systems are in error. It seems this is a continuation from distortions in the body systems. Thus our minds are faulty, prone to error, and incompletely developed. This can get out of hand and so we see many cases of mental illness.

Once we understand that the body is based on the elements of earth, water, fire, and air, we can also understand that mind is based on the consciousness element. This is necessary understanding for dealing with mental disorders. We can't treat mental illness solely with physical means. Like the four physical elements, consciousness is simply a natural element, neither strange nor special, although its capacities may seem mysterious. If we can see that it's really just an element dependent on causes and conditions, we can then study its underpinning conditions so that mind can be developed and not left to the whims of ignorance.

It's difficult to explain the entire system of mind, but we don't need to know everything there is to know about it. We just need as much knowledge as is truly necessary, such as the things the Buddha described as being dukkha. The Buddha describes dukkha first appearing when an infant begins to experience sense contact and, more specifically, feelings of pleasure and pain. In the womb, the fetus is innocent of vedanā and doesn't think anything. Within a few days after being born, the infant becomes sensitive to contacts and feeling tones arising with the eyes, ears, nose, tongue, body, and mind itself. The baby thus begins to feel satisfaction and dissatisfaction, which then leads to ideas and thinking and becomes serious enough for suffering.

In the womb, fetuses have no knowledge of "what's what," which is almost like not having a mind at all. They don't remember and think about anything until they begin to undergo sense contacts and feelings of pleasure, pain, and neither pain nor pleasure outside the womb. When these feelings develop, they respond by feeling pleased and displeased, happy and unhappy, which then conditions thinking and pondering according to their likes and dislikes. This is how the mental system gets started—with vedanās, feeling tones.

Now the question is how there possibly can be mental correctness when infants leave the womb without any knowledge and wisdom. It's difficult for small children to have properly operating mind systems; their minds are left to develop haphazardly in response to causes and conditions. The knowledge and wisdom system also depends on causes and conditions. Subject to whatever conditions are prevalent at any given time, children drift into whatever knowledge they can acquire, which usually isn't the right kind. This is why ordinary, worldly people don't understand dukkha and its quenching, and why they make so many mistakes, behave wrongly, and suffer. This is how incorrectness in the mind tree originates.

Correctness at this stage of life depends on the causes and conditions surrounding children. When infants receive the right kind of nursing and care, they will have appropriate feelings and thoughts. If, however, they are surrounded and raised ignorantly, they won't learn what they need to know at each age. If parents, nannies, or whoever brings them up merely follow their own habits and preferences, or follow misguided customs, the mental life of their children will be increasingly wrong. If regularly surrounded by things capable of leading them astray, children end up infatuated with delicious, pretty, and fun things. That's all that interests them, and they cry when they don't get what they want. Raised haphazardly in a culture that doesn't know what's right, children grow infatuated with what pleases them, hating what displeases them, and suffering when their desires aren't fulfilled.

So children grow up in darkness, in ignorance. Everyone has been a baby; what do we see when we consider our own pasts? Were we born and raised in the midst of darkness and unknowing, depending on whatever the adults surrounded us with? Please forgive me for speaking bluntly. Did our parents and others surround us with lovely, attractive things and encourage infatuation with such things so that we habitually sought our happiness from them? At best, our desires were limited to avoiding death rather than aiming to end dukkha. While good enough to survive physically, we had to bear with frustrations and dwell amid a variety of problems—in other words, dukkha. Mind got used to false thinking, which promoted wrong speech and improper activities, which naturally followed the path of dukkha rather than the path of dukkha's quenching.

As we continued to mature, passing through adolescence, then becoming a householder with a vocation, we were confronted repeatedly with the various forms of dukkha. Eventually it began to dawn on us that life has so much trouble, stress, and pain. We began to ask what we can do to get rid of it all. In this way, we gradually oriented toward Dhamma. We began to think that there must be something able to solve the problems we came to recognize. We wondered if anything can quench this dukkha, and so we went looking in monasteries, retreat centers, or wherever occurred to us.[1] So now we have studied, meditated, learned, and searched to find what we need to quench all the dukkha that has been building up since we left our mothers' wombs.

Having started late in life, often not until middle age, the process of reorienting our lives to Dhamma is very difficult and slow.

Understanding the kilesas is hard for us, as is controlling and eradicating them. Consequently, quenching dukkha is a huge challenge, because we didn't start out with the necessary intelligence since before we were born and have since increasingly fallen under the power of ignorance and affliction. We're more fit for suffering than for freedom. Now that we want to get out of this dilemma, want to purge and cleanse mind of such problems, it's quite difficult to do. This is normal. If we really can't bear it any longer, we'll keep seeking until we're fit for quenching rather than fit for suffering.

Restarting with the ABCs of Dhamma

This transformation requires a radical restart. Know the ABCs of dukkha's quenching so that you can study Dhamma properly and systematically. Don't rely on sketchy explanations given on the spur of the moment or cling to catchy sayings from famous teachers. If you do, you'll never have a coherent Dhamma system that serves you throughout life. Such knowledge won't function well and have the true effect of Dhamma. If Dhamma is delivered correctly, it's able to quench dukkha; if not, it can't. So it falls to us to do the extra study needed to complete our understanding within a well-rounded system, even if it takes restarting with the basics.

When the Buddha sent disciples to announce the teachings far and wide, he emphasized that they should disseminate the brahmacariya, the supreme way of living. That is, they were to proclaim Dhamma—flawless and beautiful in its beginning, middle, and end—in a pure, correct, and complete manner.[2] The Buddha emphasized that the disciples he sent to promulgate the supreme way of life should do so fully and properly in its entire system—after all, there were those in this world capable of knowing, understanding, and gaining benefit from such a teaching.

Nowadays, we can't blame the first disciples for our muddled and sketchy understanding. We ourselves have the duty to expand, deepen, and complete our understanding so that it is flawless and beautiful in its beginning, middle, and end. Our duty is to study correctly and comprehensively. We need to add whatever is missing, to fill in the gaps and complete the structure of the Dhamma system to be just like a living tree with its roots, trunk, branches, twigs, leaves, flowers, and fruits functioning together as a complete structure. When our Dhamma knowledge has a full, systematic structure, we then use it to maintain the living systems of body, mind, and wisdom correctly. This is the way to survive physically, psychologically, and Dhammically.

Don't be discouraged if this seems like a lot. If you take on just as much as is necessary, it's not such a lot. Consider how planting trees successfully doesn't require a PhD. Expert farmers have learned by observation and acquired the necessary skills to plant and care for each variety of tree in their orchards so as to get the best returns. They know how to cultivate the varieties of durian, mango, and rambutan in the most perfect ways. Their knowledge is full and complete enough to get excellent returns without having studied abroad for a dozen years to acquire a long tail of degrees after their names.

It is much the same with Dhamma. We don't need to study for a degree; we only need to study as much as is necessary to quench our dukkha. So begin with the ABCs, with the foundations of this field—the eyes, ears, nose, tongue, body, and mind. Start by studying all of these senses, how each of these sensory systems functions. Observe how they can be afflicted by the reactions of craving and clinging such that suffering is created. Learn to respond in the opposite way so that dukkha doesn't happen. Don't think you need to study the whole of the Buddhist scriptures; hardly anybody manages that. Even if you did, it all comes down to the essentials, knowing just as much as is necessary about the eyes, ears, nose, tongue, body, and mind so that they aren't corrupted by kilesas. Explanations other than that are just fluff, nonessential.

The eyes, ears, nose, tongue, body, and mind are the underlying systems on which everything depends. We explore what happens to them through the paṭiccasamuppāda teachings. These senses, which the Buddha described as the "starting point of the brahmacariya," are the ABCs of Buddhism. If we're not genuinely interested in this most important subject, we might make assumptions and wild guesses, jump to conclusions, or blindly follow somebody's theory, without closely observing ourselves. That's how the kilesas lead us astray, until we leave the sphere of Dhamma altogether. That's how we fall for superstitious versions of Dhamma and cling to superstitious views of life.

We need a scientific study of the actual natural system. Essentially, we have the eyes, ears, nose, tongue, body, and mind, which interact with visual forms, sounds, smells, tastes, tangibles, and mental objects. Each of these six pairs functions is in the same basic way and are the basis for sense consciousness (*viññāṇa*) arising. For example, the eyes interact with a form and eye consciousness arises; these three working together are known as *phassa*, contact. With the arising of phassas, there arise vedanās, feelings of satisfaction and dissatisfaction. Then comes taṇhā, desire fueled by those feelings. With a feeling of satisfaction, the desire is to get, to acquire. With a feeling of dissatisfaction, the desire is to push away or destroy. And so arise the afflictions of lust (*rāga*), hatred (*dosa*), and anger (*kodha*). If there's a muddle that's neither satisfied nor dissatisfied, confusion (*moha*) occurs. The kilesas arise through ignorant desire (*taṇhā*), followed by ignorant clinging (*upādāna*), all of which is dukkha. With clinging to "me" and "mine," suffering is concocted. That's the essence of the matter. It's possible to go into more detail, but this is what everyone needs to know to avoid being careless and foolish.

With sufficient intelligence and understanding, we know how these things are. Thus we learn to take care when there is sense stimulation and meaningful contact resulting in feelings of pleasure and pain. Be clearly aware; don't be foolish with phassas and vedanās. Know them as they are, as naturally "just like that." With care, we don't give them illusory meanings leading to liking likable things and disliking annoying things. Then there isn't any foolish desire (*taṇhā*), foolish clinging (*upādāna*), and foolish dukkha. The matter fizzles out right there without creating suffering.

With proper supervision, surroundings, improvement, and development, mind becomes fit for intelligence and comprehension. It's firm, and it doesn't easily fall under the power of the kilesas, the afflictions that prevent it from functioning properly. When able to live like this, our mental system is right and thriving. The mind tree is clean, clear, and fruitful.

Conversely, the minds of worldly people are weak, easily enslaved by the kilesas. Such minds are moody and corruptible, unable to resist provocations and maintain their true nature. They fluctuate under the power of their surroundings, for the sake of the afflictions, without samādhi (collectedness). These weak and wandering minds continually dissipate their energies in unwholesome habits.

The minds of worldly people are habitually weak, scattered, and distracted, but their owners aren't generally very interested. In truth, there aren't any real owners; minds themselves take ownership of their habitual ways. Such infatuated minds will be caught in the mass of dukkha until they have suffered enough of a battering to start learning their lessons. Only then will they recognize their predicament and become interested in a new direction, one that leads away from dukkha.

How long will it be before this happens? Once born, people live stuck in the mass of dukkha for as long as it takes for mind to learn its lessons. This isn't about selves that are owners of mind, or of anything else for that matter. There is only mind that is infatuated and that has fallen into suffering until becoming sufficiently aware of the suffering to realize it must follow a new path, opposite to what it has habitually followed. This is the fundamental principle for the mind system.

Mind can be chastened quickly, can smarten quickly, and can turn around quickly. This mind must help itself. Don't be discouraged that nobody can come in and help you. Help yourself. That is, the mind that is chastened by dukkha, fed up with it, and disenchanted with the things that promote it, will turn around in search of a better way. This is where the mind system begins to find its rightness.

At present, there's hardly any training aimed at correcting the mind tree because there's not enough proper teaching. The principles of correct meditation remain largely unknown. There's too much self-promotion among teachers and confused followings of students, and too much trying to please each other. Please drop confused ideas about being spontaneous and not needing a systematic practice. Nor is meditation about sitting shut off from surroundings, quiet without understanding. Mechanical practice doesn't lead to a rightly purified, stable, strong, and able mind capable of its proper work. The kind of concentration where mind sinks inside itself doesn't display the qualities of a perfected mind.

The collectedness and unification (*samādhi*) that we need is the kind we can use in performing all of life's tasks, in every branch of human endeavor. If the human mind were to operate in a truly proper way, we would have this wonderful tool at our disposal. This mind is able to do anything it needs to do in such a way that it remains free of dukkha. It won't have any trouble doing the things we must do to make a living. This mind, mental system, or mind tree requires proper nurturing and correct training, a process we call *citta-sikkhā*. Citta-sikkhā, or *samādhi-sikkhā*, is a form of education, a course of instruction for the mind system to be right, as it ought to be, and truly beneficial for humanity.

The Bodhi Tree of Wisdom

Next, we'll look at the third system, the bodhi tree or bodhi system. *Bodhi* means "awakened knowledge" or "wisdom." Pali has many terms that basically mean the same thing, such as *paññā* (wisdom), *ñāṇa* (insight knowledge), and *vijjā* (true knowing)—the third system involves all of these. How life goes depends on whether this system is false or true. When it's wrong, the knowledge system leads life into trouble. When it's right, life is without suffering. With our minds wrong since birth, lacking the necessary wisdom, we've struggled with dukkha all along as we've carried on in cycles of vaṭṭasaṃsāra. Suffering from these repetitive cycles since birth until now is the meaning of vaṭṭasaṃsāra. What happens after death is too long a timeframe to be observed and isn't sandiṭṭhiko (personally experienceable), so we'd do better to concern ourselves with what we can observe personally. Rather than focusing on physically dying and being born again, let's concentrate on the vaṭṭasaṃsāra of cycling round in dukkha, which has been happening in this particular life from the time we were born.

Mind suffers repeated dis-ease and distress in vaṭṭasaṃsāra until right knowledge starts to change the course of life. When carrying on in the old ways is no longer bearable, mind begins to turn toward nonsuffering. Hence, there is searching, seeking, and studying for the right direction. The bodhi system, the wisdom mode, begins because dukkha has been experienced and properly seen.

How will wisdom grow? In the Pali scriptures, there are at least two ways this can happen. The first is when interest arises through hearing and listening to the warnings and promptings of others. However, that isn't as powerful as being continually bitten and beaten until aching with dukkha. It really hits home when we find out for ourselves. Knowledge arising from direct confrontation with dukkha fosters insight regarding the need to turn around and head in the opposite direction. Such knowledge truly helps. The knowledge learned from outside ourselves is still beneficial, though not as effective. Still, if we seriously listen to the right warnings, we will consider their reality. If the advice seems probable, we'll try it out. If testing the advice shows that it's right, we will continue with it until receiving the full reward.

This is the reasonable way to proceed, in line with the principles of the *Kālāma Sutta.*[3] In this teaching, the Buddha advises how to respond when we hear someone claim spiritual knowledge. Rather than believing impetuously, we listen closely and consider whether what was said has proper reasoning behind it. Is it worth trying? Without having to believe it, we give it a try to see if it works. When we've tried and tested it, and gotten the desired results, then we can believe. Now believing firmly, we can continue onward until realizing the ultimate result.

Dhamma works like the strange Western medicines that we were slow to adopt around here. We were used to the large, dark herbal pills, and we didn't dare take the modern pills and tablets. When local doctors spoke kindly and with convincing reasons, a few people were willing to try the pills. When they were effective, other people were willing to try. Now many people prefer the tasteless modern pills. It's the same when someone teaches that dukkha can be quenched in a certain way. If well explained and reasonable, we are willing to consider it. Then we may try and practice it. Once it is proven effective, we increase our effort and truly quench dukkha. This is how the wisdom system is developed. The bodhi tree grows strong, large, and full of life.

In the Pali texts, the wisdom system is divided into two stages. Seeing the nature of things truthfully—that they are inconstant, unsatisfactory, and not-self—is the first stage. When these insight knowledges (*ñāṇas*) are complete, the second stage follows, which is insight knowledge concerning withdrawal and release. Profoundly seeing the impermanent, unsatisfactory, and essenceless nature of things fosters disenchantment and dispassion regarding the sources of suffering. These are the ñāṇas of disenchantment, dispassion, and release. In other words, our pains, suffering, and torments lead to insight knowledge that realizes the true nature of the things for which we suffer.

Insight knowledge can be parsed in great detail, but we only need to know about these two primary stages. The first set of ñāṇas concerns the basic facts of all things—that is, that all things are impermanent, unsatisfactory, and void of attā. More concisely, they are seen as "just like that." If such penetrating knowledges are cultivated regarding the true nature of things, then the second set appears. Insight knowledge appears as disenchantment, the fading away of clinging tendencies, and release. These are the fruits of the first set.

Observe well how our wisdom proceeds in this way. First, we must see the nasty, punishing quality of dukkha and its objects and conditions. When we see clearly that something is a condition for dukkha, or is itself dukkha, we begin to withdraw, we don't mess with it, we shift the stream of causes and conditions. Disenchanted with and weary of the things that once provoked greed, infatuation, and grasping, the clinging gradually dissolves. Disenchantment unravels that infatuation and clinging. When clinging fades and ends, there is release.

In short, our wisdom has two stages. Insightful knowing of things as they really are is the first; the unraveling through disenchantment (*nibbidā*), dissolving and fading away of clinging (*virāga*), and release (*vimutti*) are the second stage. Wisdom has these two main levels.

The Wisdom System Arises through Cultivation

As we've seen, such insightful knowledges can arise from hearing teachings, considering them, and practicing them. They can also arise without listening to anyone. They arise when an excess of dukkha provokes the necessary giving up of old vaṭṭasaṃsāra and finding of the wise alternative. This second instance explains how self-awakened Buddhas and solitary Buddhas appear of their own accord, although rarely, without anyone teaching them the final stages of realization.[4] Rather, the circumstances and suffering of their lives teach them. We should appreciate our good luck that, although we aren't clever enough to awaken on our own, we have encountered Dhamma teachings to study, investigate, observe, experiment with, and practice in search of the needed result. So don't let go to waste the good fortune that someone has passed on the Buddha's teaching to us. At the same time, don't just straightaway accept it as correct either—that would be contrary to the principles of the *Kālāma Sutta*. Rather, consider whether it's reasonable and worth trying out. If you see clearly enough that it is, then try it and experience the results of practice. Experiencing those fruits, put your full trust in this Dhamma.

Now don't fall into thinking that you haven't got the character, haven't got what it takes, and so might not be able to create paññā. That kind of thinking leads to giving up and letting things happen according to fate. That wouldn't be right, because wisdom, paññā, is a saṅkhāra, something created and conditioned. It has its causes and supporting conditions, and it follows the law of nature. Therefore, create the causes and conditions for the arising of wisdom.

Engage in a systemized form of proper conduct—that is, a yoga. The wisdom system arises through yogic development, which is systematic. A Pali text says that "wisdom firm as the earth arises from yoga."[5] Yoga is behaving and practicing correctly within a system.

When one behaves and practices rightly within that system, firmly grounded and penetrating wisdom arises. Then wisdom will appear and liberation (*vimutti*) occurs.

Wisdom and insight must be taught and cultivated systematically, not just circumstantially or idiosyncratically. Those with deep insight pack a lot of meaning in their words, even when responding to spontaneous circumstances. If we listen carefully and investigate thoroughly, we will find the system that leads to the wisdom that ends dukkha. Training along these lines is *paññā-sikkhā*. First, sīla-sikkhā, ethical training, is for managing the body and physical behavior. Second, citta-sikkhā, mind training, is for managing mind. Third, paññā-sikkhā, wisdom training, is for managing understanding and wisdom. When all three cooperate rightly and systematically, the individual task is completed because one is liberated.

The Mettā Tree for Society

However, an important question remains. Even though our personal suffering has been quenched, how are we to live in the world with others? There is a system for this, which also must be rightly followed. This is the mettā system or, we might say, the metteyya tree, the tree of mettā's support. Developing mettā is a systematic process that, just like a tree, needs to be properly cultivated and nurtured, until its flowers and fruits appear in the world. We can speak of this tree as *mettā* (friendliness, kindness) or *karuṇā* (compassion); however, *metteyya* fits best because Metteyya is the name of the future Buddha.[6] *Metteyya*, or *maitreya*, means "supporter of mettā." The Dhamma supporting mettā in this world means that people are replete with mettā, always displaying a friendly attitude. Everyone is a friend and there aren't any enemies left. That is the religion of Metteyya, a world without any enemies, not even one, and no hooligans left to trouble anyone. In Metteyya's world, all people are friends.

The traditional metaphor is that everyone is the same, equally good. Even when we're traveling far from home and don't know who is who, everyone is equally good to us. When we return home, we know that the people here are our spouses, our partners, our children, and our friends. All of them are our people. We can't distinguish between them because they are all friends, whether at home or in the broader world.

This religion teaches a final goal greater than individual liberation from dukkha. Even liberated individuals will find it difficult to live with other people in a world that includes criminals and hooligans. Personal escape from dukkha won't accomplish the fullest meaning of arahant, which is human completeness. Another system is needed to make friendliness a worldwide phenomenon. When there's nothing but friendliness, when there are no enemies, the full meaning of arahant—far from kilesas—will manifest and there won't be any problems left to solve.

Let's go over this again. There are four important systems: the sīla, samādhi, and paññā systems for the salvation of individuals, plus the mettā system for a peaceful and happy society for all. Thai Buddhists will wonder where *dāna* (giving and generosity) fits in this system. Dāna is inherent in the mettā system: loving others is giving. Generous giving eliminates personal selfishness and extends love to others; however, its range is somewhat narrow in meaning. We prefer the broader meaning of mettā as the universal friendliness that has no enemies. This would really be loving-kindness.

The world really needs this system of universal friendliness without enemies so that the salvation of humanity is complete. Remember, it requires four stages: correctness of the body; of mind; of wisdom; and of society, which is mettā. These four add up to the necessary subsystems within the complete Dhamma system.

Humanity's Rightness Is in These Four Interlocking Systems

The final point to make is that we can practice these four systems simultaneously. Each human being maintains both physical and mental correctness, possesses correct understanding, and is lovingly kind during the course of each day. Every molecule and organ of this body are right, all aspects of mind are right, wisdom is rightly complete, and behavior toward others is right. These four trees growing together harmoniously are the fully ripened Dhamma system.

Although the complete system is somewhat detailed, it isn't more profound than our intelligence can handle. Let's make this happen. Have body, mind, intelligence, and behavior toward society all be right. Each day, examine life internally so that body, mind, and intelligence are three interwoven strands of correctness, and that, externally, the fourth strand completes the package of correctness. See how intertwining the external strand with the others completes the full-strength Dhamma system infused with mettā.

The systems of body, mind, wisdom, and loving-kindness make up the trees of life. Each system has its own subsystems to be fully developed and completed, then integrated with the others for life to be rightly liberated from dukkha. Just as botanical trees thrive when their life systems operate correctly, the trees of human life are a lush, thriving grove when all its systems function smoothly. This is the universalism of Dhamma expressed by *kevalaṃ* (whole and complete) in the Buddha's original purpose of "proclaiming the spiritual life of wholeness and purity."

*

To sum up: Previously we have approached Dhamma in a sketchy, shaky manner and were unable to see it as a full and complete system. Now we can see clearly that, just as a tree is a complex system, Dhamma is a system of systems that can be cultivated until thriving and bearing the most nutritious fruit. Minus a clear and correct understanding, we can't practice properly. Study and training that aren't properly systematic are impractical because they can't be properly put into practice. Please see Dhamma as a practical system full and complete, right and proper, like a healthy ecology of trees—the body, mind, wisdom, and loving-kindness trees.

Don't dawdle or delay! Don't be lackadaisical in Dhamma study and practice without comprehensive paridassana. Don't be puffed up with incomplete Dhamma knowledge that leaves you like a tiny frog in a buffalo wallow that thinks it's lord of the ocean.

Make your Dhamma life a reality by seeing all aspects and systems properly, as they actually are, and the great matter will be settled. Know yourself. Know how it's really mind that takes itself to be a separate self and makes itself the owner of life that thinks it should be in control. Know how ignorant mind creates the "me" and the "mine" and gets dukkha as a result. And know that mind gradually turns away from the life of suffering to a life that knows it isn't a "me." The rightly knowing mind comes to accept that there's only nature carrying on in harmony with causes and conditions. The story concludes with realizing there's no "me" to be the basis for falsehood and error. Kilesas aren't reborn in the thriving trees of Dhamma life.

10

EVERYTHING IN LIFE IS SOLELY MATTERS OF MIND

Everything in life is solely about citta. All aspects of life and everything concerning life are just matters of mind. Today we'll look at this point closely.

That all life comes down to mind may seem barely credible, especially to those raised in materialist culture, so pay careful attention. This requires your full cooperation. Then you might come to understand and agree. It is difficult to see that everything that happens in life from start to finish, from the beginning right up until the realization of nibbāna, is solely matters of mind. It is difficult to accept that an additional "self," separate and lasting, doesn't need to be involved at all. People rarely arrive at this conclusion on their own.

Pristine Citta, Kilesa Citta, Citta beyond Kilesas

Originally, mind is just a naturally occurring element (*dhātu*), nothing more. For ages, due to ignorance, it has been continually concocted by things surrounding it. This is the ignorant mind of kilesas. It operates in ignorance and delusion until it gradually begins to awaken and transform into the sort of mind that isn't ignorant and confused. This mind has finished ignorance; ignorance doesn't trouble it. This sort of mind, then, realizes the utmost thing that mind is capable of—nibbāna.

Grasp these three kinds of mind, first of all. The first stage is just mind as a natural element, without right or wrong, without good or bad. There are no kilesas in this mind. This is mind just as it is in nature, nothing more. In the second stage, through ignorance it becomes foolish and full of kilesas, thus wandering and spinning around in vaṭṭasaṃsāra for a great long time experiencing distress and torment. In the third stage, mind turns around, opens its eyes, knows dukkha, and understands the punishment within vaṭṭasaṃsāra. And so it trains itself and cultivates Dhamma within until it releases from the kilesas and escapes vaṭṭasaṃsāra. Thus realizing nibbāna, nothing can fabricate such mind ever again. As a consequence, mind is completely free from all its former problems.

Please remember these three stages of mind. All of our lives begin with pristine mind. In the second stage, mind becomes ignorant and afflicted. In the third stage, mind is finished with kilesas and ignorance. That ends the story. Rather amusing, isn't it, that this story involves nothing more than natural mind, corrupted mind, and liberated mind? All of Buddhism's 84,000 Dhamma themes are expressed in just three short phrases: pristine mind, mind with kilesas, and mind without kilesas. That's all. There's no need to drag in attā (self).

Confusions about Self

We can rephrase the stages as follows: The first stage is mind without self, natural mind without any thoughts or notions of self. The second stage is foolish mind with feelings of self, "me," and "mine." Mind falls into clinging to self because of ignorance; it creates this illusion as it wanders in the world. The third stage is mind that's finished with all of that; there's no notion of self in this mind. Mind turns away from the ignorant spinning and is without self once again. That may not sound like much: mind that's never been self, foolish mind with self, and then mind turns around and stops assuming self. That finishes it.

What remains is for us to discuss the details of these three stages of mind. When we get to the details, please be careful to remember all three stages. That will make you a cooperative reader, and this story will be easier to explain and understand in detail. So remember these three minds. Discuss them, debate them, and investigate them: mind naturally without kilesas, mind with kilesas, and mind that has put an end to kilesas and realized nibbāna; alternatively, the original mind without self, mind with self, and then mind beyond self. That's the entirety of the Dhamma.

The importance and great meaning of this attā is that there's dukkha because of it. Nevertheless, the sense of self can't be avoided in life. It's so deeply entrenched that it's impossible to dislodge before arahantship is realized. Because we all acquire such self and let go of it with extreme difficulty, we often hear that there is self. And we also hear that there isn't, which can be confusing. Both understandings are discussed and taught, even within Buddhism. That there isn't really self is the main principle, the correct standard, in Buddhism. Still, we find wordings that can confuse, even in the original Pali suttas. For example, in a famous line, the Buddha says that "self is the refuge of self."[1] Self trains and practices to realize not-self. This appears to be a contradiction: Is there self or not? If properly understood, any confusion disappears because this "self" that is refuge for itself is just mind that believes itself to be a self. When ignorant, mind thinks that it's self, and that it's "my self." Self, therefore, is simply foolish mind. Who will help it overcome its foolishness? Itself! Mind spins around in the mass of dukkha, slowly awakens, becomes smarter, and finally gives up the self idea altogether. This is what the Buddha meant when saying that self is a refuge for itself.

Life and Mind Are Merely Natural Elements

To understand life without taking it as self, we will examine mind more deeply. Please be mindful of all three kinds of mind as outlined above. First, to better understand the pristine, pre-concocting mind, we will consider how mind is just a natural element like all the other elements. The Buddha said, "This person is composed of six elements."[2] These naturally occurring elements (*dhātus*) are earth element, water element, fire element, and wind element, on the physical side of things; consciousness element (*viññāṇa-dhātu*), the element that becomes mind; and, finally, space element (*ākāsa-dhātu*), the vacancy that is neither material nor mental and is the base for all things.

Please take special note that the Buddha considered consciousness and space to be natural elements. To consider all the elements mentioned by the Buddha would take too long. Here, we only need to consider the six basic elements of life, which compose the so-called person.[3]

Let's review the physical elements. This will help us understand how they and the mind element happen naturally without involving self. The elements of earth, water, fire, and wind combine together in the body. Earth element is that which takes up space. However small or large, whether a single atom or huge quantities of them, earth element is the property of taking up space. It's solid, resists touch, and requires space. Water element is the property that holds earth element together. Without water element, earth couldn't cohere in shapes and forms of any kind. Fire element is the property of temperature, which causes change and transformation to occur. Wind element is the property of expansion, which causes movement. These four properties combine together to make up the body. None of them are any kind of separate or lasting self.

Buddhists often refer to the thirty-two parts of the body that we contemplate in certain meditations. Usually, earth element corresponds with head hair, body hair, nails, teeth, and skin, while water element corresponds with blood, pus, snot, tears, and other liquids. However, this is a rather crude explanation. It should be said that earth element is hard, has resistance, takes up space, and is easy to find in head hair, body hair, nails, teeth, and skin. Water element is in the fluidity that holds things together in shapes; it can be easily detected in blood, pus, snot, and tears. Fire element can be detected in bodily warmth, and wind element is found in the air and gas that move things around in the intestines, stomach, and elsewhere. The more obvious aspects of these elements can be found in parts of the body.

The more refined aspects are in the basic properties of solidity, cohesion, temperature, and expansion. The elements direct attention to particular properties. Earth element is the property of solidity occupying space. Water element is the property of connecting and binding together. Fire element is the property of heat that causes change, such as in the digestion of food. Wind element is the property of movement, without which progress is impossible.

We will find that it's incorrect to separate the dhātus from one another. In life, the four material elements are always in combination. This is apparent in the body: the hard part is earth element; that which holds it all together is water element; that which provides temperature and keeps the body warm is fire element; and that which moves things in the body, such as the various gases that are everywhere in the body—in the muscles, even between the cells—is wind element. We can't dissociate these elements from one another. Even in the blood, which is commonly understood as being water element, all four elements are to be found: earth element manifests in the subtle solidity of the cells, fluidity is more obvious, there's temperature or heat, and there's the movement and expansive property of wind. All four are to be found in blood. The same is true of all organs and parts of the body. These are the four physical elements most familiar to Buddhists. How could they and their interactions truly be self?

Mind and Space Are Natural Elements Too

Next is viññāṇa-dhātu, the element of consciousness. Don't overthink this one. Just know that it, too, is a natural element: the property of being sensitive, feeling, perceiving, thinking, and being aware. The body is the instrument that enables these functions. The nervous system, like the rest of the body, is also composed of the four elements and is the seat of consciousness element. Mind element relies on the nervous system in order to operate. Consciousness element and the physical elements can't be separated. If they were, mind would have no means and place to operate, while the body, if lacking consciousness element and thus being unable to do anything, would have no value or meaning. Hence, the physical and mental elements must happen together for there to be life. To separate them is equivalent to their not existing.

Finally, space element (*ākāsa-dhātu*) completes the set. Space element, being neither material nor mental, is the vacancy that accommodates and supports the physical and mental elements. These other elements depend on it. Consider this analogy: the value of a container is in its emptiness or hollowness. Bowls, glasses, bottles, and other containers are useful because they're empty and hollow. If a glass or a dish is filled up with something already, can it be used? Pots, pans, jars, dishes, and basins are useful because they have free space and are hollow. So, note how the value of free space is in allowing other things to exist within it.

There are interesting Pali texts that treat all things as dhātus; there isn't anything that isn't an element. Everything is one element or another. Even nibbāna is the nibbāna element. In reality, nature is all about elements. Thus, free space is an element too. Although space isn't anything, the Buddha included it as one of the elements.

In Buddhist teachings, the elements occur naturally. No creator is necessary. What we assume to be a person is actually a combination of the six naturally occurring elements. The law of nature having created them, they each go about doing their respective duties. Working together, they cause the arising of the body and mind. For the elements to function—for the physical elements to compose a body and for mind to arise in it—space is required. Space doesn't have any form or activity to be noticed. We can't see it directly; we can only see the things happening in it. We'll take a rock as an example. A rock exists within space; without vacancy, it can't manifest. Space is there for the rock to be. However, when we look, we only see the rock, and we overlook the vacancy, even though every atom of the rock requires space.

Seeing how these six elements combine in nature, we realize that what we supposed to be a person or self can be analyzed into physical aspects, mental aspects, and free space. The body is the physical part and mind is the mental part. Both are established in vacancy, which can't be measured or counted because it has no active role. It's the physical aspects and mental aspects that create all the trouble. Separately, we refer to them as *nāma* (mental) and *rūpa* (material). Together, we speak of *nāmarūpa*, body that has mind. Each person is nāmarūpa, mind with body.

Mind is the important, most meaningful part, while body supports it. The body serves mind. In truth, the body is merely an instrument for mind to operate. We can compare the body to the components that make up electrical generators and the physical equipment through which electricity works. While we easily see the dynamos, batteries, electric machines, and light bulbs, we can't see the electricity itself. Such equipment allows the electricity to function. The dynamos and generators perform a similar function as the body; they are simply the mechanisms that allow electricity's great power to express itself. The body's value is the same, the means for mind to express itself.

The bodily side of life has four elements, and the mental side has one. The side that supports these two is space element. When we realize the natural functioning of these six elements of life, we won't need a self component to gum up the works. Now, having clarified the elements as the natural basis for life, and particularly mind, without needing to assume or posit self, we can return to the three stages of mind.

The First Stage—Natural, Luminous Mind

The first sort of mind is natural mind, mind pristine and simple, before kilesas have happened, before notions of "me" or "mine," just elements operating naturally. A sutta describes this natural mind element as basically luminous (*pabhassara*) but susceptible to corruption by visiting kilesas.[4] Mind is naturally luminous, with luster and radiance like a diamond. Yet it's corrupted when kilesas occur. Before the kilesas appear it's called "luminous mind." Such mind can't think or imagine anything, so it can't have notions or thoughts about self. There's no sense or feeling of self in this mind. It remains luminous simply because kilesas haven't occurred. However, they might arise at any time, but until they do, mind will retain its luminosity. We can't say it's purified, so we describe it as luminous. At best, it's temporarily pure. This is natural and doesn't require any training or development.[5]

Life starts out with this first stage of mind, uncorrupted by kilesas and a sense of "me" and "mine." The entire run of life has this mind as its basis. However, this mind depends on the body, and eventually it is concocted by bodily things. Relying on the body and with the many things impacting it through the senses, mind is concocted and becomes corrupted. Be careful with how the natural mind becomes corrupted mind.

To understand this more easily, consider fetuses in the womb, which insulates and protects fetal bodies and minds. Such minds are able to feel, but they aren't yet able to think. They aren't capable of liking and disliking, either, so thoughts and notions about "me" and "mine" aren't yet possible. Still, they experience and feel, though their feelings aren't strong enough to provoke craving and clinging. Fetal experience of vedanās—pleasant, painful, and neither-painful-nor-pleasant feeling tones—isn't of a magnitude capable of forming the basis for clinging. In Dhamma terms, it's as if they have no vedanās. The eyes, ears, nose, tongue, body, and mind aren't functioning fully according to their purpose. Although there are some physical sensations, these aren't full sensory experience: the eyes can't really see forms, the ears can't hear sounds very well—not enough for meaningful experiences of seeing and hearing that cause meaningful feeling tones to arise. Their noses aren't breathing, so they can't smell anything. Fetuses feed through their umbilical cords so their tongues aren't used for tasting. And their skin is more or less protected in the womb, not impacted like in life outside the womb. This is to say that fetuses in the womb don't have or use fully developed sets of the six senses. Hence, mind remains natural and pristine, before it's susceptible to kilesas and before it clings to itself as "my self."

The Second Stage—Corrupted Mind

Immediately after birth, the minds of infants are pretty much as in the womb. However, the steady growth and development that follow leaving the womb bring about functional use of the eyes, ears, nose, tongue, body, and mind according to the nature of each sense. After a month or so, infants begin to have fully functional sense apparatuses. Once the six senses are acquired, feeling tones can arise because sense contacts take place. The eyes see forms, ears hear sounds, noses smell odors, tongues taste flavors, skin feels tangible sensations, and minds receive mental objects. Great change has happened. As they take in food through their mouths, rather than their umbilical cords, they experience delicious and unpalatable. As their eyes see, perceive, and recognize things, they experience pretty and ugly. With fully functioning ears, sounds are felt to be soothing or sweet, harsh or discordant. Working olfactory organs experience odors that are satisfying and repellant. Skin experiences comfortable and uncomfortable sensations, such as warmth and cold. Then mind, once able to think and imagine, experiences objects of thought capable of pleasing and displeasing, just like with the other senses.

Please understand that this all happens quite naturally. When the eyes receive light waves that are comfortable for the optic system, those images are experienced as attractive or pretty. If the light waves strike in coarse or harsh ways, the images are experienced as unattractive or ugly. There must be suitable light waves striking the eyes to cause such pleasant or unpleasant feelings and thereby stimulate corresponding attraction or aversion toward them. Light waves experienced as attractive are enjoyed; light waves experienced as harsh are avoided.

Likewise, the ears, when receiving the appropriate sound waves, will feel comfortable, so infants experience pleasure. When the sounds aren't comforting, infants experience pain. As they come to feel comfort and discomfort via the ears, they are pleased and displeased accordingly. Such patterns are repeated with noses. When the particles of the volatile gases are such that the olfactory nerves feel comfortable, the odor will be experienced as fragrant and desirable. When there are too many gas particles, the smells are intense, even foul, hence uncomfortable and undesirable. With tongues, substances stimulate taste receptors in ways that are experienced as delicious or unpalatable. With skin, soft and gentle tangible sensations feel comfortable and rough or harsh sensations feel uncomfortable. Thus, when bathed and powdered, infants feel satisfaction and are pleased. Opposite touch experiences are disagreeable.

All this is quite natural for eyes, ears, noses, tongues, and skin to feel comfort and discomfort. None of this is taught. Life is very different once children know both poles of sensory experience—attractive and repulsive. Life outside the womb is full of pleasurable and painful vedanās regarding visual, auditory, olfactory, gustatory, tactile, and mental experiences. This aspect of experience is the same for adults.

Vedanās Lead to Greed, Hatred, and Delusion

Feeling tones, both those that please and those that displease, can make children smart or make them foolish. The children we've been discussing are all of us who have left the womb and experienced feelings that are comfortable and painful. Either way, the two kinds of vedanās make us clever or make us stupid. Regarding this, recall how the Buddha said, "The infant doesn't know liberation of mind and liberation through wisdom from when in the womb."[6] Children are ignorant of mind's liberation and liberation through wisdom from before birth. So they react with liking and disliking. They are pleased with agreeable experiences and displeased with difficult experiences. Ignorance is not understanding liberation when faced with feeling tones, so the vedanās become foolish. Ignorant of liberation, children proceed naturally, following nature's program. They end up with the kind of forms, sounds, smells, tastes, tangible sensations, and mental objects that stimulate pleasure, satisfaction, and infatuation, as well as with the kind that stimulate pain, dissatisfaction, aversion, and resistance. Children become capable of greed for things that attract them and irritable or angry with things that displease them. Can you see how this isn't the pristine mind anymore, how this is mind taken over by ignorance? Can you see how far we have come now from pristine mind?

This second stage of mind is ignorant concerning liking and disliking, and the kilesas they produce. Children don't understand liberation of mind and liberation through wisdom, that it's all "just like that," and everything is transient, distressed, and without a fixed, stable essence. Lacking such true knowing, citta reacts with pleasure and displeasure. Because of this ignorance, mind falls into affliction. When mind falls for the attractions of things experienced, greed and lust are born. When mind is drawn into aversion toward other things, anger and hatred are born. When mind is confused, suspicious, or doubtful, delusion is born. Now, our children are capable of the early stages of the root corruptions—lobha, dosa, and moha. In mind's second act, it isn't pristine anymore.

How the Five Khandhas Operate in the Corrupted Stage of Mind

Let's bring in another important Dhamma teaching to take a more detailed look at what's happening in this second stage of mind. Infants are also composed of the six elements. Out of the elements, the aggregates of clinging arise to become the basis for the kilesas. To understand how this comes about, we must observe how the aggregates come to be. Earth, water, fire, and wind make up the body; consciousness is mind element; and space element is where they all manifest. Mind depends on and acts through the body. The body operates as eyes, ears, nose, tongue, organs of touch, and mind. Whenever the senses function, we have a child's *rūpa-khandha* (body aggregate).

Now, whenever there is interaction between the eyes, ears, nose, tongue, body, or mind and external things—forms, sounds, odors, tastes, tangibles, and mental objects—there arises consciousness.

This is a child's *viññāṇa-khandha* (consciousness aggregate). Viññāṇa-khandha operates in six ways, as visual consciousness aggregate, aural consciousness aggregate, olfactory consciousness aggregate, gustatory consciousness aggregate, bodily consciousness aggregate, and mental consciousness aggregate. A child now has consciousness aggregate.

When there is sense contact of one kind or another, there arises *vedanā-khandha* (feeling aggregate). The contact either feels pleasant, unpleasant, or neither pleasant nor unpleasant, and thus our child has vedanā-khandha.

Next, a child perceives and recognizes what something is. Whatever is being experienced via the senses is recognized and regarded as being this or that. Perception recognizes colors, such as black, red, green, and yellow; it recognizes shapes and sizes, such as short, long, big, and small; and it recognizes flavors, such as salty, sweet, sour, and bitter. It recognizes mental phenomena, such as perceiving as "pleasant," "unpleasant," and "neither pleasant nor unpleasant." It recognizes male and female. It also recognizes qualities of value, such as "this has value," "this has meaning," "this is useful," and "this is important." This power of recognizing and regarding is *saññā* (perception). Now our child has *saññā-khandha* (perceiving aggregate).[7]

With sufficient recognition, an experience is regarded in a certain way, then there is thinking what to do about it. When beauty is perceived, there's thinking of getting. When ugliness is perceived, there's thinking of destroying. Thus a small child reacts in the ways that small children do. Perhaps it flattens an insect according to how it was perceived. If the insect is regarded as "my enemy," a child proceeds to squish or smash the foe. Thinking has occurred: thinking of getting, of keeping, of eating, of using, of killing, and of caring for. *Saṅkhāra-khandha* (thinking aggregate) has happened. Our small child now has saṅkhāra-khandha, completing a full set of five aggregates.

Observe that the five khandhas don't all arise at the same time. First is rūpa-khandha, without which mind is unable to function. Then mind involved with sense impacts is the activity of viññāṇa-khandha. With each impact, there is a sense consciousness: eyes meet a form and there's visual consciousness aggregate; ears meet a sound and there's aural viññāṇa-khandha; and so on. Viññāṇa-khandha doesn't arise at the exact same time as rūpa-khandha.

Once consciousness aggregate has arisen, there is phassa (contact) and feeling aggregate comes in. With vedanā-khandha, perception aggregate arises to recognize and evaluate the thing felt and how it is felt. Lastly, the various forms of thinking and reacting occur, which is saṅkhāra-khandha. The aggregates don't arise simultaneously. Rather, they are the causes and conditions for each other's arising—sometimes directly and sometimes indirectly, sometimes before and sometimes after, depending on the nature of the situation. Our child now has a full set of aggregates for clinging to as "me" and "mine."

Khandhas Are Excuses for Clinging to "Me" and "Mine"

Now that a child can feel, remember, and think, the notion of self occurs. Whenever an event draws mind's attention and interest to rūpa-khandha, thoughts of "me" within the body occur. Sometimes, depending on the case, there's thinking about "my body." With an intention for the body to do something, the body is "me." Otherwise, the body is merely "mine." Whenever the child's mind experiences a feeling tone, that mind that feels is taken to be "me" and the feeling tone is considered "mine." Mind perceives itself to be "the feeler" of that vedanā; while feeling, it conceives itself to be "me." The vedanā itself is clung to as "mine." Next, in the saññā stage, perceiving mind is taken to be "the perceiver," the "me" who recognizes and perceives. The object of perception is "mine"—my perception, recognition, or memory. Saṅkhāra-khandha is the same as the others. The thinking and intending mind clings to itself as "me" and to the thoughts and intentions as "mine"—my thoughts.

In these ways, the various khandhas are assumed to be "me" and "mine," making them clinging-together aggregates (*upādānakkhandhas*). Each of these five aggregates has a way to be clung to as being self, as "me," as attā. They also can be clung to as belonging to self, as a possession, as "mine," as *attaniya*. Each khandha is an opportunity for ignorant clinging to self and to of-self.

In the *Anattalakkhaṇa Sutta*,[8] one of his earliest teachings, the Buddha observes how everything is neither attā nor belonging to attā. He discusses the nature of the khandhas and asks whether any of them can truly be called "self." They cannot. He then asks how any of them could be spoken of truly as "possessed by self." They cannot. Only because of clinging are there distinctions of self and belonging to self.

Just so. With fully operational khandhas, mind is far from pristine. Such a supremely foolish mind repeatedly clings to rūpa, vedanā, saññā, saṅkhāra, and viññāṇa as "me" and "mine." Mind is full of kilesas, with ignorance, foolish craving, and foolish clinging as the major stockholders.

These patterns and cycles are repeated and become ever more entrenched as the child grows into adolescence and then adulthood. Causes and conditions reinforce mind's tendency to cling to "me" and "mine." By middle age, habits of thinking and assuming intensify the clinging-together aggregates until they're as thick as a human can bear. Saññā and vedanās are the khandhas that particularly concoct ignorant mind. Because they fabricate mind with increasing power, they are referred to as "mind fabricators."

Let's summarize the crux of the human story so far. Whenever mind appropriates something as being the actor or the issue, that is taken to be self or belonging to self. When mind appropriates form as the central concern, form is taken as self. When there's self, it has form. Anything associated with that form belongs to self. Mind takes itself to be self and anything associated with it in a particular case is taken as belonging to self. Mind that's concocted by ignorance is "appropriating mind."

Here's an example. A child runs into a chair. It hurts, and the child feels that "my self" was hurt by "that self," the chair; it's so foolish as to project the meaning of self onto the chair.[9] Ignorantly considering the chair to be self, a separately existing entity, the child's own body is considered to be a separate self-entity, with these two selves opposed. The chair has become the child's enemy. So it might kick "my enemy," or if the child is too small to attack, it calls on its mother to punish the chair for what it did. Foolish mothers will actually punish a chair on "my child's" behalf. Ignorant parents reinforce self belief in children by hitting a chair to stop their child from crying. How can misunderstanding do anything but increase? As with form, so with the other khandhas. As they get stronger, their value and meaning increase, and so does the clinging.

Self Exists Only in Thought

Self is illusory. Rather than really existing, it's something thought up by ignorant mind. Get this simple fact and you'll understand anattā easily. Attā is an idea. When mind thinks there is self, that's attā. Mind gives itself attā by thinking. For instance, when mind feels delicious pleasure, it assumes that somebody is having the delicious feeling. That's mind taking itself to be attā. Anything that comes along to connect with such a mind at that time belongs to attā.

In this stage of mind, there is always some self, identity, or personality associated with the five aggregates, whichever of them happens to be dominant. Whatever among form, feeling, perception, thought, and consciousness is most meaningful and prominent is grasped as attā; and then associated things are grasped as belonging to self (*attaniya*). When we see how this happens, it's obvious that there isn't really a self at all. There's just thoughts and feelings led by ignorance: misperceiving and misconceiving. Such self isn't real, it's just illusion playing out like this in line with natural law that causes mind to sense, feel, and think that there is self, "me," and "mine."

Pristine mind has been lost. Mind is now full of foolishness and affliction, the core of which is self. Life is full of things self is greedy for, that self hates, that self fears, and that self doubts. Mind spins in fascination with self and what benefits self. Now mind is full of ignorant self. Although it keeps changing, it thinks it's self. In human terms, because mind feels this way, and the feeling really happens, the self identified with feeling seems to be real. For itself, it is real. It's real because people think it is. That's what gives self its power. In

Dhamma terms, these are illusory appearances. Because we haven't been smart enough since in the womb, we fall for the appearances and pretense of self.

Original luminous mind has been lost. With clinging, we assume this situation is who we are. That is, until dukkha awakens us. The journey beyond affliction challenges mind profoundly.

11

THE JOURNEY TO BODHI MIND WITHOUT SELF

When mind forgets its original nature and becomes cluttered with self, the second stage grows steadily heavier. In this, the ignorant wandering of mind thinking it's self usually gets worse before it gets better. The cycles and habits of selfish kilesas deepen and strengthen. Understanding this is a big part of waking up.

Kilesas Get Worse in the Second Stage

A review of the tendencies and effluents will illustrate how kilesas ignorantly build momentum and become increasingly entrenched in the second stage of mind.[1] Once foolish mind has created the kilesas, familiarity with them develops into habitual patterns. With each arising of greed, a bit of familiarity is left behind and the inclination toward greed grows. So it is with each instance of anger, delusion, and their offshoots, all leaving deposits in their wakes. This inclination toward corruption is referred to as *anusaya*. We can name three of them: *rāgānusaya* is the tendency toward greed and lust; *paṭighānusaya* is the tendency toward anger and intending harm; and *avijjānusaya* is the tendency toward ignorance.

The more a particular kilesa occurs, the more powerfully its corresponding anusaya accumulates in the subconscious. Once the accumulation of anusayas is big enough, pressure builds and flows out as effluents (*āsavas*). The anusayas flow out as the effluent of sensuality (*kāmāsava*), the effluent of becoming (*bhavāsava*), and the effluent of ignorance (*avijjāsava*). When mind has accumulated a lot of an anusaya, the pressure pushes out as an āsava, which is like pouring more water into a leaking jar. If there isn't much water in the jar, the leakage is small, but if we fill the jar with water, the strong pressure comes out in spurts. Lots of anusayas means lots of messy āsavas. This makes us greedy, angry, and confused easily and quickly.

Thus affliction and corruption of mind is expressed in three ways: the ordinary occurrences of affliction, the kilesas; the familiarity with and tendency toward affliction, the anusayas; and the leaks and spurts of affliction, the āsavas. Understanding these patterns shows us what we must do in practice. In each opportunity for reactive affliction that doesn't happen, an anusaya decreases. This means that the anusayas diminish every time kilesas are avoided or prevented. As the accumulated tendencies diminish, the pressure to leak weakens. Hence, leaving alone an opportunity for greed weakens rāgānusaya; not allowing anger when provoked reduces paṭighānusaya; and being mindful, clear, and intelligent weakens avijjānusaya.

With luminous mind already lost and corrupted mind dominant, the condition worsens for as long as skillful practice is lacking. Unless we work effectively to reduce the anusayas, mind is increasingly encrusted with the stains of kilesas, anusayas, and āsavas. Are these the treasures we've accumulated in life?

Mind Is Trapped in Cycles of Dukkha by Powerful Kilesas

When ignorant mind acts under the power of a kilesa, that deliberate action is karma. The result of a karma is vipāka, which increases the strength of the motivating kilesa. The basic cycle is that afflictions lead to actions which in turn have results. If a result satisfies, this feeds attractive, greedy kilesas; if a result annoys, this strengthens aversive, resentful kilesas. If left to fate, the fruits of karma are stronger afflictions and corruptions of mind. Kilesas and suffering will increase unless mind turns to the path of knowledge and awakening.

For the most part, human minds act out of greed, hatred, and delusion. Karma is motivated by these unwholesome roots. The cycles perpetuate with each reaction to the results. To clearly see how scary this is, observe the vaṭṭasaṃsāra of concocting kilesas, performing of karmas, and receiving the results: kilesa-karma-vipāka, kilesa-karma-vipāka, over and over. The results of karma happen here in this life; there's no need to talk about results in future lives. These powerful cycles spin right here, day and night, nobody knows how many rounds each day. This sort of mind is crude and lowly, not at all pristine.

Incredibly foolish mind—darkened by ignorance, thick and dense with kilesas, intensely clinging to self—spins around and around in vaṭṭasaṃsāra. Many Buddhists prefer the simple language of spinning from one life to the next and then the life after that. They understand vaṭṭasaṃsāra in terms of the birth and death of bodies over years and centuries, cycling through numerous coffins. Alternatively, we can emphasize the symptoms of these cycles: birth, aging, illness, and death. That's vaṭṭasaṃsāra too. The point is to realize how trapped in suffering such minds are. While the lifetime-to-lifetime version is popular, it's difficult to directly experience right now. I prefer to talk about the vaṭṭasaṃsāra that is personally experienceable today, such as the cycle of a kilesa creating an action of mind, followed by mind experiencing the result, which is reacted to with further kilesas. This vaṭṭasaṃsāra of intensifying afflictions is what should frighten you. Can you see how spinning around in cycles of kilesa-karma-vipāka is a truly fearsome affair?

Every Realm Stinks with Dukkha

What do we find in this vaṭṭa cycle? Nothing but dukkha. For mind trapped in vaṭṭasaṃsāra there is only distress and struggle. In whichever realm it's spinning, there is dukkha. When mind thinks sensually, it suffers in those ways. When it thinks in terms of pure materiality, it suffers in more refined ways. When mind thinks in nonmaterial terms, it suffers in more abstract ways.[2]

In personal terms, beings—such as demons, animals, and ordinary humans—wandering in and infatuated with the sensual realms endure the dukkha of whichever sensual realm they are stuck in. The *brahmas* (gods) wandering in and infatuated with the more elevated realms of pure form, stuck in nonsensual pleasures, endure the sort of dukkha that is subtle, hard to comprehend and see, yet just as entrapping. Lastly, the brahmas wandering in and infatuated with immaterial realms, experiencing the happiness of formless meditations, experience the subtlest dukkha. All existences are dukkha, whether sensual, pure-form, or formless.

The Buddha is recorded to have said, "Even the tiniest bit of excrement stinks." A bit so small that it can't be seen still stinks. Think about this: even the smallest, most refined existence is still dukkha. Unable to see this, people keep wandering and circling through existential dukkha. Ignorant mind changes from one realm of existence to another, all while depending on the same physical body. In Dhamma language, ignorant mind cycles through many existences each day. All of them involve dukkha.

In the ordinary language of most people, these realms are understood to be actual places: hells and heavens populated by all sorts of beings. I don't object to that, and I don't wish to argue about it. Rather, I prefer to talk about things that we can understand through personal experience. Currently, we may feel most disturbed and troubled while seeking sensual comforts and pleasures. Hence, dwelling in a consumer paradise pleasing to all the senses is still dukkha, because of the clinging to them—the senses, the pleasures, and the dwelling—as "me" and "mine." We cry when separated from them and are infatuated even when satisfied.

In the superior realms of the pure-form and formless gods, clinging to self still creates dukkha. This can't be helped, because the better the quality of existence, the greater the desire to avoid death. Pali texts state that the brahamas are the beings who most want to avoid death, because their existence is most happy, comfortable, and refined. More than anyone else, they don't want to die. However great the desire to avoid death, the fear of death is just as great; and the greater the fear, the greater the dukkha. Human beings aren't as afraid, as we have less to lose. Still, none of the existences of ignorant mind are an escape from dukkha.

This is as far as we can go with the second stage of mind. The pristine mine had nothing; then it became full of kilesas and dukkha. We have surveyed the various ways in which original mind is lost and ignorantly corrupted mind takes its place through appropriating the khandhas; with the proliferation of kilesas, anusayas, and āsavas; and with the relentless spinning of the karma cycle. Such mind flounders in the ocean of dukkha.

The Third Stage—Mind's Path beyond Corruption

Mind in the third stage emerges from the mass of suffering and leaves self behind. Third-stage mind wanders and spins in dukkha: tasting this dukkha, tasting that dukkha, tasting all kinds of dukkha. Think about it: What happens with all this wandering and cycling? Mind gradually comes to know dukkha keenly, feels dukkha snapping and biting, and learns from the experience. In biting, dukkha teaches. It goads us into learning about and from our foolishness. When we have borne dukkha in the various realms of becoming long enough, it educates us. The distress, dis-ease, and persistent dukkha of vaṭṭasaṃsāra spark recognition that this state of affairs can't go on. Mind gradually understands that dukkha comes from clinging to things as belonging to self and as self. Though at first vaguely and faintly, it realizes that this problem of dukkha originates in attachment to self. This realization grows, correlating with the Buddha's statement, "The five clinging-together aggregates are the core of dukkha." Once there's clinging, there's suffering.

When beings ache and groan long enough—as if falling into hell five hundred times—won't they eventually become smarter? Beings immersed in the mass of dukkha start to feel fed up with it and begin to look for an alternative. We begin to suspect our own foolishness, our kilesa habits, and our clinging. We start to cultivate the character that searches for the way out of dukkha.

Once we reach the point of being really fed up with the dukkha that has punished us, we finally are interested in hearing about its quenching. Then we seek out the wise, listen to their teachings, and come to understand dukkha and its causes. We come to the Buddha's teachings through a disciple of the Buddha or some other true person. Unlike those who haven't faced their suffering, we hear about the four noble truths and understand easily because we have experienced dukkha in abundance.

Because of their confusions and infatuations, young people, for the most part, don't pay attention to the noble truths. They haven't been bitten and beaten sufficiently. However, as soon as someone has had enough, they are interested. They listen and can understand when they hear about the four noble truths. This explains the difference between those who can't understand when hearing Dhamma and those who understand easily. One sort of person is already chastened by the experience of dukkha. The other sort, still ignorant, doesn't get the message no matter what they hear.

At the time of the Buddha, it was perhaps easier for people to understand because they didn't have so many deceptive things to deal with. Nowadays, we face many more confusing fabrications that tempt people into the mass of dukkha. The Buddha's time didn't have all the modern-day stimulating pleasures and enjoyments. People had better opportunities to hear the Dhamma, and it was easier for them to understand. Now, massive creativity is put into churning out ever stranger and more enticing bait to lure us into problems. Hence, people in this era find it difficult to listen to and understand the quenching of dukkha. In this day and age, Buddha-Dhamma remains mostly sterile.

Take a look at our big, crowded cities. All of them are packed with things that deceive the ignorant, draw them into infatuation, and keep them suffering. Such things aren't just in our homes and shopping centers; they have infiltrated our temples, retreat centers, and Buddhist organizations. This is why it's so difficult nowadays for people to recognize dukkha well enough to become weary with it. So help out a little. Don't let your children fall into the same traps. Don't provide them with deceptive things.

I've said over the national radio that parents are the ones who make their children ignorant. I advised parents to take their children to the shops that sell toys, tasty treats, and such, then explain to them how all these beautiful, expensive things are there to make us stupid. Then, perhaps, their children will grow up less foolish and infatuated. Give them the chance to see such things as they really are—a waste of money, no more than that. Such children will be less easily deceived and better suited to hearing and understanding Dhamma. They in turn will grow into young men and women, into fathers and mothers, more capable of absorbing and passing on the Dhamma.

Path of Insight That Mind Takes beyond Dukkha

The third stage of mind, with its better understanding of life and dukkha, is ready to listen. We seek wise teachers who can teach how things are: how dukkha is and what the causes of dukkha are. We discover that there have been and still are people whose dukkha is quenched. We find someone who has discovered the quenching of dukkha and practices for its quenching. We realize that here is the Dhamma that quenches dukkha. Mind now knows the Buddha, Dhamma, and Sangha, and follows a different trajectory.

Receiving teachings on virtue, samādhi, and wisdom—the eightfold path—mind puts them into practice. Practicing sīla, samādhi, and paññā, it knows what Buddha, Dhamma, and Sangha are about. Investigating the noble truths, true knowing arises. Previously, knowing was false, ignorant. Practicing rightly, mind realizes the opposite knowing that everything is not lasting, hard to bear, and not-self.[3]

There are many insight knowledges collectively known as *dhammaṭṭhiti-ñāṇa* (insight knowledge into the natural reality of things). These include insights that know impermanence, suffering, selflessness, emptiness, thusness, and dependent co-arising.[4]

These insight knowledges regarding how things naturally manifest are more usually referred to as seeing the three characteristics of all conditioned phenomena (*tilakkhaṇa*). Mind beginning to see the tilakkhaṇa is waking up; it's starting to dispel ignorance and despise kilesas. Seeing the danger in the kilesas, it understands the harm in clinging to self and spinning around in vaṭṭasaṃsāra. Rising above such phenomena, it realizes the nibbāna-ñāṇa (insight knowledge inclining toward nibbāna), which is the transition to fully seeing visaṅkhāra. There is insight knowing that leads to disenchantment with the world and its concoctions; that seeks release; and that releases all objects of clinging.[5] These are the primary nibbāna-ñāṇa, the set of knowledges that open the door to nibbāna and realize the deathless. The third stage is this incredible change of mind.

Problem concerning Self in Buddha's Phrasing

Before we end, we must return to a problem of language. I've emphasized that for mind to release, it must be without the sense of self. In this liberation, nothing feels like it belongs to self. While the Buddha consistently pointed out how everything is not-self, even he spoke of self at times. You will recall that he said, "Self is the refuge of self" or "Self is a refuge for itself."[6] Why did he say this? Because communicating with ordinary people is difficult without referring to self. As the Buddha stated in the next lines, Dhamma is the true refuge, actually. Self being the refuge of self means that mind with Dhamma is refuge, but this mind is clung to as being self. When mind is still foolish, it assumes there's self, and this "self," although it's of ignorant mind, must help itself. Who can help it, if not the suffering mind itself? Hence, foolish mind must help foolish mind. After mind's foolishness grew steadily heavier the longer it wandered in vaṭṭasaṃsāra, it began to open its eyes to helping itself. When no self is fabricated, it's only a matter of mind. If mind is taken to be self, such self is a matter of mind that must be dealt with continually until mind has no self and finishes.

The problem is that having self creates problems belonging to self.

If mind is finished with self, there are no problems for anyone. Then problems don't exist for mind because mind has no self to endure dukkha. If there's no sense of self, we people can't suffer. Dukkha is born and can exist because mind feels it has self: self to be born, self to age, self to get sick, self to die, self to achieve, self to fail, self to win, self to lose, self to profit, self to go bankrupt. These are matters of mind that has self, that has problems. When there's no more self, all those problems fall away completely.

Therefore, the words "self is the refuge of self" are correct enough. This mind must be its own refuge, so long as mind is assumed to be oneself. If mind isn't taken to be self, mind itself is the refuge for itself. If mind is taken as self, we necessarily say that self must be the refuge for itself.

Buddhism understands self to be illusory, created by mind through its foolishness. Certain other religions understand self differently. They speak of true self that is above and beyond mind, as something other than citta within this *attabhāva* (self-condition, selfhood). (Even Thai Buddhists use this term *selfhood*, as if it were something real, which is confused.) They practice so that their kind of self, something other than citta, is liberated and merges with the eternal self. That's self in certain non-Buddhist creeds.

There's no such self in Buddhist teachings. There's no need for self, only citta. When mind thinks there's self or that it has self, it's got a self, according to foolish mind for as long as it's foolish. When mind loses its stupidity, it has no self. There's only pristine mind, pure mind, mind reaching visaṅkhāra, accessing nibbāna. Nibbāna is nibbāna. Nibbāna isn't self; it's just nibbāna. When mind has no causes and conditions, it quenches. The story ends there without needing self to reoccur.

Other teachings believe that mind attains a permanent self in a particular place. We don't find this in Buddhism. Those who believe in a God have citta as a self that goes to be with God, with Kaivalya, with Paramātman, according to the terms and teachings of those religions. In Buddhism, however, we say that mind realizes visaṅkhāra, citta "reaches" the state in which nothing can concoct. It finishes, ends, empties. The final end is nonmind, so empty of self that mind itself isn't anything. Then self doesn't exist because mind is no longer foolish. This nonfoolish mind continues until it quenches in the final moment and ends. Unending emptiness—that is, nibbāna, the supreme emptiness—is fully realized.

This is what is meant by "mind only"—nothing, nothing else, nothing of anyone beyond matters of mind. All things are matters of mind. Everything happens at mind, from mind, arising with mind, accomplished by mind. All dhammas, excepting none, are matters of mind.

When Not Foolish Mind Isn't Self

Our method for explaining Buddhism points out that there's nothing except matters of mind, nothing besides citta. When stupid, it's self. When not stupid, it isn't self. When foolish, it suffers. When not foolish, there's no dukkha. At first, mind is pristine, without kilesas, without stupidity. Once body is conceived in the womb and there are eyes, ears, nose, tongue, body, and mind, it begins to practice foolishness little by little. Foolishness increases steadily because of the deceptions of eyes, ears, nose, tongue, body, and mind. Foolish mind doesn't have wisdom, and so it's mind full of dukkha, full of self.

First mind is pristine mind, second mind is foolish mind, and third mind is mind no longer foolish. This mind is superior to pristine mind in that it doesn't return to suffering. Pristine mind can still fall into dukkha. Matters of mind have these three stages. If anyone understands, I won't have played my flute for turtles.

I'd like to provide a simile here, for comparison only, illustrating the nonreality of self. There were primitive people living in the forests who had never seen an automobile. Seeing one run, stop, turn, and back up, they thought the automobile was alive. On the other hand, the engineers and mechanics who built the automobiles would never have thought of one as living. They knew how automobiles ran because they built them and so knew they weren't alive. Automobiles aren't alive, automobiles have no attā, but they can easily be mistaken as being living beings with self by those who have never previously seen one.

Mind is the same. While still foolish, it sees these concoctions as being self, until it smartens up—smart like automobile engineers—and realizes it's not-self. Some of us nowadays might see airplanes flying and think they're living selves. Once there's understanding of how sufficient and fitting causes and conditions fabricate an experience that seems to be self—subtle, refined, and wonderful, the same as if truly self—there's realization that it really isn't self after all. Life is anattā; mind is anattā.

Nowadays mind can think anything, all sorts of things. Mind can think its way to the moon. Mind can think of reaching nibbāna. It tends to cling to all that as self, when in fact none is self. It's all just the nature of thinking and imagining mind. Whatever causes and conditions influence it, it thinks in that direction. With correct conditions, it thinks in ways that don't suffer. With wrong influences, it thinks in ways that suffer.

It's all just about mind. Nothing else besides citta. Pristine mind is neither foolish nor clever. It becomes foolish mind; it wanders in foolishness, reaping the harvest of being foolish. It starts to smarten up—the sort of intelligence that doesn't fall back into foolishness. It quenches self making, it calms wandering and spinning. It enters arahantship and realizes nibbāna. It travels foolishly until foolishness is finally abandoned. Originally not foolish, it was susceptible to being tricked into being foolish, and finally is never foolish again. It knows what needs to be known.

Mind Reaches Visaṅkhāra, Returning to Unending Luminosity

Mind is realizing path, fruit, and nibbāna on successive levels. Disenchantment and dispassion liberate it as stream enterer (*sotāpanna*), the first level of nobility; as once-returner (*sakadāgāmī*); as nonreturner (*anāgāmi*); and as perfected human being (*arahant*). Mind is now without afflictions and corruptions. At the start of life, mind was pristine yet liable to becoming entangled. Now the kilesas can't happen. The original purity of mind isn't the same as this purity at the end. That early purity was conditional, pure only because clinging hadn't occurred. In the third stage, mind is pure through training and cultivation such that the kilesas can't arise ever. It's now pure going forward without ever returning to the way it was.

We say that mind has reached visaṅkhāra, has realized the nature beyond concocting, where nothing can fabricate ever again. Pristine luminosity cannot be obscured or tarnished. The story ends with stage three.

From a speck of dust, a tiny morsel of corruption, to the realization of unconcoctable nibbāna, it is all a matter of mind. Not really about self. This is exactly what we want everyone to see: there's nothing that isn't about mind.

12

ANYTHING AND EVERYTHING ARE MERELY NATURAL ELEMENTS

Throughout this book, we've been looking at important Buddhist principles necessary for seeing with the eye of Dhamma. For example, in the previous two chapters, we examined how everything is about mind or has to do with mind. We can summarize these minds as follows: At first, there's just pristine mind without any feelings, thoughts, or kilesas. Such mind also lacks understanding of life. Subsequently, there's ignorant mind working through the senses, receiving contacts, having feelings, and clinging. This foolish mind suffers. Finally, mind loses its foolishness, having tasted so much dukkha in vaṭṭasaṃsāra, and grows intelligent. Overcoming ignorance, this mind comes to know what's what and is released from suffering. These three stages represent the whole story of Buddhism concisely: pristine mind then foolish mind and then liberated mind. If you thoroughly understand these stages, you have understood all of Buddhism.

Some people, however, aren't ready to understand that everything is mind. Some of us are more suited to another approach. For them, in this chapter we'll look at *dhātus* (natural elements) and how everything is just a dhātu. When seeing clearly that all things whatsoever are basically just elements, there's no clinging to anything as being self or belonging to self. Thus mind is liberated. This, also, ends the story.

The Meanings of Dhātus

What are dhātus? Dhātus are the most basic units discovered when things are analyzed into their component parts. A step-by-step deconstruction of something—anything—will conclude with dhātus. Once the dhātus are reached, that's enough; to break them down further would go too far. In Thai, Pali, and Western languages, the meaning is the same: *dhātus* and *elements* refer to the final, useful units found when systematically deconstructing things.

Exploring further, we find that dhātus have two levels: pure elements and compounds of elements. To illustrate the two, we can review the example of pure elements as understood in modern chemistry, which numbered ninety-something when I was young, now number more than a hundred, and may increase as new ones are discovered. According to chemistry, when there's a single element not combined with another element, that's called a "pure element." When two or more elements are joined together, that's referred to as a "compound." The chemical properties of a compound are different from those of the elements that make it up. For example, oxygen and hydrogen are pure elements; when conjoined in a certain way, they become the compound we know as water, which behaves differently than the two gases. When we speak of water, we mean a compound of elements. When the compound is broken down, we have two pure elements, hydrogen and oxygen. In another example, elements appear as pure dhātus, such as copper, and as compounds, such as when copper is mixed with tin creating brass. Pure metal dhātus, such as gold, silver, and copper, can be combined in the alloy red gold, which is used in making jewelry.

Dhātus, both pure and in compounds, make up human beings and everything associated with us. Because our ingenuity concocts the elements into so many different compounds and strange new mixtures, we have a vast array of enticements for clinging. The possibilities are endless. Along the way, we become enamored with compounded elements. Even so, these are merely examples of the physical elements, which is the meaning of *dhātu* in ordinary language. There's a deeper meaning that we must understand.

The Dhamma Meaning of Dhātus

The elements of Dhamma are far more numerous than those in the periodic table. We discover them differently and their meaning is more profound. These elements of experience also appear purely and in compounds, and in ever more strange mixtures. Still, all of them are natural elements. Even if the concept of nonphysical elements is strange for you, please give it your careful attention.

To see their importance for our Dhamma understanding, and to intuit their not-self character, let's consider some of the trickier compounds. When the elements concoct in complex ways, they take on certain meanings. For instance, things eaten and consumed are essentially elements, as are their eaters and consumers. This is exemplified in the *Dhātu Paccavekhaṇa*, a reflection on the basic requisites of life, which I was taught when I first ordained. It teaches us that robes, almsfood, lodgings, and medicines are all dhātus, natural elements. Likewise, we recited that the wearer of clothing, the eater of food, the user of lodgings, and the taker of medicines are just elements too. The individual who consumes is merely natural elements that have combined to become a person who wears, eats, uses, and so on.

Although you won't find them in the periodic table, elements of this sort are important in Buddhist teachings. In the Dhamma system, whenever something is compounded into having a certain meaning or value—such as being something eaten, used, or worn—that's a dhātu. Further, the compound taken to be an individual or person—taking on the meaning of the eater, the user, or the consumer—is just an element too. *Element* here is more broad, profound, and marvelous than in ordinary usage. Nevertheless, all dhātus share the meaning of being just natural elements.

Worldly language describes the material elements, whether those of the periodic table or our daily experience. Dhamma language, the spiritual language of mind, however, describes many more dhātus, including ones most people haven't heard of. Some of these are pure, and others are compounds, similar to the chemical elements. Some of the basic dhātus are eye element, ear element, nose element, tongue element, body element, and mind element. Their mates are elements too: form element, sound element, odor element, flavor element, touch element, and idea element. If you have never heard about them before, please begin meditating on these elements of experience.

Each of the five aggregates that arise on the foundation of the senses—form, feeling tone, perception, thinking, and sense consciousness—is an element: form element, feeling element, perception element, thinking element, and consciousness element. The actions carried out by aggregates—good, evil, and neither good nor evil—are also elements: skillful karmas, unskillful karmas, and neutral karmas. The significance of actions are elements like everything else: goodness element, evil element, and indeterminate element. These are just some of the elements that are seldom discussed yet are important in the workings of mind.

All the characteristics and qualities of mind are also dhātus. Take the kilesas, for instance: greed is an element, aversion is an element, and delusion is an element. The sensations arising from meaningful experiences are also elements. When something tastes delicious, there's deliciousness element. When something tastes unpalatable, there's unpalatable element. These elements arise according to designations and assumptions, with the meanings and values given to things. Colors such as red, green, and white are such elements in experience, although the underlying reality is just light waves of differing wavelengths causing the visual experiences and perceptions. Please understand that all experiences and perceptions, all encounters with meaning and values, are just dhātus.

There are still more elements related to mind. The element of sensual wandering (*kāmāvacara-dhātu*) can dominate mind so that it's infatuated with sensuality. The element of pure-form wandering (*rūpāvacara-dhātu*) can dominate mind so that it's infatuated with nonsensual form. The element of formless wandering (*arūpāvacara-dhātu*) can dominate mind so that it's infatuated with formlessness. Each of these can dominate and infatuate mind. The highest dhātu of all is *nibbāna-dhātu*; even nibbāna is an element, one free of the wandering and infatuation of the lower dhātus. In the language of Dhamma, it's all elements. It's a clean sweep: there isn't anything that isn't a dhātu.

We Are Just Elements Too

When we analyze ourselves into earth, water, fire, air, space, and consciousness, we find that each of these components is just an element. When we analyze the body into its constituent organs and parts, each individual part is just an element too. When taken altogether as a "person," that person is still just an element. The aim of all this is to show that there isn't anything that isn't an element, so as to avoid the wrong understanding that clings to things as being self.

Concerning the quenching of dukkha, the important elements will be the six that we learned about in chapter 10. As the Buddha said, we—each individual—are a combination of earth element, water element, fire element, and air element, along with space element and consciousness element. If you want a good understanding of Buddhist teachings, you ought to remember the names of all six elements, which are earth element (*paṭhāvi-dhātu*), water element (*āpo-dhātu*), fire element (*tejo-dhātu*), wind element (*vāyo-dhātu*), space element (*ākāsa-dhātu*), and consciousness element (*viññāṇa-dhātu*). The physical parts of us are made up of the four physical elements; the viññāṇa-dhātu means mind that feels, thinks, and imagines; and the vacancy in which all these things manifest is space element.

Space element requires a little more study than the others, as it's the least tangible and subtlest of the six. The simple explanation is that there must be empty space for something to happen in. This rock next to me, for instance, couldn't be here if the space were already taken. Look closely to see the fact that anything we might experience is based on space element. Without space, nothing can manifest. If all space is occupied, if there's no vacancy, nothing else can happen. So we need to acknowledge how valuable space element is. A container, such as a cup, is useful because of its available hollowness; water can be poured into it. This value makes space meaningful, and it is why it's referred to as an element, as ākāsa-dhātu.

All living things, animals and plants, are compounds of the same six elements, and I've observed that all living things must have mind element, the dhātu that is sensitive, to a greater or lesser degree. Plants possess the consciousness element, or mind element, appropriate for plants. A tree's mind element is rather basic, while that of animals and people is more complex. If an expression of life is highly developed, its mind element is correspondingly developed; if less developed, its mind element is correspondingly less developed. While the sensitivity of a plant can't be compared to that of a human being, nevertheless, plants clearly are sensitive, as we observe in plants that move away from danger or close under certain conditions. Animals are correspondingly more sensitive, as we see in their fleeing danger, fighting, and avoiding pain. The physical elements aren't sufficient for life; consciousness element is necessary too. And space element plays its crucial part.

I review this teaching because most of you don't see life as compounds of elements, especially when thinking about yourselves. We don't see that it's all just dhātus. We take experience personally, we identify with things, and we cling. Yet seeing and thinking are just mind element seeing and mind element thinking in response to the influences of environmental impacts.

Mind Mixed Up with Ignorance Element Makes Dukkha

Avijjā (ignorance) and vijjā (right knowledge) are elements too. Ignorance is the lack of true knowledge (*vijjā*), and mind naturally begins with it. Mind lacking wisdom is naturally ignorant. We won't say it's stupid, just that it lacks knowledge. And so mind element experiences but the experiencing isn't correct, which is why we say it lacks right knowledge. How it experiences is mixed up with ignorance element and merely goes along with the instincts. So it feels it has self.

Rather than understanding everything as naturally operating elements, whatever mind senses is seen as having self, as having individual existence. The root cause of all our problems is right here: we face all this suffering because the various things experienced by mind element are foolishly misapprehended as selves. That these things are mere elements is missed. Such mind clings to the personal meanings of self: sometimes as lovely and lovable, sometimes as ugly and hateful. It's deceived by and fascinated with the lovely things in one way and the ugly things in another way. Thus we feel passion, anger, hatred, fear, anxiety, longing, jealousy, envy, and so forth, according to whatever is being experienced and the personal feelings.

The origin of suffering, of our problems, is that mind element is foolish when mixed up with ignorance element, which is just another dhātu. It's mind that's foolish, but we blame the person for being stupid. However, such an individual doesn't fundamentally exist. There's no separate person in the six elements. It's just that mind becomes stupid when getting mixed up in ignorance element. When we speak conventionally, we speak of "me"—me as "person," me as "individual." Further, when mind is associated with ignorance element, it foolishly clings to things around it as "mine." This adds to the suffering, which ends up "belonging to me," which is just mind foolishly possessing it.

The "me" isn't original. Originally, there are only the six elements; there's no self element or person element. The six elements of body, mind, and space work together, each in its particular role. Mind element functions relying upon the physical dhātus, and space is where they happen.

Once mind is mixed up with ignorance element, it becomes completely deluded and clings to all sorts of things as being individually existing entities. It's passionate about what's lovable, it hates what's unlikeable, it's angry with what's irritating, and it's afraid of what's startling. Then the aftereffects of such behavior accumulate, manifesting as the tendencies toward passion, hatred, anger, fear, and so on. These basic tendencies expand in various directions, turning into longing, worry, envy, jealousy, and the like. For example, envy and jealousy can grow out of greed.

All of these kinds of kilesas result from mind being mixed up with ignorance element. If an experience is unpleasant, uncomfortable, or difficult, the compound of mind element and ignorance element is displeased, which is considered painful and thus produces disliking element, which leads to anger element, hatred element, fear element, and the like. Each time the compound acts in these ways, it creates *dukkha-dhātu*, the dukkha element. If the current experience happens to be pleasant and congenial, the mind and ignorance compound is pleased, then considers this to be happiness, and thus produces *sukha-dhātu*, the pleasure element, for mind to foolishly indulge. Or if the experience is of the indeterminate sort, the mind and ignorance compound feels uncertainty and doesn't know how to discern whatever is being experienced and thus produces *adukkhamasukha-dhātu*, the neither-painful-nor-unpleasant element, to be foolish about.

Compound, Fabricated Elements and the Unfabricated Element

With so many elements—everything being an element of experience—it's a challenge to keep track of them all. Fortunately, we have an excellent way to organize our investigation of them. The Buddha distinguished all the *saṅkhata-dhātus*, the compounded elements, which are saṅkhāras, and the *asaṅkhata-dhātu*, the element that is unconcocted and unconcoctable. He also talked about dhātus in sets of three, which will help us distinguish the asaṅkhata-dhātu from all the saṅkhata-dhātus.

The first threesome considers only the saṅkhata, conditioned and compounded, side of things, the dukkha side. These are the sensual elements, form elements, and formless elements. When a sensual element dominates mind, it's crazy about sensuality. When a form element dominates mind, it's crazy about pure forms free of sensuality, such as pure material properties that are the bases of the jhānas.[1] When a formless element dominates mind, it's crazy about the formless, unconcerned with sensuality or with pure forms. According to the texts, formless things are exemplified by space, consciousness, nothingness, and neither perception nor nonperception. If you aren't ready to understand these four, you needn't worry about them now, but know that there are immaterial, formless objects of mind, such as those experienced in the higher reaches of absorption. Be aware that things don't have to have form or shape to be mental objects. When a formless element dominates mind, and it's infatuated with something formless, don't mistake this for realization of nibbāna. These formless experiences are still fabricated saṅkhāras.

No matter how many hundreds, thousands, or tens of thousands of dhātus there are, arranging them in these three subgroups of saṅkhata-dhātus helps us understand them. Human beings are usually under the influence of one or the other of these three kinds of dhātus, with the majority stuck wandering around with sensual elements. On occasion, out-of-the-ordinary people find absorption in a form element, as is the case with certain ascetics, hermits, and sages. A really first-rate ascetic will be fascinated with the formless, as was the case with two of the Buddha's teachers. Formless elements are the highest of the concocted elements. Beyond it is nibbāna, a matter of unconcoctable element (*asaṅkhata-dhātu*).

These three kinds of elements encompass all saṅkhāras, everything dependent on conditions and subject to fabrication. They are the territory of beings that wander in the realms of existence. People find themselves caught up in all three; at some time or another, they wander in each of the various realms of existence and are classified accordingly. Ordinary people mostly end up with sensual elements, in their fondness for sensual pleasure and also when falling into the woeful realms. They dream of being *devas* in sensual paradises. Ordinary humans, along with other animals, mostly exist on these cruder planes. However, certain people who train themselves as hermits and sages take pleasure in forms and formlessness, having lost interest in the sensuality of their earlier days. When their training gives them access to these more refined pleasures, their satisfaction and happiness become infatuation, and they won't want to go beyond. They say that the gods of the pure-form and formless realms have longer life spans than anyone, longer than can be calculated, because their realms are profoundly satisfying and fascinating.

Quenching Is a Natural Element Too

Another trio of dhātus also includes noble beings, in addition to ordinary worldly beings. In other words, this set includes both saṅkhata and asaṅkhata. Now, the three groups are form elements, formless elements, and quenching elements. *Rūpa-dhātus* are the elements that have form, which includes sensuality, which depends on form. The sense experiences of visuals, sounds, odors, flavors, and bodily sensations all depend on rūpa as their basis and so can be included with rūpa-dhātus. Of course, the pure, nonsensual forms are rūpa-dhātus too. The second group of elements in this trio are the arūpa-dhātus, mind's feelings, notions, thoughts, and moods, which are formless. As noted, these formless elements are also concocted by causes and conditions, thus subject to continual change. Lastly, *nirodha-dhātu* is the element in which both form and formless elements quench, otherwise known as *nibbāna-dhātu*. Indeed, nibbāna element can also be called *nirodha-dhātu*. When both rūpa and arūpa encounter nirodha-dhātu, they quench and cool—that is, they cease fabricating. *Nirodha* means the "remainderless quenching" that manifests with quenching the causes and conditions for concocting. If the quenching is only temporary, it goes by other names, such as "setting"—as with the sun in the evening only to return at dawn. The full quenching of nirodha means that supporting causes and conditions completely cease influencing and fabricating.

As we've noted, when mind element is mixed up with ignorance element, it's foolishly mired in vaṭṭasaṃsāra. Ignorance element is the necessary condition for mind element to cycle around in vaṭṭasaṃsāra. Hence, this avijjā-dhātu has to be quenched if suffering is to end. Quench the ignorance element that supports vaṭṭasaṃsāra by bringing in *vijjā-dhātu* (true-knowledge element) to replace it.

Mind combined with insight element has the property of clearly seeing the truth of all things. Most especially, it knows itself to be merely elements. Egoistic mind is just an element. Everything associated with it and concocting it are elements too. So seeing all experience as natural elements, the sense of self isn't born. Thus mind changes radically. It wakes up from being ignorant and fascinated. Mind becomes thoroughly intelligent, knows clearly, and joyfully blossoms, in accord with the meaning of *buddha*, being fully awake. Before mind was sleeping; now mind is awake.

Quality of Mind Can Be Fabricated Limitlessly

Self-knowledge means that mind comes to know mind. Mind that thought it was "me" has come to know itself. Don't forget that Buddhist teachings are about not-self, and that anything and everything is a matter of mind. Therefore, know that when we sometimes say "me" or "we," and sometimes say "mind," we're talking about the same thing. Now mind knows itself as merely elements: composed of elements, associated with elements, with elements as cause, and with any results being elements, too, all of them carrying on naturally.[2]

Elements mingle and interact, creating unending series of new results. Consider the elements we've discussed: visual element, sound element, odor element, flavor element, and touch element; goodness element, evil element, and neither-good-nor-evil element; sensual element, pure-form element, and formless element—each kind, each group, and each set fabricating among themselves without any limit. Whenever something enters and interacts, something new is created. This is just like what happens in the kitchen, where relatively few ingredients are concocted into great varieties of food.

The qualities and capacities of mind can be fabricated limitlessly. Lots of attractive things can attract and fascinate it, just as lots of ugly, unseemly things can repel it. There are so many that it's difficult to stop. Not understanding these things properly, we're led astray by them—led into liking and disliking, loving and hating, longing after and fearing, possessing and destroying, and so forth. Because mind is foolish, it doesn't know itself and all it experiences as merely elements. Even the most fabulous deliciousness is only an element. Not seeing this, mind falls for delicious and desire more. This feeling intensifies and becomes a kilesa, so strong in its desire that it might kill for what it wants. Or desiring everything, we seek power over the world. Concocting easily gets out of control, and people end up attacking each other viciously.

The way out of such violence and suffering is the heart of Buddhist teaching that sees everything as elements. As the Buddha said, "The person is a combination of the six elements." Understanding the elements properly is to know everything we need to know, because when we realize that there are only elements, there's no more clinging to anything.

The Buddhist View of Elements Is Unique

We should know how our religion differs from others, especially what's most unique about it. As far as I know, the teaching that points to everything being merely elements is unique to Buddhism. I have yet to meet another religion that teaches this. Our extensive Buddhist scriptures explain how life is combinations of earth, water, fire, air, space, and consciousness—the six dhātus. The power of idappaccayatā, the natural law reigning over all phenomena, causes the elements to continually interact and combine in plant, animal, and human forms. This concocting occurs through the law of idappaccayatā. Each happening gives rise to other things.

Other religious systems don't have this kind of explanation. The Christian religion, for instance, says that God took a handful of earth, breathed life into it, and instantaneously created Adam, the first man. Then God took one of Adam's ribs and created woman, Eve. Eventually the pair reproduced. This illustrates beliefs that human beings were created by God, who conjured us from earth element. How different is that from the Buddhist explanation? It's important for us as Buddhists to know the heart of our religion: aware that everything is just natural elements constantly concocting, combining, and separating under the power of causes and conditions.

In scientific terms, we can distinguish two kinds of religion: creationist and evolutionist. Creationist religions aren't concerned with natural elements; they teach that creator gods, the most powerful selves, made everything. Buddhism teaches an evolutionist perspective, that developments occur in accord with natural principles over time. Elements combine, develop, and naturally evolve life. I point out this distinction, first, to highlight the evolutionist character of Buddhism and, second, to remind everyone to examine yourselves carefully and see that you're just elements too. Don't get too carried away with the "me" and "mine" imagined and created by mind influenced by ignorance element.

Modern education that teaches about the periodic table of material elements can be helpful here. Deeply examining the elements of modern science can be a good start to understanding how everything is merely elements. We learn how elements are made of atoms that combine into molecules and further become all material things. So study modern materialist science enough to begin seeing that there are only elements compounding and interacting. Buddhism, then, goes deeper, while using a similar approach, and shows us that it's all just elements—material, mental, space, and beyond—without anything to cling to as self.

The Birth of Elements Is the Birth of Dukkha

Once we know that the heart of Buddhism is that there's nothing but elements, the next step is to see that the arising of dhātus is the arising of dukkha. Please remember this important sentence: the birth of elements is the birth of suffering. The difficulty here is with the word *birth*, in that most of us understand birth only as physical birth from a womb. To understand Dhamma, we need to recognize a subtler meaning of birth. In Dhamma language, the birth of an animal is when that life is fully functional according to its proper meaning. In the same way, the birth of earth element, water element, fire element, and wind element means that these dhātus are performing their respective functions. In doing so, all four elements interact and combine in ways proper to being a human body.

The same applies for mind. When body functions according to its purpose, that's birth. Although there's a body, if it's not actively functioning, we don't speak of birth. When mind functions according to its purpose, that's birth too. Although there's mind, if not actively sensing, thinking, or reacting we don't speak of birth either. The Dhamma meaning of birth refers to functioning in accordance with something's nature. The Buddha's words that the birth of the elements is the birth of dukkha mean that the elements are functioning as active body and mind, such that sensing, thinking, imagining, and feeling occur and out of which ignorance and foolishness are born. This arising of the elements is the arising of dukkha.

We won't understand this teaching if we approach it superficially. If we assume that the elements were already created in the past and have always been with us, we will wonder how the existence of these elements could be dukkha. To believe that the dhātus were already born and have continued to exist is to be grossly mistaken, thinking only in worldly language, oblivious to Dhamma language. The dhātus of Dhamma language are born when actually performing their respective functions, which is to combine and compound as body and mind experiencing this, that, and the other, in such a way that craving, clinging, and the other afflictions arise. Birth doesn't mean the natural interaction of physical elements. Birth means these interactions concocted with ignorance that create suffering. In short, the Buddhist principle is that everything is just dhātus, and the birth of dhātus is the birth of dukkha.

Seeing All Things as Merely Elements Ends Clinging

To practice seeing that all things are just natural elements is the highest Dhamma practice. Realizing that earth, water, fire, air, space, consciousness, goodness, evil, happiness, suffering, and everything else are merely natural elements is the pinnacle of Dhamma practice. As simply dhātus, none of them have self-existence or are anyone's self. Realizing this is to realize anattā, the pinnacle of Dhamma practice.

I've mentioned the most excellent ancient custom of teaching newly ordained monks the *Dhātu Paccavekhaṇa* on their very first day. We were taught to learn by heart and recite "*Yathā paccayaṃ pavattamānaṃ dhātumattamevetaṃ* . . . " (These things are natural elements, endlessly concocted by conditions . . .).[3] Yet it's sad that people merely memorize and repeat the words, as if a holy magic formula, without ever really understanding them. Repeating the Pali words without learning what they mean misses the heart of their religion. What a shame that people can ordain for a time, then return to lay life, still not understanding the heart of Buddhism, even when they have accurately memorized and repeated the words.

When all things are seen as natural elements, there's no more clinging to them, which is release, liberation, being freed beyond suffering. Clinging to something with the meaning of self is to be stuck there. To cling is to stick. When there's no more clinging, there is release from bondage to things that stimulate dukkha. This happens when all things are seen as they truly are—just dhātus.

Those things with *assāda*, a delicious quality, easily trick us into clinging. Because delight arises in contact with them, there is clinging to the delicious feeling, the pleasure, and ignorant mind immediately assumes that it's "me" who is delighted, who is having this delicious experience, and that the delight is "mine." The assumed "I who is delighted" is the meaning of attā, self; while the delicious thing and feeling clung to are attaniya, clung to as "mine." Foolishness takes things to be self and of self. When foolishness intensifies into stupid, stupid mind clings intensely as "me" and "mine." This confusion happens when proper understanding of the elements is missed. When ignorance element dominates mind, mind can't know the truth of mere dhātus.

How well do we understand this? Due to ignorance, we may think that we understand when we really don't. The basic principle to consider is that if we're still infatuated with something—whether expressed as greed, aversion, anger, or fear—we're still ignorant of the elemental nature of that thing. Later, when there's no longer any greed, aversion, anger, fear, anxiety, longing, and the like, we can say that we truly see in the elemental way. In seeing everything as elements, there's no greed for any of it. There's no anger aimed at anyone when seeing that there are only elements. There's no fear of ghosts and ghoulies when we know they are really just natural elements. There's no anxiety over and no longing after anything when everything is seen to be only dhātus.

Please evaluate yourselves in this way. Don't think that because you have stayed a long time in a monastery, or come to visit many times, or attended numerous retreats, that you know all about the elements. Be careful; you might not understand at all. Better to observe if there's any confusion over and falling for feeling tones, or not. Is there any infatuation with pleasurable vedanās, painful vedanās, or neither-painful-nor-pleasurable vedanās remaining? If there's no infatuation or reactivity, then there's real understanding of the elements.

When ignorance of dhātus leads to infatuation with their pleasures and delights, we undergo incredible stress and difficulty for their sake. This is more or less equivalent to being beasts. These words may sound overly strong, and some people may be offended, but the difference between people and other animals isn't much when it comes to suffering for the sake of pleasures and delights. Animals compete violently for mating privileges when it's the season. Humans aren't above that behavior. Ignorant of how everything is just natural elements, we, like beasts, enslave ourselves to pleasures and suffer the consequences.

Know the Dhamma-Dhātu, Realize Anattā, and Find Release

To sum up, all of us should increase our ability to study, observe, see, and insightfully know the elements. Our understandings and insights regarding dhātus are too few, still incomplete. Be more committed to understanding, seeing, and knowing them as merely elements of nature, totally lacking any meaning of self. Realize anattā, not-self, by seeing the true nature of dhātus. Right here, for once, see the *dhamma-dhātu*, the natural-reality element, and stop seeing self. The Buddha spoke of the natural-reality element as independent of everyone and everything: it is our salvation.

Previously, in the first stage of life, we were ignorantly unaware that we, and everything around us, are really just elements. Thus we were deceived by ourselves and things around us into suffering. In this second stage, suffering has bitten enough that we've begun to know it and started to wake up about dhātus, not falling for them as self. The third stage is about release, transcendence, and liberation.

Being fully Buddhist, awakened, is to see all things as they really are, as natural elements void of any meaning of self. Please reflect: Right now, are we fully Buddhist? If we unconsciously still see things in terms of self, we aren't yet truly Buddhist. *Buddha* means one who knows, who is awake, who is joyfully without dukkha. Buddha is one who has awakened from the sleep of ignorance. To know all things as selfless, natural elements is the only way to be perfectly Buddhist. If at first you don't believe me, at least think about this and contemplate the elements. We fall for the delicious pleasures and delights concocted by their endless interactions and then behave badly. We're sunk in the mass of dukkha because we don't understand dhātus.

Now, our project of covering all of Buddhism in a single volume has examined how there isn't anything that isn't a dhātu. Pristine mind is pristine elements. When ignorance element takes over, dukkha-dhātu predominates, even when ignorance mistakes it for sukha-dhātu. Distress and suffering follow these misperceptions and infatuations. Subsequently, mind wakes up and knows all things as they actually are. This is like being born anew: mind is no longer infatuated with anything. This mind is free and liberated. Through deepening realization of nibbāna element, kilesas are quenched, self-illusion is quenched, concocting is quenched. This is the supreme nibbāna element, the highest of the high; nevertheless, it's just an element. There's no mistaking it for self, for something self attains or realizes, or for something that self experiences. It's just nibbāna and nothing more is needed.

13

CONTEMPLATING SAṄKHĀRAS AND VISAṄKHĀRA

In the previous chapters we contemplated how all of Buddhism is contained in "everything is a matter of mind" and "all things are merely natural elements." In reviewing all the various kinds of mind, we have covered all of Buddhism. The same is true of examining how everything, from the tiniest mote of dust to the supreme reality of nibbāna, is simply a dhātu. This chapter explores all aspects of saṅkhāras and their opposite, visaṅkhāra, which again is the entire scope of Buddhism.

In this contemplation, we begin with a thorough understanding of *saṅkhāras*, which means "concoctings" and "concoctions." The opposite is *visaṅkhāra*, which means "nonconcocting" and "that which isn't concocted." In the whole Buddhist system, nothing else is talked about apart from these two concerns. First, the issue of things that are fabricated as beings and persons such that there's suffering; and, second, the opportunity of no fabricating so that there's no suffering, which is nibbāna. If we understand these two words, *saṅkhāras* and *visaṅkhāra*, we know everything. There's nothing that isn't either one or the other: saṅkhāras, concoctions and the results of concocting; and visaṅkhāra, nonconcocting and its fruit, the peacefulness of nibbāna.

In the Thai language, *sankharn* is usually taken to mean the physical body, as in, for instance, "ceasing of *sankharn*," which is a euphemism for dying.[1] Beyond that, most of our people have no idea what saṅkhāras are about. Hence this fundamental Dhamma teaching remains grievously misunderstood. It isn't necessary to die to quench saṅkhāras. Why that is so will be explained shortly.

Saṅkhāras has a variety of meanings in the Pali language. The activity of concocting itself is saṅkhāra. The agents that concoct other things, that cause other things to arise, are also saṅkhāras. The results of concocting are saṅkhāras too. And there is yet another, special, meaning—the power of concocting. The power, means, or ability to stimulate and fabricate things can be called saṅkhāra as well. Hence, there are several meanings found in the Pali texts: the concocting itself, the concocter, the concocted, and the power of concocting. Be aware, therefore, that sankharn as usually expressed in Thai is too narrow in meaning, implying the body only. The Pali term, however, has all meanings having to do with causing things to happen.

While we're on the topic, we should consider the Buddha's phrasing when he "released the concocting of life" (*āyusaṅkhāraṃ ossaji*).[2] Here, *saṅkhāraṃ ossaji* means relinquishing or casting off the power of concocting. When applied to *āyu* (the life principle), the meaning is to stop concocting life. When the Buddha determined that his *parinibbāna* (death) would be in three months, he relinquished *āyusaṅkhāra*, the means of continuing life. He set aside, once and for all, the concocting that had been supporting the life process. Here, then, saṅkhāra means that which concocts the continuing of life rather than the body itself. The continual extending of life is what stopped. When we stop that concocting, the continued fabrication of life will stop too.[3]

Everything but Nibbāna Is Saṅkhāra

Now, what are saṅkhāras about? Just about everything. With the exception of nibbāna, there isn't anything that isn't a saṅkhāra. Animate and inanimate, within us and outside, causal things and resultant things, actions and their fruits—all without exception are saṅkhāras.

The term *saṅkhāras*, because it appears in various contexts and in various places in the Pali texts, is easily misunderstood. For instance, *saṅkhāras* is one of the twelve terms in the well-known formulation of paṭiccasamuppāda (dependent co-arising). It is found within the first pair of dependent co-arisings responsible for the arising of dukkha. Avijjā is the condition for saṅkhāras. Saṅkhāras are then the condition for viññāṇa, which is then the condition for nāmarūpa, and so on through the twelve-mode formula. However, in reality, all twelve modes are saṅkhāras—things concocting and being concocted. Avijjā, saṅkhāras, viññāṇa, nāmarūpa, āyatana, phassa, vedanā, taṇhā, upādāna, bhava, jāti, and dukkha: all of these are saṅkhāras, both fabricated by conditions and fabricating further conditions.[4] However, the Buddha here used the word *saṅkhāras* in a special sense, for the second mode of dependent co-arising, the "power of concocting"; thus ignorance conditions the arising of the power of concocting, which then conditions consciousness to function as mind cognizing things, which conditions nāmarūpa, and so on. So be aware that *saṅkhāras* in this context is being used in a specific sense, while on the more general level, all of the twelve conditioning factors are saṅkhāras.

Similarly, in the *pañcakkhandhas*, the five aggregates—rūpa-, vedanā-, saññā-, saṅkhāra-, and viññāṇa-khandhas—the word *saṅkhāra* occurs once, as the fourth aggregate, again in a more limited sense. Yet all five are saṅkhāras in the general sense. Rūpa, vedanā, saññā, saṅkhāra, and viññāṇa all fabricate other things and are themselves fabricated, so be aware that all five aggregates are saṅkhāras. It's just that the fourth is specifically named *saṅkhāra*, which, again, causes some people to misunderstand that only the fourth khandha is a saṅkhāra. The Pali language can present these kinds of difficulties. It can be perplexing if not properly studied and comprehended.

Now we'll look in more detail at the literal meaning of saṅkhāras in the Pali language, particularly from the time of the Buddha as recorded in the original discourses. *Saṅkhāras* is best translated by the

Thai *prung*—meaning "mixing, concocting, and compounding."[5] What sort of activity is this concocting? In ordinary language, concocting is to take various things and put them together to produce something new, such as cooking food from various ingredients. In the kitchen, for example, many ingredients are mixed together to produce a curry. Such cooking is saṅkhāra, involving the aspects of the concocting agents, the fabrications created, the mixing and concocting activity, the power of concocting, and the stimulants of concocting.

Another example is a person's body. When we examine a body closely, we find saṅkhāras throughout; there's continual mixing and compounding in that body. We find concocters that fabricate other things: the liver, the kidneys, and other organs produce bile, urine, lymph, pus, and so forth. In these interactions we find the power to stimulate concocting, the ways of fabricating, the concocted products, and the ongoing processes of concocting. Our bodies are full of what the Pali language collectively calls *saṅkhāras*.

When we look around us in the wide world, there's nothing but continual concocting. Sunlight creates things; water concocts things; the earth, water, fire, and air elements produce things. These aren't one-off occurrences. The mixing, stimulating, and influencing goes on and on with things being causes and conditions for more causes and conditions continually. For instance, when there are rain clouds, the rain falls, moistening the ground and making the roads slippery. With moisture in the soil, plants and creatures of various kinds arise. Rain collects in pools and marshes creating habitat for fish and other aquatic creatures. In case of rainfall making a road wet and slippery, someone falls down, cracks their skull, and must go to a doctor, who then has complicated work to do. These are examples of how concocting works successively.

Look carefully and you'll find concocting everywhere. A tree grows from its causes and conditions, then supports the existence of other things through its fruits and material for nests, which in their turn are transformed into other things. Although *saṅkhāras* is a smallish word, it points to an enormous range of activity covering the entire cosmos. In every world, in every universe, there's really nothing but concocting. This single word *saṅkhāras* encompasses all things, with a single exception—the reality that is the opposite of concocting.

Concocting Is a Matter of Nature

Saṅkhāras involve the continual destruction of things so that other things arise. This concocting is a particular characteristic of nature operating in its saṅkhata mode: naturally creating things for nature's sake. This is the function and activity of conditioned nature. The other side of the coin is the asaṅkhata side of nature—unconcocted, unconditioned, uncompounded—nibbāna alone, without any form of concocting. Although it's difficult to explain, we are capable of understanding it.[6]

Everything else is fabricating, compounding, endlessly changing nature. All this activity of nature, by nature, and for nature is on the saṅkhata side. "Of nature, by nature, for nature" sounds like democracy, but it is far more real than that slogan. This natural concocting is totally real.

Who does all this concocting belong to? It's simply the concocting of nature. With fabricating there are results and consequences. Without it, nothing could happen. If, for instance, someone believes that the sun existed before anything else, we would have to ask what created the sun. Something had to create the sun and that something is nature—of nature, by nature, for nature. With the sun's creation, other things followed, such as the planets and our very own earth. First, our planet was molten; it cooled and atmosphere developed; then life-forms came to be—bacteria, plants, the vegetable and animal kingdoms, human beings, deities, and so forth. It's all flows of concocting with the many fruits of concocting. If not for concocting, there wouldn't be anything, not even the sun. Without the sun, this world and its creatures couldn't happen. Even if you don't know every detail, recognize these processes of concocting in everything you see. We need not go into all the scientific explanations; however, understanding the fundamental reality of saṅkhāras is crucial.

Saṅkhāra Is in Itself Dukkha

It's time to focus attention on the problematic sort of concocting that creates dukkha. This starts with the basic fact that without fabricating, nothing happens. On the physical level, without concocting, plants, animals, and people aren't born. On the mental side, without concocting, consciousness doesn't occur and so living beings don't occur. Without concocting, nothing arises.

When the power of concocting operates materially, causes and conditions compound and shape the dhātus of earth, water, fire, and wind into countless material things. When this power operates inwardly, that which is sensitive and aware, citta, experiences through the sense media—eyes, ears, nose, tongue, body, and mind. Citta tastes the objects of experience—sights, sounds, smells, tastes, tangibles, and ideas. There are consequences of experiencing these sense contacts, especially kilesas. With the arising of kilesas, karma—deliberated action—occurs. With action under the influence of kilesas, the results of action follow: there will be sukha or dukkha, happiness or its opposite, distress, to be followed inevitably by more concocting.

Because of the desire to be happy and not wanting to suffer, these patterns continue to happen. There is a continual stream of concocting, the results of which appear as our happiness and unhappiness, our well-being and suffering. This is true for people as well as animals and even plants. This fabricating continues, becoming this world and many worlds, many solar systems, and many universes and chiliocosms, all of which are concocting phenomena. Their basic fiber and substance is wrapped up in creating. There's no stopping or stilling. The concocting may be too subtle to see with our eyes, or perhaps we aren't clever enough to notice. We look without seeing the reality of concocting, without observing that everything is in flux.

When concocting stops, suffering ends. How does that happen? This doesn't require something extreme, such as dying. Rather, we put an end to the fabricating in our minds. Just experience whatever objects present themselves to the senses without creating feelings of liking and disliking, then there won't be any problem. If there is wisdom, the concocting that occurs through liking and disliking can end. If such concocting doesn't stop, there will be clinging to pleasure and aversion to pain, with dukkha created by that clinging and resisting. Hence, the concocting is itself dukkha. Dukkha is inherent in the concocting because its continual change and transformation leaves no freedom and no peace. There is no freedom when we are under the power of concocting. A Pali text states this succinctly: "*Saṅkhārā paramā dukkha*" (Concocting is supreme dukkha).[7] This includes all aspects and meanings of dukkha. When the concocting stops, dukkha stops.

Let's consider several meanings of the word *dukkha*, based in its etymology. First, the general common meaning is "pain." The second meaning is that of being ugly and hateful when truly seen. When something is carefully observed and seen to be continually concocting, changing, and flowing, it's seen as ugly. If you know how to look at even any old rock in your immediate environment, you will recognize how its transitoriness is deceptive, how it tricks you, which is what's ugly about it. *Dukkha* has this meaning of "when seen, it's ugly." The third meaning is that of being hatefully empty, disgustingly void of any substance worthy of clinging to as self. This ugly emptiness is an important aspect of dukkha. *Dukkha* has these three basic meanings: painful, tormenting, and difficult to bear; ugly and hateful when truly; and disgustingly insubstantial.[8]

All saṅkhāras have all three aspects of dukkha. Animate, sensitive saṅkhāras—that have feelings and thoughts—experience the dukkha of pain. Inanimate saṅkhāras—lacking sensitivity and feelings, such as rocks—display the characteristic of being ugly and hateful when seen truly. On top of all that, all saṅkhāras—whether animate or inanimate—are void of any substance that could be called "self." This absence of essence and selfhood is described as hatefully empty, because of how it thwarts and frustrates us.

Please remember these meanings as you explore the full meaning of *dukkha*. Living, conscious saṅkhāras necessarily experience the dukkha of enduring discomfort, pain, and difficulty. For them, maintaining life and surviving involves many hardships that must be endured. Inanimate saṅkhāras, lacking consciousness and sensitivity, when seen truly are dukkha in that their reality is ugly. All kinds of saṅkhāras are void of anything that could be called "self," despite our desperate clinging.

This "self" is something mind itself imagines, assumes, and misapprehends. Through ignorance's influence, mind takes this as "my self" and that as "mine." Such mind then suffers because it perceives, conceives, and believes things to be self. At a minimum, clinging to self is like being weighed down by heavy burdens. Clinging to things as self is dukkha because nothing is under our power and control. Mind suffers because it lacks the power to make things happen how it wants; the illusion of control is constantly frustrated. Such concocting is just more dukkha.

Visaṅkhāra Is Emptiness of Dukkha

Now we may look at the opposite side of things, nonconcocting, visaṅkhāra. The tiny prefix *vi* transforms *saṅkhāra* into *visaṅkhāra*—free of, without, and beyond concocting. Visaṅkhāra is equivalent to nirodha-dhātu (quenching element), nibbāna-dhātu (cooling element), and asaṅkhata-dhātu (unconcocted element).

The Buddha referred to this absence of concocting in saying "*nibbānaṃ paramaṃ suññaṃ*" (nibbāna is supremely empty). Further, nibbāna is the ultimate emptiness because it is free of kilesas, free of clinging, free of everything problematic, and free of dukkha. Yet it is not nothing at all. It is pure emptiness, the true essence of Dhamma. The Pali texts also record the Buddha saying "*nibbānaṃ paramaṃ sukhaṃ*" (nibbāna is the ultimate happiness), in more worldly language, easier for worldly people to understand. People are attracted to happiness. Saying that nibbāna is the final end of dukkha doesn't interest people so much; it doesn't sound useful to them. Saying that nibbāna is the ultimate happiness interests them much more. Hence, the Buddha sometimes described nibbāna as the supreme happiness, but not often. In fact, this saying occurs just twice in the original texts, while descriptions of nibbāna as being the final end of dukkha are found throughout them, expressing the deeper truth of Dhamma language.

The wise say that nibbāna is the end of dukkha—that is, nonconcocting. However, if we want to interest ordinary people, we have to say things like nibbāna or nonconcocting is the ultimate happiness. People generally are already interested in happiness, having had some experience and knowledge of it, so words such as *ultimate happiness* more easily get their attention. People who follow up and start to practice eventually realize that not clinging to anything—not fabricating anything—is free of all meanings of dukkha and sukha. In emptiness of suffering and happiness, there's total freedom from fabricating.

Embrace the principle that concocting is itself dukkha. In itself, concocting is troublesome, confusing, and turbulent. It brings pain for living beings and renders both the living and nonliving despicable. All saṅkhāras are concoctings that are inherently dukkha.

Concocting Happens Because of Ignorance

Now, we may ask, what makes concocting possible? Concocting occurs because of ignorance. In speaking of human experience, the Buddha observed that fabricating happens due to avijjā. Once we're born as human beings with eyes, ears, noses, tongues, bodies, and minds, we are continually impacted by visual forms, sounds, odors, tastes, tangible sensations, and mental objects. Invariably, there is ignorance regarding these, so that nothing is understood truthfully. When forms stimulate eyes, when sounds stimulate ears, when odors stimulate noses, and so on, there is concocting because of ignorance. This is the ignorant fabricating of craving, clinging, and all the afflictions, thereby creating dukkha. This troublesome concocting of human beings is due to ignorance.

Some people wonder about nonhuman things, such as animals, and material things, such as rocks. What makes them concoct? That's a difficult question to answer. Still, we must say that it's a matter of nature itself, although something that we can't know. Our ignorance simply doesn't allow us to know just why it is nature's function to fabricate—how concocting is by nature, for nature, and of nature. In all that nature, there's the lack of true knowing (*vijjā*) and only nonknowing (*avijjā*). Because these things lack the capacity for mental cultivation, we say that nature changes constantly through the power we speak of as avijjā. This sort of nonknowing should be understood as things we cannot know. What do we call this? God? Mystery? We lack true knowing regarding such things and so they continually change through the ongoing concocting. They aren't sentient or human, they can't sense or think, but they keep changing, keep creating.

Even inanimate, insentient forms of nature are concocting within themselves. For instance, we can't be sure where this rock next to me came from. Probably it came from the hill behind us and gradually came to be here. What caused it to be here in this way? The concocting of nature, such as rain, weather, and storms, broke it away from whatever it was a part of before and deposited it in this place. Eventually this stone will dissolve into grains of sand and then into specks of dust. Who knows what will become of it after that! Yet we don't need to know or study all of it. Scientists know that dust, stones, sediment, and mud aggregate as rock and then dissolve again into dust, earth, and mud, and later aggregate in new ways, only to be broken up, and so on. Near here is a large sedimentary rock in which can be seen many kinds of small, tiny rocks that came together to form it. Such rocks break up, recombine, break up some more, and so on, until making up a mix of many kinds of little rocks. Who makes this happen? Is it God? If we believe in God, we will say that God makes it all happen. If we don't believe in God, then nature created it.

To sum up, living things change and transform continually in ways appropriate to them; inanimate things change and transform continually in their own ways too. Living things are concocting in their ways and inanimate things are concocting in theirs. We say that all of it happens because of ignorance, through the power of lacking vijjā (true knowing).

Seeing the Streams of Transformation

Recall the quite surprising saying of the Buddha that children "have no understanding of *cetovimutti* and *paññāvimutti*, since within the womb." From before they were born, babies understand neither liberation through the power of mind nor liberation through wisdom. In other words, due to avijjā, the lack of wisdom, babies don't know that falling into concocting brings suffering. Nonetheless, concocting can stop through the power of mind or through the power of wisdom. Lacking such understanding of liberation, fetuses start concocting in the womb. Once born, they continue fabricating through childhood, through adolescence, through middle age, and into old age. People are intimate with ignorance the whole way. Ignorance doesn't know the way of liberation, so the concocting is continual, which in itself is dukkha.

See clearly how mind hasn't realized nibbāna; see this wherever you look, in the ever-changing streams of concocting. Look around everywhere—at rocks, at trees, at animals, at other people—to see the streams of continual fabrication. However, we may not have enough wisdom at this time to see things that way. So we see things as sometimes stopping, sometimes moving, sometimes going, sometimes coming, sometimes gaining, sometimes missing, sometimes profiting, sometimes losing, sometimes hot, sometimes cold, or any of the other pairs of opposites—all of which have meanings for mind to cling to.

Be clever and follow in the Buddha's footsteps. Be able to look at anything and see only streams of change and transformation. Looking around outside, whatever is seen with physical eyes is seen to be streams of change flowing continually. Looking within ourselves, see only streams of change and transformation. Looking outside, inside, at ourselves, at others, nearby, far away, coarsely, subtly—just streams of change.

Not clearly seeing the streams of change, we see things with meanings that create one of two reactions—liking or disliking. If something is pretty, we like it; if it's ugly, we don't like it. If it's sweet sounding, we like it; if it's harsh sounding, we don't like it. If it's fragrant, we like it; if it's foul smelling, we don't. Seeing things in these ways, we are continually concocting. From liking and disliking we fabricate greed, anger, hatred, fear, anxiety, longing, jealousy, envy, and so on and so forth in our human hearts. In almost all cases, these end up in some form of neurosis. If we don't properly understand the things we experience, we end up developing mental abnormalities. Such are the results of not understanding cetovimutti and paññāvimutti, liberation of mind and liberation through wisdom.

In recent decades, doctors report an increase in the occurrence of mental illness, probably due to the excess of things capable of provoking concocting. People in the modern world, it seems, are more prone to mental disorders than people of yore. We ought to study these matters so that we can understand how all the fabricating carries on, so we don't get caught and end up mired in clinging.

We encourage everybody who comes here to Suan Mokkh to sit in the forest, like the Buddha did for awakening. We encourage people to learn from things in the forest that appear to concoct less than we do. For instance, the trees tell us, "Stop, stop for a while, don't make such a fuss, don't go concocting all over the place." Sometimes they even warn us, "Don't get too crazy." The trees and stones tell us to take it easy, not be so crazy busy, and cool down. But we don't listen to them. We don't hear them telling us to stop all the disturbance, fabricating, and insanity.

However that may be, observe that when we sit among the rocks and trees, we stop to some extent without trying. We naturally cool down to some degree. Keep company with the trees and stones, with nature generally, and we'll naturally concoct less. This is why people go to the forest for awakening. None of the great prophets were enlightened in a university or the middle of a busy city. Every great teacher awakened in a forest, desert, or other quiet place characterized by stopping and cooling. The Buddha was born in a forest, awakened in a forest, taught and sojourned here and there in the forests, and realized final nibbāna in a forest. These are natural places that display less concocting. If we associate with such things, we too become cool and at ease.

Some visitors mutter that when they enter the trees here they feel a peace and coolness that can't be described. They don't realize that when sitting amid the stones and trees, the power of concocting diminishes. They feel comfortable and at ease in the forest, much different than at home in the towns, where there are lots of disturbances. People have good reason to like visiting the forest, because it facilitates slowing down and cooling. If they examine this further, they will realize that their anxious suffering comes from clinging, from too much concocting. Then they might aim to concoct less, limit the fabricating, and not be so influenced by ignorance.

The Office of Concocting

Now let's contemplate where the office of concocting is. When concocting a curry or sweetmeat, the workplace is the kitchen. Where is the office or workplace when concocting dukkha? In other words, where is the office of dependent co-arising and the clinging-together aggregates? The straight answer: in mind, when the mental territory is mixed up with ignorance. Whatever the territory's boundaries and limits, the workplace of concocting is within mind that still lacks necessary understanding. When mind is composed with true knowledge, it doesn't fabricate, it's not an office.

Our minds can have vijjā, and they can lack it. Perhaps we've studied and acquired knowledge, but it's disappeared when needed. Mindfulness is insufficient; the knowledge doesn't arrive in time and therefore that mind is ignorant. Even though the Tipiṭaka has been studied and aniccaṃ, dukkhaṃ, and anattā are understood, knowledge doesn't arrive when needed because mindfulness is too weak to stay on top of the situation.[9] Such mind is necessarily foolish, and it concocts under the influence of avijjā. It suffers no matter how much it has studied the Tipiṭaka. Thus we can say that the territory of mind blended with ignorance is where the office of concocting is found.

Even in luminous mind, original mind as yet uncontaminated by kilesas, there's opportunity for ignorance. Because such mind has not yet trained, there's always an opening. Hence, even luminous mind can be an office of concocting. As long as it's ignorant, it's the office for fabricating new products—kilesas and dukkha. Please examine how mind without proper knowledge is ignorant mind and the office or kitchen for cooking up new dukkha.

The Ingredients of Concocting Are Already in Mind

The things that go into mind's concocting are like the ingredients used in the kitchen. They can be turned into anything because they're already in this inner world of mind. The immediate ingredients are the *ārammaṇas*, the objects of sense experience that arise depending on the sense media of eyes and visual forms, ears and sounds, nose and odors, tongue and flavors, body and tangibles, and mind and ideas. Based on the inner and outer sense media, the objects take on meaning and gain power. The forms, sounds, smells, tastes, touches, and mental objects that interact with the eyes, ears, nose, tongue, body, and mind create contacts, which are the spices and utensils for fabricating mind. Here, feelings of pleasure, displeasure, or neither-nor stir the pot further. Hence, the sense media, the sense objects, sense contacts, and feeling tones are all ingredients of concocting.

For those who believe in karma that results in future lives in other realms, these too are ingredients of concocting. Such beliefs are ethically beneficial when we believe that good and bad actions create results in future lives. Such actions are fabricated and fabricating. Still, for the sake of ultimate truth, we emphasize the ingredients that are sandiṭṭhiko, directly and personally seen. This requires seeing right here and now how sense objects concoct, how phassa's arising fabricates, how vedanās' arising creates, and how the arisings of taṇhā, of upādāna, of dukkha concoct. These are the ingredients, spices, and mechanisms of concocting.

To use more scientific terms, we can say that there must be sufficient and fitting time and space to create agreeable, delightful, satisfying experiences. If too much time passes, the experience isn't beautiful, sweet-sounding, or satisfying. The shape, appearance, and size must be fitting for delightful, pleasing experiences. The occupying of space outside must be fitting and the time for concocting must be fitting. This is like cooking a curry, which requires that the ingredients and the cooking time be right, otherwise the food is inedible. When the material components come together in the right amount and at the right time, a sense object is concocted as the basis for delight. It has a flavor that provokes desire, greed, and infatuation. This is how the kilesas are successfully fabricated. On the other hand, don't think you can concoct your way to preventing the kilesas from happening. Rather nonconcocting stops them.

The Methodology of Concocting

Now let's look at the behavior or methodology of concocting, particularly as it applies to us. This doesn't have much to do with inanimate things. As regards humans, concocting has been around since we were conceived from the mixing of egg and sperm. At that stage, there's no mind to feel like self, yet there's creation. Embryos develop and become the seat for consciousness element. With viññāṇa-dhātu in the mix, fetuses feel and are sensitive. Relying on all six elements—earth, water, fire, wind, space, consciousness—the little lives begin in the womb. Sensitivity and mental life develop. This concocting increases in ways that improve the earth, water, fire, and wind elements. Consciousness develops further as the functioning of the system improves. Fetuses begin to experience sensations through their senses. Finally, infants are born, which is yet more concocting, and mind further develops in dependence on the things that surround it.

These infants, as we've noted, don't have the understanding needed to be free of dukkha. Not knowing any better, they think in ways that cause dukkha. Eventually another kind of concocting occurred. Intelligence realized they couldn't go on with all this dukkha creation. Certain people started to understand that nonconcocting would be better and searched for the way of nonfabricating. Feeling that living the household life was difficult and too caught up in production, they left home for the forests, caves, and mountains, seeing solitary life among nature as more conducive for avoiding fabrication. Finally they discovered the way and life of nonconcocting. Thus those people we know as noble ones appeared, culminating in the Buddha fully realizing nonconcocting.

As long as there's concocting, there's dukkha. When concocting stops, there won't be dukkha. Even while experiencing sense objects via the eyes and so on, while one person concocts, another doesn't. With sufficient intelligence to not fall for sights, sounds, ideas, tangibles, and the rest, we can stop fabricating. Things stimulate the eyes, ears, body, mind, and so forth, but we don't react. This is the meaning of *quenching saṅkhāras*. Many Buddhists, including in Thailand, have confused this with death. The Dhamma-language understanding means to stop concocting while continuing to live. In this, there's no suffering, which is supreme happiness, undying nibbāna. That's what visaṅkhāra (nonconcocting) is about.

The three stages of mind can now be reformulated: pristine mind before concocting, mistaken mind that does nothing but concoct, and mind that realizes not concocting is best. Pristine mind can't do anything, mistaken mind acts egoistically, and unfabricated mind responds naturally. This is the story of human life, from the beginning until the realization of nibbāna: original mind, ignorant mind, and, finally, mind knowing the ultimate—nonconcocting.

Neither Saṅkhāras nor Visaṅkhāra Are Self

Now we can discuss the term that causes people so much trouble—*anattā* (not-self).[10] According to the original teachings of the Pali suttas, both saṅkhāras and visaṅkhāra are anattā. That is, both concocted phenomena and the unconcocted are not-self: neither can hold up as "me" or "mine." How could saṅkhāras that change and flow continually be self? How can constant fabricating be self? And even the unfabricated—so cool and peaceful—can't be grasped as self either. It's simply a natural element, the nibbāna-dhātu, the quenching element. Don't grab it as attā. Just as the four basic physical dhātus are naturally occurring elements that can't be upheld as self, so too the naturally occurring unconcocted element. It cannot fulfill attā. To grasp it as self is confusion, which concocts reactions and new consequences, such as clinging to "me," "my self," and "mine," along with the coarser afflictions.

The Buddha said that "all dhammas are not-self," which includes visaṅkhāra as a dhamma. We're more familiar with the words that compounded things are unstable, impermanent, dukkha, and therefore can't be attā. Moreover, even that which isn't compounded, transient, and dukkha is anattā, because it's only natural. There's no real way that any of these can be taken to be self, because whatever they may be, they're really just natural elements.

Taking things to be "me" or "mine" bites us: we suffer from wrong thinking, misguided desires, and foolish clinging. Whatever we fabricate, whether valuable or without value, bites when we cling to it. Try not clinging to anything, neither good nor bad. Bad things should be left alone, while beneficial endeavors can be performed without clinging. Valuable things may be acquired and used as needed, but don't cling or you'll wind up with anxiety and distress. Before the Buddha appeared, people clung to the highest of the brahma worlds as being the ultimate good. Then the Buddha realized and taught that nothing is worthy of clinging. He pointed beyond the brahma worlds to nibbāna—beyond good and bad, beyond merit and demerit, beyond karma and karmic results. Nibbāna is visaṅkhāra, the unconcocted nature beyond producing such things.

In Buddhism, nonconcocting is recognized as the fourth kind of karma. Before the Buddha, three kinds of karma were taught—good, evil, and a mixture of good and evil—and that these three would bear fruit in good results, bad results, and mixed results. The Buddha, however, realized that karma can be cancelled. We can live above karma, we can end karma, through the karma that stops concocting good and evil. The noble path is the karma that stops concocting. When nothing is fabricated, there's no good, no evil, and no mix of the two. There are no results to worry about. This teaching is the heart of Buddhism.

Stop Concocting with Good and Evil

Anyone who clearly sees the path of noncocting won't be afraid to say that both good and evil are ultimately disgusting. Anyone with the usual understanding wouldn't dare to say such a thing, for fear of ridicule and condemnation. So I've been cursed for saying that both good and evil are despicable. Those who didn't know any better accused me of heresy. So it is with clinging to conventions.

I dare say such things because good and evil exist within the realms of concocting. They are each bases of clinging, and when clung to, both bite their owners. When there's no concocting, there's no good and no evil. Above and beyond this pair is nibbāna, where there's no dukkha at all. Swat them aside with "both evil and good are equally obnoxious." Here, *obnoxious* means unlovely, unworthy of affection, contemptible. Falling in love with good or evil wounds us badly. Nobody loves bad things anyway, but people love the good, to the point of going crazy over it. People wallow in distress because clinging to goodness drags them into the mass of dukkha. So don't cling to either the good or the bad in relation to "me" and "mine." Stop concocting preferences for and against.

All forms of concocting, including concocters and concoctions, are saṅkhāras endlessly streaming and characterized by dukkha. Visaṅkhāra is the opposite, without any ignorance remaining, without any meaning of "me" or "mine." Thus nothing is fabricated into greed, hatred, anger, fear, or any other torments of the heart.

But who is truly interested in the fact that the end of dukkha is in nonconcocting? Who really cares about visaṅkhāra? Who cares about being independent of good and evil? There's no good or evil outside the boundaries of the realms of fabricating. This transcendent release is the fourth kind of karma, a special teaching found only in Buddhism. However, hardly anyone teaches the kind of karma that ends production of good and evil. We carry on about bad and good karma, teaching people to cling to and be trapped in goodness, which wounds people.

Clinging to the good gets so out of hand that it fosters neurosis, which doesn't come about with clinging to evil. Anxiety, worry, jealousy, and envy come from clinging to the good, which can disturb intensely enough to cause mental illness. Being trapped under the power of goodness forces intense concocting, which creates so much continuous distress that we can't take it. Not getting the good that we want leads to mental illness and, in some instances, death.

Visaṅkhāra Is Coolness, the End of Dukkha

For as long as we are infatuated with the concocting side of things, we won't give a hoot for what's beyond concocting—visaṅkhāra. This makes both saṅkhāras and visaṅkhāra the two things that we really need to know.

Whereas saṅkhāras are all the things involved with dukkha and the causes and conditions for its arising, visaṅkhāra is nibbāna, which has no causes and conditions, isn't concocted, and can't create dukkha. When dukkha has no way of arising, that's nibbāna, the peaceful coolness free of fabricating. If there's concocting, even that of goodness, it isn't really cool. There's still the mental turbulence of the good sort, which is hot with clinging, although not overtly showing the symptoms. Actually, goodness doesn't cause the trouble. Nor does evil. But clinging to them hurts.

Hence, arahants don't cling, not even to goodness. Although good things come to them—such as material support, respect, and reverence—it never troubles them or makes them suffer. That's living on the visaṅkhāra side, where concocting ends. When in the midst of concocting, it's difficult to know when the long ages of saṅkhāras started and when they will end. Yet visaṅkhāra ends it immediately. Concocting's end is cool: there's no heat of greed, hatred, and delusion. When no longer stoking these fires, life is cool. Saṅkhāras are the hot life of concocting, while visaṅkhāra is the cool life of nonconcocting. This pair covers all there is to know in Buddhism.

Understand Saṅkhāras Properly to Realize Visaṅkhāra

If we don't understand the word *saṅkhāras*, we can't understand Dhamma either, especially the supreme dhamma—visaṅkhāra. Thai Buddhism provides a good example of this. At wakes and cremations, monks chant these famous lines from the *Mahāparinibbāna Sutta*:

> *Aniccā vata saṅkhārā, uppāda-vaya-dhammino;*
> *Uppajjitvā nirujjhanti, tesaṃ vūpasamo sukho.*[11]
> All saṅkhāras are impermanent,
> their nature is to arise and decay.
> Once arisen they quench, their stilling is happiness.

The words *tesaṃ vūpasamo sukho* and "stilling of saṅkhāras" are widely misunderstood to mean that lying dead in a coffin is bliss. Properly, *tesaṃ vūpasamo sukho* means that stopping all saṅkhāras is happiness, which doesn't require ending physical life. How could death be the meaning of happiness? For the Buddha, supreme happiness is stopping the concocting, wherever and whenever. The Buddha makes this statement as a general principle in regard to a wide range of saṅkhāras, not for chanting at funerals.[12] However, they were repeated at the Buddha's passing away by the god Sakka. This derivative usage gave rise to our custom of chanting the verse during death rites. This and similar traditions confuse people into thinking *saṅkhārā* only means "the body," a mere subset of saṅkhāras. For the Buddha, stopping applies to all concocting, which is dukkha. Hence, stopping the concocting is sukha, true peaceful happiness.

When monks recite *aniccā vata saṅkhārā*, the meaning is that all saṅkhāras, mental as well as physical, are impermanent. All things that are created and that concoct other things are impermanent, not just the body. Their nature is to arise and pass away.

> *Aniccā vata saṅkhārā, uppāda-vaya-dhammino;*
> *Uppajjitvā nirujjhanti, tesaṃ vūpasamo sukho.*

If you ever hear these words at a cremation, remember that they speak of the happiness of stopping all concocting, not merely the stopping that prepares us for cremation. Don't fall for the confused logic and think that putting ourselves in coffins makes happiness.

In other instances, the Buddha spoke of visaṅkhāra and related terms as the stopping of all ignorant concocting. If everyone stopped concocting their lives, that would be emptiness, coolness, peace, and freedom. When no longer concocting actions, and not creating the resultant karmic problems, people wouldn't have to cycle around as a result of karma. The nonarising of kilesas and dukkha is the visaṅkhāra side of life.

Saṅkhāras are concocting; visaṅkhāra is nonconcocting. Saṅkhata is to be concocted; asaṅkhata is unconcocted. With only these two kinds of things in the universe and, therefore, in Buddhist teachings, our seeing with the eye of Dhamma journey comes down to nonconcocting with true understanding (*vijjā*). Whether eating, using something, going somewhere, or preserving something, whatever we need, or whatever we must do, do it with vijjā. Don't assume that there is "me" or "mine" involved, and there won't be any foolish concocting. Live and act with mindfulness, intelligence, and wisdom so that these activities are beneficial rather than troublesome. Of course, any resultant convenience, benefit, or well-being isn't "mine," it's all just natural affairs.

Mind really only wants but one thing—to be without dukkha. The "me," the "myself," isn't anything other than mind foolishly thinking of itself as "me" and of things as "mine." As long as there's ignorance, mind thinks in these deluded terms. On realizing the ultimate, there's only mind, but without such thinking. Such mind is released from all clinging to "me" and "mine." This is "*visaṅkhāragataṃ cittam*" (mind that's realized the unconcocted).[13] Remember, the Buddha spoke these words and lived for another forty-five years.

Animals can quench concocting in their animal ways. Humans should be able to do even better—that is, we should be able to quench the mental saṅkhāras, the inner concoctings that create sukha and dukkha. These are subtle, difficult to understand, and require careful study. When such mental concoctings don't arise within the streams of mind, there's coolness. Later, when the time comes for the body to die, bodily saṅkhāras simply come to an end in an ordinary way. They perish without mind concocting notions of "me dying" or "this dying body being mine." This is what it means to be released from the shadow of death. Mind lets go of thinking that it's "me" who dies, who lives, who loses and gains, who fails and succeeds, and so on. Mind emerges from any and all concocting—there's no more dukkha.

For Cool Life, Partner Mind with Visaṅkhāra

To conclude, if we haven't understood the word *saṅkhāra*, we aren't able to understand Dhamma either. Understanding only the physical fabrications, we don't understand the mental and spiritual fabrications and confuse the quenching of saṅkhāras with physical death. Thus we don't know how supreme happiness can be realized and we continually concoct in pursuit. So get to know the mental concocting enough to stop fabricating. Things not known and not understood will deceive and seem to be the opposite of how they really are. Deceived by ignorance, we'll see only "me" and "mine" in everything we experience. When mind destroys ignorance, wisdom replaces it and there's no more misunderstanding that there's a "me" or a "mine." Mind that wisely quenches the concocting and afflictions is cooled. That's nibbāna.

The choice is up to us. We each have the right to choose between satisfaction with the hot life of concocting or the cool life of nonconcocting. The Buddha's teaching offers us the choice, and it's our responsibility to choose. If we choose wrongly, we'll take things that look safe and happy but are in fact dangerous. Instead of a beautiful flower, we grasp a deranged weapon. The genuinely safe choice is based in understanding saṅkhāras—concocting, concoctions, and concocters—which leads to visaṅkhāra. With nonconcocting as mind's partner, there's no clinging and no danger. Then life is always cool and problem-free.

✳

My hope is that you will understand saṅkhāras and visaṅkhāra better than before and make progress in the path of nonconcocting, the path of deathless nibbāna.

14

THE END OF THE JOURNEY

This chapter concludes our examination of the universe of Dhamma. The contemplations along the journey of seeing with the eye of Dhamma offer a comprehensive tour of Buddhist teachings. We will bring together the highlights in this last chapter.

For easy remembering and to insure against disorganization in our study of Dhamma, all of Buddhism, from start to finish, can be summarized in just a few lines:

> Natural elements concoct together until the phenomenon "mind" arises.
> Everything is mind, or arises from mind, and all minds lead to the highest mind, the mind of awakening (*bodhicitta*).
> From bodhicitta comes the realization of nibbāna, and that's the end of the story.

Please observe how much is covered by this summary and yet how concise it is.

All Things Are Dhātus, Concocting into Mind

The first line means that everything is dhātus, natural elements that interact and concoct, in ways such that mind arises. It's important to understand that there isn't anything that isn't a natural element. All physical and mental phenomena are really just elements. In simple village language, we can say that from a tiny speck of dust all the way to nibbāna, everything is elements. There are all the material elements (*rūpa-dhātus*), starting with a valueless speck of dust, and the mental elements (*nāma-dhātus*) making up the conditioned elements (*saṅkhata-dhātus*). Then there's nibbāna-dhātu, which is the unconditioned element (*asaṅkhata-dhātu*). In Buddhist teaching, none of this entire range of natural elements can be taken as "me" or "mine," simply because they're all just dhātus.

We start with six basic elements. Earth, water, fire, and wind elements are rūpa-dhātus, the material side of life. The consciousness element is the nāma-dhātu side. Space element is neither material nor mental (although scholars tend to put it in the nāma category). Ākāsa-dhātu, the element of free space, isn't exactly a mental thing and so can't be considered nāma; it ought to be recognized as the element that's neither rūpa nor nāma. So there are six elements that are material, mental, and neither.

If we wanted to include the nibbāna element within these six, it would fit in the category of space element, since nibbāna is also void of both rūpa and nāma. However, the early texts don't categorize it so. Moreover, the space element is usually understood as being a saṅkhata-dhātu (concocted element). In that case, nibbāna-dhātu couldn't be included with it. Nevertheless, as people tend to understand space element in different ways, there's no universal agreement. To keep matters reasonably simple, let's consider the six basic elements to be saṅkhata-dhātus, while beyond is the asaṅkhata-dhātu, the unconcocted element, nibbāna.

Let's review how the six elements interact, step by step. They combine as nāma and rūpa: the earth, water, fire, and wind elements make up the physical (*rūpa*); consciousness element is the mental (*nāma*);

and ākāsa-dhātu serves as the empty space necessary for nāma and rūpa to operate. These six cover all of life: through their combining together, the things described as physical and mental arise, with the latter in the leading role. The earth, water, fire, and wind elements combine to become the bodies of people, animals, trees, and so on. The intangible viññāṇa-dhātu does its duty as mind in being sentient and sensitive. The ākāsa-dhātu serves as the free space where the other elements establish themselves. Material things can only establish themselves in places where there aren't any other material things, while nāma, mind, can establish itself only in a place currently free from nāma. Free space is thus the basis for all things.

Emptiness is a wonderful word with meanings that shift in various directions. Here, it becomes something of value. Without empty space available, this planet couldn't have happened. Simple vessels—such as cups, bowls, and jars—have a use value because of their vacant space. If they weren't hollow, they wouldn't have any worth. But because they are hollow, because they provide empty space, they are useful for holding other things. Please understand that this space, this hollowness, is nothing, yet it is still important. This is why space is classified as an element. Although it can be observed in many things outside us, it's better to observe space element within ourselves.

A person, what we assume to be a person, consists of earth, water, fire, and wind elements, along with mind element, and then space element in which they manifest. If we analyze the body into atoms, each and every atom must be established in empty space, while mind requires space that is empty of mind for it to concoct into being. Anyone who is unfamiliar with space element ought to get to know it. Not only is it mentioned in the suttas but we can also see its reality for ourselves. Relying upon space element, the physical elements and mind element combine intimately and naturally, so that we get a person, such as each of us. When natural elements combine as nāmarūpa, mind takes the leading role.

The second line of our summary points to how everything has to do with mind, which takes the lead in all things. The many and various experiences of life will continually concoct, change, and transform mind until it reaches the exalted level of bodhicitta (mind of awakening). Mind develops steadily until it's focused on bodhi and no longer focused on self. This comes about through seeing the concocting of dhātus and the ceaselessly changing mind.

The third line refers to bodhicitta flowering and fully realizing the clear knowing of awakening (*bodhi*). Through knowing everything in accord with reality, bodhicitta has developed fully and realized nibbāna, which is also a natural element. Mind attains nibbāna-dhātu, the element free of concocting, which is unchanging and has no dukkha. When the interactions of these elements conclude in nibbāna, it's no longer a story of self and that's the end of the story.

Although Self Doesn't Exist, Foolish Mind Clings to Self

Fundamentally, there isn't a separate self to be found in any of this: body isn't self, mind isn't self, and even nibbāna isn't self. Why is that? Because these are really just natural elements. See everything as elements and you won't concoct anything unnecessary.

Although mind isn't self, when foolish it thinks that it is. This is important to see. Problems arise because mind, which is really just a natural element, creates notions and thoughts of self when ignorance element interacts. Then mind assumes self, takes itself to be self, and takes the things it experiences to be selves too, depending on circumstances. It's all about mind and the phenomena it experiences, and then its ignorant clinging to things as self. Foolish mind can latch on to anything as self, as separate abiding entities. Such mind clings and grabs, which is heavy, so there is oppressive suffering.

All dukkha arises from clinging, from grasping with mind. Physical things can be grabbed with the hands; mental phenomena are clung to with mind. When combined with ignorance element, this mind isn't able to know things as they truly are and thus is naturally prone to regarding them in terms of self. This is easily observed. When mind gets something it wants to eat and experiences deliciousness, foolish mind concocts the thought that "I feel delicious"—there's a self who consumes this tasty feeling and is identified with it. Then the deliciousness is taken to be "my deliciousness." Actually, there is only mind, without any self. However, with its great ignorance, when seeing beauty, hearing melodiousness, smelling fragrance, tasting deliciousness, touching comfort, or thinking pleasantly, mind interprets these pleasing, delicious experiences as "I feel delicious." The tasty feeling comes first. Once experienced by mind, it then concocts the thought that "I am" this tasty experience or "I'm having" it. This "me" wasn't there before the particular experience; it's only just occurred. The "me" idea is a reaction to the experience; it didn't create the experience.

This is at the heart of the most important matter in life. If we don't know this, we won't understand how we suffer. If we do know, we understand that dukkha happens because mind is ignorant and clings to things as self. Mind first clings to itself as "delicious me" and then to the deliciousness or tasty thing as "mine."

Foolish Khandhas of Clinging

Sometimes mind experiences incidents connected with the tactile body, as when the body collides with something and is injured. Mind then takes the body to be "me" and the pain as "mine." At the same time, it projects the meaning of "self" onto whatever it collided with, perhaps blaming that thing and getting angry at it. Sometimes, mind experiences pleasant and unpleasant feeling tones (*vedanās*). It then takes either itself or the feeling to be "me." When mind clings to itself as "me" experiencing a feeling, then the feeling becomes "mine." Sometimes mind recognizes something via perception (*saññā*). It perceives and regards the object as being this or that: saññā regards it as "person," "animal," "woman," "man," "child," "wife," "husband," or whatever the object seems to be. Mind takes the perceiving or that which perceives—mind itself—to be "me" and the perception to be "mine." Sometimes there is thinking (here called *saṅkhāra*). The thinking follows according to the perception. Mind clings to the thinking as "me" or to itself, the thinking mind, as "the thinker." When the thinking operates fully, mind and the thinking become one and the same, which is clung to as "me," and the specifics of whatever it's thinking about become "mine."

On some occasions, mind takes sense consciousness (*viññāṇa*)—such as direct awareness of a visual form via eyes or a sound via ears—to be "me." The consciousness of the moment, whether visual, auditory, olfactory, lingual, tactile, or mental, is grasped as "me." Some Buddhists are confused about this, being influenced by pre-Buddhist teachings that there's a *winyan*, a kind of permanent self that is conscious through the eyes, ears, nose, tongue, body, and mind door.[1] Although this isn't Buddhist understanding, some teachers have mistakenly taught such a winyan as Buddhist. Don't make consciousness into a pseudo-Buddhist principle of self, when it's actually just mind's stupidity. Properly, Buddhism teaches that ignorant clinging to form, feeling, perception, thinking, or consciousness as self creates suffering.

In truth, this story is about the mental fabricating of and with the various elements. The things that stimulate mind—visual forms, sounds, odors, flavors, tangibles, and mental objects—are all elements. The eyes, ears, nose, tongue, body, and mind are elements too. See them all as natural elements rather than as selves. They combine and work together naturally, yet the main player—mind—is still capable of foolishness. When concocted by ignorance element, it becomes foolish mind and creates self.

Everything Is about Mind

Let's now explain some of the details and subtleties of mind. Everything is about mind. For instance, whenever a visual form is seen with the eyes, mind functions visually. The form is seen because of the interaction between eyes and the form, which creates eye consciousness. Cakkhu-viññāṇa directly sees and clearly knows what sort of form it is. So we say that the "seer" is really just mind.[2] Don't carelessly assume there's a self that sees; it's just mind operating normally, as visual consciousness in this case. Mind is the seer, the subject of seeing. The seeing is mind too. And the activity of seeing is nothing more than natural functioning of mind.

Further, the thing seen—a tree, for instance—is mind too. Through the activity of seeing, mind creates a tree in the visual pathway. It's not that the tree outside somehow enters mind. Rather, mind creates an image within itself corresponding to something outside, which can't actually enter mind. But mind creates an image of it. The visual system sees a tree that is a subjective creation of mind, not the objective tree itself. In other words, the thing seen is also just mind. This is like the film in a camera that records the image taken in by the lens. An image is created there to be seen.

People usually don't believe it when I say this sort of thing. Scientists who accept only material phenomena probably won't believe it either. However, if we're interested in the reality of mind, all aspects of experience become mind. The seer is mind, the seeing is mind, and the seen is mind. It's all mind. There's nothing else.

It's the same with the ears and sounds: the hearer is mind, the hearing is mind, and the sound heard is mind too. With the nose and odors, the smeller is mind, the smelling is mind, and the odor is mind. With the tongue and flavors, the taster is mind, the tasting is mind, and the flavor experienced is mind. With the body and tangible sensations, the toucher is mind, the touching is mind, and the tactile sensation is mind too. With purely mental experiences, mind knowing an object, the knowing, and the known are all mind. It's all mind of one type or another in each particular moment and each sense concocting.

In saying that everything is mind or is about mind, I'm making a universal statement. If this is understood, then it's understood; if not, then it isn't. If I'm blamed for talking nonsense that nobody can understand, so be it. But I don't know how to explain it in any other way. Anyway, it's up to each of you to consider this matter carefully and find out for yourself that everything is mind.

All that we've got, as people, are phenomena experienced through the eyes, ears, nose, tongue, body, and mind. All of them are related to mind or are mind itself. The Buddha, on a deeper level of understanding, is mind too—mind awakened to Dhamma and knowing it's awake. Dhamma is what mind realizes, which awakens mind. Dhamma is concocted by mind, in mind's awareness through a particular mind, until Dhamma becomes just mind itself. Sangha is minds awakened through following the Buddha. See, there's nothing—not even the most wonderful—apart from mind.

Four Characteristics of the Fruits of Mind's Concocting

If we look at the results of concocting—whether good, evil, or whatever—all are about mind. One characteristic is considered *pāpa* (evil) because it's wrong and disturbing. Another characteristic is considered *puñña* (good) because it feels right and pleasant. A third characteristic is considered *āneñja* (imperturbable) because it doesn't seem to be good or bad. These three characteristics are matters of mind. Above and beyond such characteristics is described as lokuttara because it's beyond the power of these three and yet still a matter of mind. Correspondingly, mind is named in many ways: *kāmāvacara-citta*, mind wandering in sensuality; *rūpāvacara-citta*, mind wandering among pure forms; *arūpāvacara-citta*, mind wandering in formlessness; and *lokuttara-citta*, mind that is above all such wanderings.

Let's look more closely at the four descriptive terms used here: *evil*, *good*, *āneñja*, and *lokuttara*. Evil (*pāpa*) refers to mind that is crude, wrong, and wicked. Good (*puñña*) refers to mind that satisfies its worldly wishes and is happy in a worldly way. However, the foolish happiness and limited goodness of ignorant persons are still subject to corruptions. Āneñja is when all meanings of evil and good are relinquished: the absence of agitation and perturbation over good and evil. This refers especially to nevasaññānāsaññāyatana, the meditation experience of neither perception nor nonperception, which is āneñja deluxe. Imperturbability has also been used to describe all four arūpa-jhānas, and some teachers even include the fourth rūpa-jhāna.[3] If we consider evil to be bitter and goodness to be sweet, ānañja is neither bitter nor sweet. Mind in such samādhi isn't interested in good and evil. Still, it is aware of feeling and perception. Beyond all of that is lokuttara, which is above worldly characteristics, above the meanings of the world, and above the influence of the values normally ascribed to forms, sounds, smells, tastes, tangibles, and mental objects.

Because these words may be new or strange for some readers, let's go through them once more. The basest is evil mind. Higher than that is good mind, which is right and happy according to worldly understanding. Puñña is the opposite of pāpa. Next is imperturbable mind, which is neither good nor evil but nevertheless is still saṅkhāra, still concoctable, and still under the power of causes and conditions. Ānenjā mind is hardly ever mentioned, and mainly in relation to the arūpa-jhānas, which have no sense of good or evil. Ānenjā mind is disinterested, neither sweet nor bitter. Beyond the influence of such characteristics, without any concocting at all, is lokuttara. To know these four is to know the full range of experience.

In addition to the Dhamma language we've been using—*pāpa*, *puñña*, *āneñja*, and *lokuttara*—we may consider the conventions of popular language to make these easier to understand. Couched in worldly terms, the four levels are the hells, the human world, the divine worlds, and nibbāna. The hells are the lowest and worst, while humankind is on a better, higher level. Higher still are the devatās (celestials), and beyond them the brahmas (gods). Highest of all is nibbāna. If we consider these as material worlds, the hells are the lowest, deep in the earth. The human world is above them, on the planet's surface. Higher again are the six levels of devas, and then the subtle formless worlds of *rūpa-brahmas* and *arūpa-brahmas*. Leaving all of those behind is nibbāna, beyond even the most refined divine worlds. Simple metaphors for the four levels are underground, earth's surface, in the sky, and the deep emptiness of outer space. These metaphors aren't meant to be taken literally; they're for the sake of easier understanding. Their purpose is to help us see that there's nothing that isn't mind in one form or another, no matter how base or exalted.

From Concocted to Unconcocted, All Are Matters of Mind

Whether underground, on the surface, or in the sky; whether evil, good, or imperturbable; whether human or divine; that entire spectrum contains saṅkhata-dhātus, elements capable of concocting. Beyond them all is, in Dhamma language, nibbāna, the asaṅkhata-dhātu, the element that can't be concocted. The elements are divisible into two categories: those that concoct and are concocted, and that which doesn't and isn't. We can group the good, evil, and imperturbable together as saṅkhata-dhātus—elements that are conditioned or concocted. Nibbāna is the asaṅkhata-dhātu, the element beyond concocting.

The concocting of elements by causes and conditions spins around in the mass of dukkha. When that concocting stops, the asaṅkhata-dhātu quenches dukkha completely. As the Buddha said, "Concocting itself is dukkha; ending the concocting is the supreme happiness." *Tesaṃ vūpasamo sukho* is recited in rituals for the dead to remind us that stopping the saṅkhāras is true happiness. If concocting still occurs, dukkha remains. We contemplate the elements to see those that concoct and the one that doesn't. Mind's path is from saṅkhata to asaṅkhata. Just that.

Mind is a natural element belonging to the saṅkhata group. Mind is continually concocted and concocts in response until developing into bodhicitta, mind of awakening, through which it crosses over to the asaṅkhata-dhātu side. Hence, we can say that everything concerning mind is about the path from concocting to nonconcocting. If you've never heard this before, you might be put off by it. To avoid that, we can also phrase it as the journey from dukkha to the remainderless quenching of dukkha. The plethora of details and developments all come down to "from dukkha to the remainderless quenching of dukkha." The 84,000 dhammas of Buddhism can be condensed into this one brief statement: from dukkha to the remainderless quenching of dukkha. Or, from saṅkhata to asaṅkhata. And that's the end of it.

This is the core message of our "little" *Seeing with the Eye of Dhamma.*

My objective has been to distill central Dhamma teachings into such concise terms. Recall what I said earlier, that from natural elements concocting together comes the many aspects and kinds of mind until bodhicitta arises. From mind of awakening, nibbāna is realized and the job is done—the demons are dead. From dukkha to the end of dukkha is all there is.

Nurturing the Trees of Practice

How do we practice in order to go from saṅkhata to the asaṅkhata, from dukkha to the quenching of dukkha? I compare such practice to planting and nurturing five trees. We'll examine this tree by tree, as it were, from the bare beginnings of practice up to the end, until nibbāna is attained.

First is the body tree—both the physical body and things connected with it. Second is the mind tree. Third is the bodhi tree, concerning intelligence, which isn't identical with mind but depends on it. Fourth is the metteyya tree, the tree of loving-kindness. Each tree must be planted and nurtured correctly according to its needs. In chapter 9, I mentioned four trees; here we'll add a fifth, the speech tree. Speech is usually considered under body and so could be included with the body tree. And while I'd rather not increase the list, there are good reasons for adding this tree of communication.

Now let's review each tree in more detail. The body tree is about physical well-being, which requires that physical behavior, activity, and concocting be healthy and correct. This applies to the body itself as well as things associated with it, such as the household utensils and tools we use and also the house itself. We act skillfully regarding the physical, material things of life, which expand to everything associated with the body. To borrow from the *Pāṭimokkha*, the Buddhist monastic training code, this tree includes being correct in our manners and the places we regularly visit. We behave respectfully within the customs and cultures of where we are and spend time in places that are in keeping with our ethics and spiritual values. If we're successful in these, we'll have planted and nurtured the body tree so that it prospers and flourishes, bringing calm and stability to the physical side of life.

The speech tree, now distinguished from the body tree, means correctness of speech and other means of communication among people. If we were all alone, there would be no need to communicate, and speech wouldn't happen. Our reality, however, is that we are many people who must live together and interact; therefore, means of communication are essential, including writing, drawing, music, singing, and all the other ways we exchange information, thoughts, and emotions. These must be correct so that our communication activities are wholesome karma. Our culture, customs, and traditions of speech and communication must be skillful and blameless. This is how to cultivate and nurture the speech tree successfully. However, if you prefer, consider it a major branch of the body tree.

Next is the mind tree, the system of mind and things associated with it, such as the nervous system. Although the mind tree depends on the body tree, the two can't be treated as the same. Cultivating this tree involves meditation and samādhi (stability and unification of mind), which are essential to this tree's well-being. Cultivating samādhi cultivates mind. Meditation is often assumed to mean sitting still and not thinking anything. However, the Dhamma meaning of samādhi is mind that's pure because it isn't afflicted by kilesas and nīvaraṇas (hindrances). When mind is purified (*parisuddho*), it's firm, steady, and undistracted (*samāhito*). Then it is ready for anything, alert and active (*kammaniyo*). Such mind is ready to do its proper duty, which is to see clearly (*vipassanā*). Correct samādhi has these qualities, which meditation nurtures and matures into a healthy mind tree. Merely sitting quietly isn't sufficient.

Please review the fruits of cultivating this tree. First of all, samādhi itself has great benefit. In samādhi there is happiness. It's also capable of special powers, though we don't need to go into that here, as powers and miracles are not the main intention. (Nevertheless, we can't deny that the well-trained mind can do special things.) More to the point, mindfulness is perfected so that mind is always present, circumspect, and incapable of error. The samādhi mind with perfect mindfulness is ready to develop path, fruit, and nibbāna to ever higher levels. This tree also has a social and cultural aspect: in any community in which cultivating samādhi is valued, people will be strong-minded, stable, pure, gentle, and cultured. Such a society of evolved human beings would be the full expression of mental rightness, of the well-cultivated mind tree.

And now the bodhi tree: the training of intelligence, knowledge, and wisdom in mind. Real knowledge in the Dhamma sense refers to clear seeing and realization. So let's consider the differences among three words: *knowledge*, *understanding*, and *realization*. Knowledge is acquired through study, while understanding comes through thought, reasoning, and reflection. Insight and realization, the final stage, occurs through seeing clearly and directly into the reality of things. This is knowledge in the ultimate sense. Ordinary knowledge is normally obtained through learning. Understanding develops through the use of thought and reasoning. Realization completely surpasses both knowledge and understanding, as it can't be acquired through book study or by mere thinking. Realization is above reasoning and requires thorough, intimate experience of real things. When something is experienced profoundly and sufficiently, realization occurs, which is referred to as *bodhi*: the knowledge from clearly seeing things as they actually are. Book learning and reasoning aren't enough.

Understanding and Realizing Nibbāna

Knowledge reaches its climax with the realization of nibbāna. When mind is trained properly, it grows in intelligence, knowing, and understanding, which culminates in intimately knowing nonclinging and nonconcocting in regard to all things. This is realization of nibbāna, which is free and empty of afflictions, thus free and empty of dukkha. Even momentary freedom from dukkha is a kind of nibbāna. Momentary nibbāna happens naturally without any particular effort. It happens that, sometimes, environmental conditions are appropriate for the nonarising of kilesas. Mind is naturally cool and there's no dukkha. This is easily experienced when sitting quietly in a place where there's nothing to provoke the corruptions. Sometimes it happens when mind just wants to stop, to be still, to rest; it doesn't feel like getting involved with the usual disturbances. When the kilesas don't arise, there's no dukkha. Momentary nibbāna occurs naturally and with everyone, much more often than we realize. Without these moments of peaceful, cool mind, we would go mad. We would break down and perhaps even die without such momentary respite from afflictions and suffering. Fortunately, mind possesses this natural ability to relax and let go.

During the twenty-four hours of a day and night, for how many hours is mind hot with kilesas? And for how many hours is mind cool and free, empty of kilesas? Strengthen appreciation for this momentary freedom from affliction. Even though it's temporary, you'll get to know the flavor of both kilesas and their absence. Contemplate the contrast. With kilesas, it's hot like falling into hell—taste what that's like. When enjoying something delicious, it's like being in heaven—taste what that's like. And when there's no kilesas and there's nothing disturbing—taste what that's like. These comparisons reveal the radical difference between affliction and nonaffliction.

Diligently observe, study, and get to know the life of coolness in this world. Such observation ought to be a daily custom, a tradition, and an integral part of our culture. Then each member of each family would know coolness because they would live together in a way that makes it difficult for the afflictions to happen. When the kilesas hardly disturb life, it's correspondingly cool. This is the natural temporary form of nibbāna that deserves to be known.

By practicing sīla, samādhi, and paññā on the highest level, mind is trained until realizing perfect, complete nibbāna. When the afflictions, the effluents, and the underlying tendencies have ended such that they never return, that's true, full, perfect nibbāna. This highest nibbāna isn't realized through customs or culture but through the highest level of Dhamma. This total nibbāna is the absence of concocting, the condition that doesn't fabricate anything, the quality that doesn't create afflictions and suffering.

Every kind of nibbāna is a dhātu. The temporary form is called *sāmāyika-nibbāna*, which is a natural element. True nibbāna—either *saupādisesa-nibbāna* (coolness with fuel remaining) or *anupādisesa-nibbāna* (coolness without fuel)—is a natural element.[4] Thus even beginningless, endless, deathless nibbāna is just a natural element and can't be grasped as being self. In this way, our bodhi tree is trained, nurtured, and cultivated for the highest realization of nibbāna. Take good care of your bodhi tree as it buds, blossoms, thrives, and brings forth the fruit of nibbāna.

Our personal duty ends here. However, our duty to society hasn't ended because dukkha doesn't happen to just one person. The story may have completed on the individual side; on the social side, however, it isn't finished yet. Suffering and problems don't exist only for individuals; there are the suffering and problems of society too. Nature has arranged matters such that we can't live without society. Nobody can exist all alone; we all depend on and live in society. Therefore, it's our duty to act for the benefit of society at large. This much remains to be cared for, and so we'll need to plant and nurture the final tree, the metteyya tree.

Every religion has a metteyya (*maitreya*) concept. Although others have their own names for it, the basic meaning is the same: exalted through mettā, friendliness, amity, and benevolence. No longer troubled by personal issues, the problems of society still disturb us, so we need to plant this tree to finally end human problems. *Metteyya* means supporting friendship, encouraging friendliness, and cultivating universal amity. We plant this fifth tree for friendliness in society.

The reason why we need to plant and nurture this tree is to some extent self-interested. In worldly terms, we have kindness and act for the benefit of others because we can't live in this world alone. This isn't completely pure. Hence, the worldly and ethical reason for bearing in mind the benefits and well-being of others is so that we can live comfortably together. This is why we have the ethical (*sīla*) teachings. In terms of ultimate truth, our reason is that we're all comrades in birth, aging, sickness, and death. Because we are already friends in birth, aging, sickness, and death, we must act for the benefit of others.

I find it intriguing that all religious systems, as far as I've been able to study, have one particular component in common—the messiah to come. In our Buddhist system, we have Maitreya, who will appear in the future. In the Hindu system, they have Kalki, the tenth avatar of Vishnu, who has yet to appear. The Semitic religions—Judaism, Christianity, and Islam—also have their messiahs to come. Jesus referred to himself as the Messiah and was killed for it, because there were those who wouldn't accept him as such. That all religions have an equivalent of Maitreya to come in the future means that our human duty isn't yet completely fulfilled. We must help bring it about.

Fulfilling our duty toward our fellow human beings is the final tree we need to plant and nurture, the metteyya tree. Our Theravada story of Metteyya already involves a tree—*Kalpavriksha,* the wish-fulfilling tree. Whoever has a need goes to the wish-fulfilling tree to have it satisfied. Hinduism has a similarly named tree—*Kalpadruma.* In either case, it's believed that this tree, as yet, remains far off in the future. Breaking with these conventions, I say that it isn't far away. It's right at the end of our noses. The religion of Maitreya is right at the tip of one's nose; all it takes is for everyone to love everyone else and it appears immediately. When through training, education, advertising, and teaching everyone knows how to love everyone, our world will be filled with wish-fulfilling trees. Wherever we go, everyone will be ready to help us. Feeling only love and generosity toward one another, people are ready to give and help wherever and whenever. This metteyya tree won't just be in a few special locations; it will be everywhere in a full, worldwide blossoming of the metteyya tree.

No political ideology could bring about such a state of affairs. Their utopias are dishonest, as all such ideologies are based in selfishness. A genuine metteyya religion must be based in love for our fellow human beings, all of them, both workers and investors. This comes from seeing the harm of selfishly not caring about others, which only increases kilesas and dukkha. People who can't open their hearts to others, don't care about others, and aren't able to help anyone merely torment themselves. They only injure themselves with their narcissism, envy, possessiveness, and their ever-increasing dukkha. Loving others, sharing with others, and serving others is happiness. Providing food to the hungry is more satisfying than eating oneself.

We each still need to cultivate the metteyya tree, training our minds little by little to have love for others. When everybody loves everybody else, the world of Maitreya appears and then, wherever we go, we meet only friends ready to lend a helping hand. People will always be looking out for others in this and that way. This human duty can't be ignored. Hence, let we Buddhists do our part and remember that when our own personal goal is achieved, we then need to think about the good of others. Mutual benefit, the good of all, is what binds us together. The Buddha regularly spoke of three kinds of benefits: our own benefit, the benefit of others, and the mutual benefit that binds the human race together as one. All three are connected, and fulfilling them is the end of the story. We practice to realize all three.

Relying upon the Body, Mind Leads

Whether cultivating five trees or four, it's all about mind. Life is about training and cultivating mind. These trees are planted in mind for the development of mind. The fruits of these trees are in mind and for mind. This is why we say that everything is accomplished through mind. Life, the body, thoughts, self-images, happiness, and distress—everything depends on mind. Phenomena can only happen in mind, not anywhere else. Nevertheless, we don't take mind to be self, because mind can't exist by itself. Mind is necessarily associated with the body, so the body must be developed correctly too. We don't prefer one over the other, mind alone or the body alone.

We call this "Dhamma-ism" in response to those who accuse Buddhism of being a form of idealism. Buddhism is a middle way focused on Dhamma, rather than a one-sided system like materialism or idealism. Dhamma-ism gives importance to both material and mental phenomena, to rūpa and nāma, which must both be correct and in balance. Nāmarūpa cannot be separated into two components, into nāma divorced from rūpa—the two only function in tandem.

Separating mind and body actually causes death. While mind is cultivated with the body as its foundation, mind operates as the leading partner. This is like machines in which certain parts have a regulating and controlling function while others do the work. Hence, we attribute special importance to mind. After all, anything and everything is accomplished through mind. Even the body relies upon mind and dwells under the power of mind.

As We Conclude Our Journey

This journey of *Seeing with the Eye of Dhamma* concludes with just three sentences:

> From natural elements come mind.
> From ordinary mind comes bodhicitta.
> From bodhicitta, nibbāna is reached.

The story ends with the monster slain; with the kilesas defeated. When mind grows into bodhi and then realizes nibbāna, all the evil afflictions die. Dukkha quenches and the matter is brought to a close. That ends the story this book aims to explain.

Please take to heart this short, easy summary. We must cultivate through these stages: from hell underground, to the human world on the earth's surface, to the deva worlds in the sky, and beyond the sky to the void of deep outer space. Metaphorically speaking, evil is underground, ordinary goodness is on the surface, the goodness bordering on imperturbable is in the sky, and beyond that is outer space, which represents nibbāna. This comparison isn't meant to be literal; it provides a picture of the stages through which mind must journey.

Underground, earth's surface, sky, and space are matters of mind. One moment mind is underground, and another moment mind is in the sky. Mind cycles through these stages with great rapidity, often erratically, repeatedly experiencing the form of birth described as *opapātika*. This mode of birth is instantaneous, doesn't involve parents, and is fully formed. Mind is born this way all the time—now here, now there. Sitting wherever you are, you can spontaneously be born in hell, in the human realm, in one of the deva heavens, or even in a brahma world. This "rebirthing" keeps happening until bodhicitta—mind that isn't seeking further birth—arises. Without self, having destroyed the self-illusion, there's nobody to be "reborn." It ends empty and free.

Nibbānaṃ paramaṃ suññaṃ (nibbāna is supremely empty): free and empty of kilesas, free and empty of dukkha, is nibbāna. This pithy condensation of the Buddha's words points to the ultimate freedom that's empty of self. This is emptiness of the highest meaning. When there's no "me," there are no kilesas; when there are no kilesas, there's no dukkha. So we say that nibbāna is voidness supreme, the end of all spinning around in vaṭṭasaṃsāra.

I hope that you will understand this supreme theme and aspire to emptiness, to stopping, to no longer seeking further concocting, and to finishing with cycling round and round. Even if your spinning around was only in goodness, it could never quench dukkha. The final resolution of the dukkha problem is to stop cycling between evil and good, to rise above good and evil, to no longer swim in the stream of good and bad karma.

Buddhism doesn't teach us to wander around with good karma; rather, it teaches going beyond the cycling round in streams of good and bad actions. Practicing for the realization of path, fruit, and nibbāna is the ultimate karma taught by Buddhism, as it ends ordinary karma. Lower religious systems only teach about doing good and dwelling endlessly in goodness, then continuing with goodness in some other place postmortem. Because of their misunderstanding, they want to go to some good place, such as a heavenly city believed to be full of goodness. However, true Buddhists aren't interested in such places, in reappearing somewhere else, in getting stuck there. They aspire to living above everything with mind free of self, empty of clinging to "me" and "mine." Rather than dwelling somewhere, Buddhism aims at dwelling above all things: above karma, beyond both good and bad actions, and so above all forms of dukkha.

This is the ultimate aim of life: to escape from all bondage to things that enwrap mind. Beware of benefits: they bind more tightly than evil and misfortune. If we go crazy over goodness, it kills. It entraps in torment. "Benefit" received can be a most wicked thing, as *payojana* means "to bind tightly and completely." Any benefit we are caught in makes us suffer for its sake. Hence, we rise above benefits to escape their bonds. Nibbāna is total freedom from all binding benefits.

So don't think of nibbāna as "benefit." That both violates its true meaning and rebels against actual nibbāna. Nibbāna is unbound and doesn't bind anyone; if there are ties, it isn't nibbāna. Describing it as good or beneficial is confused. Genuine nibbāna is above "the good" and any binding benefits. Nibbāna is release into boundless freedom, into emptiness.

I hope that everyone will aim for the true goal—that is, to get out from the spinning, from concocting, from being bound tightly by the various things we experience. Such life is full of afflictions, craving, and suffering. Instead, take interest in the unconcocted element that offers freedom and coolness beyond all ordinary benefits. It may seem strange at first, but it's the true meaning of life.

*

This concludes our contemplative journey of seeing with the eye of Dhamma. May this journey be of great fruit, from a life of hot anxiety to a life of peaceful coolness, for you personally as well as for others.

LECTURE DATES AND CHAPTER CORRESPONDENCE

Lecture 1	1st January 2526 (1983)	Introduction and Chapter 1
Lecture 2	8th January 2526 (1983)	Chapters 2 and 3
Lecture 3	15th January 2526 (1983)	Chapter 4
Lecture 4	22nd January 2526 (1983)	Chapter 5
Lecture 5	29th January 2526 (1983)	Chapter 6
Lecture 6	5th February 2526 (1983)	Chapter 7
Lecture 7	12th February 2526 (1983)	Chapter 8
Lecture 8	19th February 2526 (1983)	Chapter 9
Lecture 9	5th March 2526 (1983)	Chapters 10 and 11
Lecture 10	12th March 2526 (1983)	Chapter 12
Lecture 11	19th March 2526 (1983)	Chapter 13
Lecture 12	26th March 2526 (1983)	Chapter 14

GLOSSARY

Throughout this book, we have adhered to Ajahn Buddhadāsa's understanding of the many Pali terms he used. His usage, at times, differs from that of other teachers and translators. This glossary will highlight such terms, along with important concepts found in the chapters and terms for which familiar English translations may be disappointing. Ajahn Buddhadāsa derived his understanding primarily from the original Pali sources, informed to a lesser degree by the explanations of commentaries compiled many centuries after the suttas. In conveying Ajahn Buddhadāsa's understanding of these terms, I draw on his own explanations scattered throughout his lectures and which have been collected in a Dhamma glossary to his major Thai works (*Dhammānukrom Dhammaghosana*, rev. ed., ed. Pinit Raktonglor [Chaiya: Dhammadāna Foundation, 1997]). A few terms are discussed in detail because of their importance or confusion concerning them.

Alphabetization follows the order of the English alphabet, as many readers may be unfamiliar with the Pali alphabet.

If you don't find a term in this glossary, please use the index to look it up in the main text.

ānāpānasati. Mindfulness with breathing in and out; the system of psycho-spiritual cultivation practiced and taught by the Buddha.

arahant. Worthy one; one who has gone beyond craving, clinging, and the **kilesas**. Arahants have fulfilled the spiritual duty of ending **dukkha**. The Buddha is the most exalted of arahants.

ariya. Noble. Also, the noble ones well advanced in cultivation of path, of which **arahants** are the fullest expression. Stream enterers (*sotāpannas*) signify a life that has entered the stream that flows inevitably to **nibbāna**.

asaṅkhata. Unconcocted and unconditioned; not made, born, or liable to concocting.

āsava. Effluents, leaks; outflows from the unconscious tendencies toward **kilesas**. Their end is synonymous with awakening and liberation from **dukkha**.

attā. Self; separate, individual, abiding entity. A convention, appearance, and assumption rather than a reality. See "Key Terms" in the preface.

avijjā. Ignorance, lack of **vijjā**; not knowing what ought to be known (passive ignorance) and knowing incorrectly (active ignorance). Avijjā is often delineated in terms of not understanding the four ennobling realities. Lack of insight regarding inconstancy, unsatisfactoriness, and selflessness is also avijjā. Views and opinions are more active avijjā. Ignorance underlies and permeates all **kilesas**.

āyatana. Sense media, sense domains. The six inner media are the eyes, ears, nose, tongue, body, and **mano**. The six outer media are the forms, sounds, smells, flavors, tangibles, and mental experiences that correlate with the six sense doors.

bhava. Being, existence, becoming. In Dhamma language, to identify with, to take personally, to conceptually "be" or "have" in a particular way.

bhāvanā. Cultivation, development of body, moral action, **citta**, and **paññā**. Often in a compound with **samādhi** meaning cultivation through the power of samādhi. See "Key Terms" in the preface.

brahma. Highest, supreme, sublime. Applies to realms of existence (pure-form and formless) and the gods who dwell in them. Associated with the form and formless **jhānas**.

brahmacariya. Supreme way of life; the way of life that is sublime, excellent, and able to solve all human problems. Ajahn Buddhadāsa uses it in the original sense of the path leading to the utter quenching of **dukkha**, such as described by the noble eightfold path.

Buddha. Awakened One; one who knows, is fully awake, and has blossomed into wholeness. Buddha represents life that has seen deeply into our human reality, engendered profound compassion, given up all clinging to self, awakened from the sleep of the **kilesas**, and selflessly shown the way to beings in search of liberation from **dukkha**.

Buddha-Dhamma. Dhamma of the Awakened One, Natural Truth for Awakening. Not meant to be an ism.

Buddhasāstra. Buddhology, the science of awakening: Ajahn Buddhadāsa's coinage for **sayasāstra**'s replacement.

Buddhism. *Buddhasāsanā*. Originally, the Buddha's teaching, message, and dispensation.

citta. Mind, psyche, heart; the name we give to the capacity to experience and which thinks, has moods and emotions, reacts, understands, realizes, and is either caught within craving and clinging or is liberated and awakened. **Viññāṇa**, sense consciousness, and **mano**, mind that experiences sense objects, are not equivalent to citta, though usage is seldom strictly separated. In the text, the definite article has been avoided as "the mind" implies something singular and independent that is too easily taken as "the self." See "Key Terms" in the preface.

dhamma. Phenomenon, natural thing; a natural principle or quality.

Dhamma. Nature, law, duty, truth, reality, Dharma; a full understanding of everything signified by this term unfolds through a lifetime of practice. Can also mean teachings that express and point to Dhamma.

dhātu. Natural element; the basic units into which things can be analyzed. The elements in **Dhamma** teaching, as distinct to the material elements of modern chemistry, are the properties, values, and meanings that mind recognizes and apprehends, and out of which experience is compounded.

dukkha. Suffering, distress, dis-ease; the unnecessary pain we undergo because of craving and clinging regarding the essentials of life. Through clinging to any aspect of life as "**me**" or "mine" we create suffering.

idappaccayatā. Conditionality, the "fact of having this as condition"; the basic reality of conditioned, impermanent things, that they are dependent upon and conditioned by other things. *Paccaya*, condition, encompasses all forms of influencing relationship. "Conditionality" is more inclusive than "causality" or "cause and effect," especially the limited linear causality commonly assumed by those unfamiliar with Buddhist teachings. Ajahn Buddhadāsa considered idappaccayatā to be the most fundamental natural law, the Buddhist counterpart of God.

jāti. Birth. Ajahn Buddhadāsa usually takes jāti to mean the mental or spiritual birth of a fully formed ego, identity, or personality, which is often self-centered. Material or biological birth isn't the main issue in **Buddha-Dhamma**. Even if interpreted as "rebirth," jāti is best seen happening every day.

jhāna. Absorption; deep levels of **samādhi** in which mind is singularly focused on a particular aspect of inner experience. The Buddha-to-Be was familiar with the four form jhānas and the four formless jhānas that can develop out of the first four. After awakening, the Buddha used them for rest and recreation, and taught them as foundations for deeper insight and contemplation.

kalyāṇamitta. Noble, splendid friend. More than "teacher," includes mentor, role model, inspiration, and spiritual guide. Originally used in reference to the Buddha, the best friend anyone could have.

kāma. Sensuality; the basis of sensual pleasure and the object of sensual desire.

karma (Pali, *kamma*). Action; volitional actions of body, speech, and thought. The fruits and consequences of actions are *kamma-vipākas*. Karma does not mean "fortune" or "fate." Nor does it mean the "law of cause and effect."

kilesa. Afflictions, corruptions, reactive emotions, egoistic states. Most often categorized as three: lust (*rāga*) and greed (*lobha*), hatred (*dosa*) and anger (*kodha*), and delusion (*moha*). The term *kilesa* is rare in early suttas, but the three categories and other examples appear frequently. As time went on, kilesas became a powerful label for what ails humanity. There are many groupings and categories of kilesas, including the *anusayas* (underlying tendencies), **nīvaraṇas**, and **āsavas**. Ajahn Buddhadāsa often used kilesas in a narrower, more specific way: the full-blown reactive emotions that devour us like tigers. See "Key Terms" in the preface for fuller discussion.

lokuttara. Beyond the world (*loka*), transcendent; not caught within worldly conditions, independent of loka, that which naturally disintegrates. Often paired with *lokiya*, worldly.

magga-phala. Path and fruit; the activity of quenching the causes and conditions of suffering and the fruits, results, and consequences of that activity. More colloquially, completion and success in any activity. See "Key Terms" in the preface.

mano. Mind, mind-sense; mind as a sense door interacting with a mental phenomenon, **dhamma**. Cf. **citta** and **viññāṇa**.

"me." Thai, *tuakoo*. Ajahn Buddhadāsa used this term to convey a sense of self-centeredness or narcissism that arises from a fully developed sense of self. Its belongings are "mine" (Thai, *khongkoo*).

mettā. Kindness, friendliness, benevolence, love; wishing health and happiness to all beings. In Thai usage, mettā overlaps with *karuṇā*, compassion for the suffering of beings.

nāmarūpa. Mind and body, mind with body, body-with-mind, name and form. Used to reference living beings in nonpersonal terms.

ñāṇa. Insight knowledge; the wisdom accumulated through insight. Sets of nine and sixteen are listed in the later Abhidhamma literature and include path knowledge and fruition knowledge.

nibbāna (Sanskrit, *nirvāṇa*). Coolness; the end of all suffering and misery, of all things that burn and scorch, and of the egoistic reactions that cause them. Nibbāna has become the most common name for **Buddhism**'s supreme reality, although other names are common in the suttas. Often portrayed as a distant goal to be realized after many lifetimes of striving, Ajahn Buddhadāsa highlighted the possibility of "nibbāna at the tip of the nose" and its accessibility for everyone in this life. Cf. **asaṅkhata** and **visaṅkhāra**.

nirodha. Quenching, cessation; that something does not perform its usual function, is unable to perform that function, or has no function. Nirodha doesn't mean the utter ending, obliteration, or extinction of something. When something, or a life, quenches, it is no longer a basis for or capable of flaring up into craving, egoism, and **dukkha**.

nīvaraṇa. Hindrance, obstacle; the moods and attitudes that interfere with **samādhi**, hence blocking insight and feeding ignorance. For Ajahn Buddhadāsa, they are half-baked forms of **kilesas** that pester like gnats rather than devour. While more easily noticed during meditation, they can interfere with any activity or situation.

pabhassara. Luminous, radiant; describes **citta** before being clouded by passing **kilesas**.

paññā. Wisdom, discernment, understanding, intelligence. The range of this term is wide, including book learning and profound spiritual insight. Ajahn Buddhadāsa uses *paññā* as an umbrella term encompassing more specialized terms such as *vipassanā*, **ñāṇa**, and **vijjā**.

paramattha. Supreme meaning, ultimate purpose.

paridassana. All-round seeing; seeing comprehensively, viewing all of the important aspects of something. Coinage from *pari*, "all-round," and *dassana*, "seeing, vision."

paṭiccasamuppāda. Dependent co-arising (depending upon + together + arising); detailed analysis of **dukkha**'s arising. The subject of Ajahn Buddhadāsa's *Under the Bodhi Tree*.

phassa. Sense contact, sense impression; the functioning together of inner and outer **āyatana** and corresponding sense consciousness, **viññāṇa**. There are six kinds of phassa, categorized according to the six senses. **Vedanā** and **taṇhā** occur dependent on phassa. Ajahn Buddhadāsa distinguished between ignorant contact and mindful, wise contact.

samādhi. Unified, calm stability of mind. Primarily characterized by nondistraction, samādhi is clean, unhindered, clear, bright, unified, agile, and imperturbable. It provides the strength and stability for meditation practice. Classically exemplified by the **jhānas**, samādhi is always present to some degree when we function with focus and coherence, which can be refined and deepened into "good enough samādhi" and the **jhānas**. Samādhi supports both *samatha* (serenity) and *vipassanā* (insight).

samāpatti. Accomplishment, attainment: used in reference to meditative states, the **jhānas** and *saññāvedayita-nirodha*, the cessation of feeling and perception.

sammā. Right, correct; appropriate to the middle way of ending **dukkha**.

sammādiṭṭhi. Right view, right understanding; the guiding factor of **magga**.

sammatta. Rightness, correctness; Thai, *kwaam-thuk-tong*. In suttas there are ten, the eight factors or rightnesses of the noble eightfold path plus right knowing and right release. See "Key Terms" in the preface.

sandiṭṭhiko. "To be seen personally by those who practice," to be seen clearly and known truly within oneself in a way that is subjective, intuitive, and immediate. A defining quality of **Dhamma**.

saṅkhāra. Concocting, concoction; fabricating, fabrication; conditioning; the power to concoct various things into existence. *Saṅkhāra* has three primary uses in the suttas: most broadly, all concocted, created things; as a *khandha*, aggregate, thinking-emoting; and in the **paṭiccasamuppāda** teachings, the volitional influences that give rise to sense consciousness. See "Key Terms" in the preface.

saṅkhata. Of the nature to concoct and to be concocted.

saññā. Perception, regarding, naming; perceiving and regarding things in terms of concepts and past experiences. Often, the names attached to experiences take over from direct experience and become stories.

sati. Mindfulness, recall, recollection, remembering, awareness, attentiveness; keeping attention on what's happening at present, whether internally or externally; bringing something into awareness for reflection, investigation, or contemplation; keeping something in awareness in order to be fully present with it; delivering the appropriate wisdom to an experience in the nick of time. Liberating right mindfulness is guided by **sammādiṭṭhi** and backed up by skillful effort. Sati is hindered when lacking a solid ethical foundation.

sati-sampajañña. Mindfulness with clear comprehension; mindful, ready wisdom; applicable wisdom ready for use in the given situation.

sayasāstra. Superstition, the science of sleeping in ignorance; misunderstanding how natural law and duty operate, attributing causal efficacy where it doesn't actually exist, and behaving accordingly, although there may be partial understanding. See "Key Terms" in the preface.

sikkhā. Training. Usually threefold **sīla**, **samādhi**, and **paññā**. Equivalent to **magga**.

sīla. Ethics, virtue, morality; the aspect of path and cultivation concerning verbal, physical, and economic behavior. The five precepts are basic training in sīla.

suññatā. Emptiness, voidness; to be empty of **attā** and *attaniya*, anything having to do with attā. More or less equivalent to *anattā* (not-self).

taṇhā. Craving (lit., "thirst," "hunger"), ignorant desire. Usually categorized as three: sensual; existential, to be or have; and nihilistic, to not be or not have. Sometimes as six, according to the six senses. Taṇhā doesn't include wise skillful desires, wants, and aspirations.

Tathāgata. Untranslatable epithet the Buddha used for himself and other indescribable "beings." Variously explained as "one who is thus come" and "one who is thus gone." Ajahn Buddhadāsa explains Tathāgata as one who has fully realized and lives in **tathatā.**

tathatā. Thusness, suchness; **dhammas** that are "just so," "simply thus," "just like that," "merely such." Tathātā is nondualistic, outside of positive and negative valuations and categories.

Tipiṭaka. Three Baskets: Vinaya, monastic code; Suttas, discourses of the Buddha and leading disciples; and Abhidhamma, an early level of commentary that attempts to analyze and express the Dhamma in impersonal terms. The name comes from the baskets in which palm leaf manuscripts were kept.

upādāna. Clinging, grasping. The suttas list four kinds: clinging to **kāma**, to precepts and practices, to views, and to concepts of **attā.** The last, the conception of self, clinging to **"me"** and "mine," is the core of the others and is of central importance in **Buddhism**.

upādānakkhandha. Clinging-together groups, aggregates of clinging. These five—body, **vedanā, saññā,** thoughts, and **viññāṇa** taken personally—are the core of **dukkha.**

vaṭṭasaṃsāra. Spinning in circles, recycling through birth and death; repeating the same old rounds of *saṃsāra*, wandering continuously through birth and death, over and over.

vedanā. Feeling tones; pleasurable, painful, and neither-pleasant-nor-painful feeling tones that occur with sense contact. Vedanā is generally distinguished in this threefold manner and also according to the six kinds of **phassa** on which they are based. Commonly translated as "feeling," vedanā does not mean physical sensations or emotions. Vedanā is the simple subjective feeling tone of an experience, whether pleasant, agreeable, comfortable, attractive, or beautiful; painful, unpleasant, disagreeable, uncomfortable, repellant, or ugly; or neither one way nor the other, which may feel neutral or ambiguous. Emotions, like other forms of experience, involve vedanās and may feel pleasurable, painful, or ambiguous.

vijjā. True knowing, clear knowing. Ignorance is the absence or distortion of vijjā. Replacing ignorance with true knowing leads to liberation. Vijjā and **paññā** are effectively synonyms, as is **ñāṇa**. They arise from skillful cultivation and *vipassanā*, clear seeing, insight.

vimutti. Liberation, emancipation, release; to be freed from the influences of **kilesas** and from suffering.

viññāṇa. Sense consciousness, discriminating consciousness; to cognize sense objects via the six pairs of sense media. Viññāṇa distinguishes particular objects within each sensory sphere. Readers should be careful to understand consciousness as used in the Pali suttas and not confuse it with the various associations in English usage.

vipāka. Result of **karma**.

visaṅkhāra. Nonconcocting; the reality that cannot be fabricated. Cf. **nibbāna**.

NOTES

Guide to abbreviations appearing in these notes:

DN Dīgha Nikāya (Long Discourses of the Buddha)

MN Majjhima Nikāya (Middle Length Discourses of the Buddha)

SN Saṃyutta Nikāya (Connected Discourses of the Buddha)

AN Aṅguttara Nikāya (Numerical Discourses of the Buddha)

KN Khuddaka Nikāya (Miscellaneous Discourses of the Buddha)

These are the five collections of Pali suttas listed in their traditional order. Good English translations are widely available in print (only some portions of KN) and online.

Introduction

1 The original Thai title was *Little Dhamma Book*, which made sense in the original context much more than for English readers who are new to Ajahn Buddhadāsa's style. *Seeing with the Eye of Dhamma* conveys the core theme of this book, as you will see.

2 The many Pali terms used throughout the book are explained in the glossary. Please refer to it often.

Chapter 1: The Ordinary Conditions of Human Life

1 *Lobha*, *dosa*, and *moha* (greed, hatred, and delusion) are the chief categories of these unwholesome, reactive concoctions of thought and emotion that tarnish and corrupt mind.

2 This takes for granted that our work is ethical. "Work" here is broader than simply "job."

3 Some of the original audience were local villagers, many of whom were rubber planters and tappers, while others may have worked for hire. For the majority of the audience who were middle class, the implication is that if laborers can work with this attitude, then more privileged workers can too.

4 *Kamma* is the Pali equivalent of Sanskrit *karma*.

5 The Thai text has *tuaton*, a standard term in Thai Dhamma discourses equivalent to Pali *attā*. *Tuaton* is less troublesome than our English *self*, with its diverse usage in mainstream psychology and Western philosophy. Still, "self" is the most acceptable translation for *tuaton*. In this book, I'll add adjectives such as *separate*, *lasting*, *independent*, and *individual*, when appropriate. Whenever you read *self*, please keep these adjectives in mind.

6 *Sayasāstra*, "sleepology," the science of remaining asleep.

7 Here and in later chapters, Ajahn Buddhadāsa uses the traditional phrase *magga-phala-nibbāna* in reference to the highest level of practice and realization.

8 *Buddhasāstra*, "Buddhist science," the science of awakening.

9 AN 3.65 is widely known as the *Kālāma Sutta* in Thailand, but sometimes as *Kesaputtiya* or *Kesamutta Sutta* in Pali editions.

10 Among the virtues of Dhamma recited daily in Thai monasteries and homes: *Svākkhāto bhagavatā dhammo sandiṭṭhiko akāliko ehipassiko opanayiko paccattaṃ veditabbo viññūhī* (Homage to the Dhamma proclaimed by the Blessed One, immediately seeable, timeless, inviting, leading ever deeper, and personally experienced by the wise).

11 These three levels of knowing are *pariyatti*, *paṭipatti*, and *paṭivedha* (study, practice, and direct experience).

Chapter 2: To Cultivate Mind Is to Develop Life

1 *Bhāvanā* is a Pali term, while *pattana* (derived from Pali *vattana*) is a Thai neologism from the 1950s, coined for the international development ideology that was the West's response to Soviet Communism during the Cold War. While the underlying meaning of the two terms is the same, they have been used in different realms of experience, that is, *bhāvanā* for religious and spiritual life, and *pattana*

for the social and economic sphere. Ajahn Buddhadāsa wanted his compatriots to understand the psychological and spiritual aspects of development, not just the material ones.

2 KN Mahāniddesa 1.41 (Guhaṭṭhakasuttaniddesa) and 1.116 (Jārasuttaniddesa).

3 Here, the Thai *naatee* is translated by both "duty" and "function." *Naatee* is an important aspect of Ajahn Buddhadāsa's understanding of *dhammas* (phenomena, realities, qualities) and Dhamma (natural truth). We name things according to their function and purpose. When conscious intention is involved, we speak of "duty."

4 The senses, contact, feeling tone, craving, and clinging are central to the *paṭiccasamuppāda* teaching. See Buddhadāsa Bhikkhu, *Under the Bodhi Tree: Buddha's Original Vision of Dependent Co-Arising* (Boston: Wisdom Publications, 2017).

5 The same applies to books about neuroscience. Theories about how the senses and brain work aren't equivalent to actual contemplative experience.

6 Most commonly, *vedanās* are categorized as pleasant, painful, or neither-painful-nor pleasant.

Chapter 3: Samādhi within the Path of Cultivation

1 *Sayasāstra* is the main theme of chapter 6.

2 *Sāstra* is a loan word from Sanskrit, explained by Ajahn Buddhadāsa as a "sharp weapon for cutting through." In modern Thai, the word commonly is used for modern fields of knowledge such as history, mathematics, humanities, liberal arts, and some scientific fields (whereas *vidya* is used for sciences such as biology, chemistry, neurology, and psychology). Here, it's being used as bodies of knowledge and ways of knowing.

3 The noble eightfold path is composed of right view, right aspiration, right speech, right action, right livelihood, right effort, right mindfulness, and right *samādhi.*

4 Here, Ajahn Buddhadāsa shifts to a meaning of *samādhi* common in Thailand. The aspects of the term in Pali and Thai are fluid; our translations reflect this fluidity.

5 Suan Mokkh is near the southern Thai town of Chaiya, which has ancient monuments and roots.

6 The *nīvaraṇas* are discussed further in chapter 5. See "The Hindrances Are Weaker and More Common" (p. 78).

7 *Tathatā*, thusness, is one of the ignored Pali terms that Ajahn Buddhadāsa rejuvenated within Thai Buddhism using the phrase *chen nan eng*, "just like that." Alternative phrases found in this book are "just so" and "just how it is."

Chapter 4: The Result of Mental Cultivation Is Path, Fruit, and Nibbāna

1 Ajahn Buddhadāsa uses "path-fruit-*nibbāna*" in reference to the highest level of practice and realization. In mid-twentieth-century Thai Buddhism, the Pali terms *magga* (path), *phala* (fruit, result), and *nibbāna* (coolness) were combined to signify completion and fulfillment of practice. In this common usage that Ajahn Buddhadāsa draws upon, the specific meanings of these terms are influenced by Abhidhamma and commentaries. There, *magga* refers to the mental event of path severing kilesas, *phala* refers to the result of those *kilesas* being severed and destroyed, and *nibbāna* refers to the coolness and peace realized when *kilesas* have no purchase. Within the scheme of the sixteen *ñāṇas* (insight knowledges) taught in insight meditation circles, there is a *ñāṇa* that realizes each of them. Colloquially, *magga-phala-nibbāna* came to mean success in any endeavor or enterprise, including ordinary worldly affairs. Ajahn Buddhadāsa's usage balances the colloquial and the technical.

2 In the progression of *jhānas* (absorptions) and *arūpas* (formless states), these two are the most refined formless objects of *samādhi*.

3 This is the term used by the Buddha when addressing the group of householders in the *Dhammadinna Sutta* (SN 55.53).

4 At the time of these lectures, Ajahn Buddhadāsa was well aware of rapidly increasing ecological harm and changing weather patterns in Thailand, whereas acknowledgment of climate change and catastrophe was only beginning in the wider world.

Chapter 5: The New Life of Path, Fruit, and Nibbāna

1 Often, Tan Ajahn uses *kilesa* in a broad sense that includes all unwholesome qualities from the subtlest ignorance to the crudest destructive passions. This is in line with Theravada tradition. Here, however, the sense is more restricted and compared to the subtler *nīvaraṇa*. In this discussion, greed, aversion, delusion, and the like refer to fully developed destructive passions. Please see the editor's preface and the glossary for further explanations and examples.

2 AN 4.41.

3 Students of Ajahn Buddhadāsa were familiar with his detailed teaching of *ānāpānasati* (mindfulness with breathing in and out) based on the discourses of the Buddha, especially the *Ānāpānasati Sutta* (MN 118). For readers interested in a full explanation of *ānāpānasati*, see Buddhadāsa Bhikkhu, *Mindfulness with Breathing: A Manual for Serious Beginners* (Boston: Wisdom Publications, 1988).

Chapter 6: How Superstition Influences Mental Cultivation

1 Ajahn Buddhadāsa often contrasted *buddhasāstra* (Buddhism proper) with *sayasāstra* (Buddhism confused by superstition). *Sāstra* originally meant a sharp weapon for cutting through obstacles, hence, systematic knowledge or science (*vidyasāstra* in modern Thai). Buddhism, properly, is an ethical-spiritual science of awakening, Buddhology. Its opposite, sleepology, is all the false knowledge and its derivative behaviors that keep us spiritually asleep—that is, ignorant.

In this chapter, Ajahn Buddhadāsa gives examples relevant to his diverse Thai audience in the 1980s. Readers today might reflect on superstitions of our own cultures and times, such as materialism and individualism, beliefs such as "the wisdom of the market," and understanding health as primarily deliverable by chemistry and technology. Western readers may harbor old beliefs inherited through our family trees and Asian cultural practices that, even if beneficial, have not yet been verified in direct spiritual experience and can become superficial distractions. Please use the Thai examples to look for one's own unacknowledged superstitions.

2 *Sala phra phum* are small idealized models of a traditional Thai house mounted on a pillar four to five feet off the ground somewhere in the family compound. Small offerings of rice, water, fruit, savories, and incense are placed there, usually daily, when people are also giving alms to monks wandering the village or neighborhood. The "spirit" protects the home. Shrines to ancestors are usually inside.

3 These are the first three of the ten fetters (*saṃyojanas*) that bind beings to existence.

4 Retreat centers are not immune to the superstitions of the cultures in which they operate.

5 Nowadays, a few clicks and a credit card will supply fantasies and magical solutions to profound existential challenges.

6 Jewel Temple: The Chaiya area where Ajahn Buddhadāsa spent all his life, except for a brief study period in Bangkok, has many temple ruins from the Srivijaya period (seventh through twelfth centuries C.E.). Some sites also have modern buildings, in active use.

7 Readers from outside Southeast Asia might enjoy these Thai examples as impetus to reflect on how their own forms of Buddhism are infiltrated by capitalist individualism, celebrity worship, and "superstitious psychology," in addition to Indian beliefs not proper to Buddhism.

8 The Thai word is a compound of *sakdi* (success, completion) and *siddhi* (power), meaning efficacious power, the power to create success. It's usually translated "sacred" or "holy."

9 At the end of traditional services and observances, water is poured from a special vial, usually brass, over one's fingers into a corresponding bowl while words are recited to share the merits of the activity with ancestors and kin; devas, animals, ghosts, and spirits; sun, moon, and planets; and all beings everywhere.

10 The third-century B.C.E. Indian emperor, whose empire was based on Buddhist ideals, at least on the practice of *sīla*, proper human behavior.

11 *Brahmajāla Sutta* (DN 1).

12 The quotations are found in many discourses that express *idappaccayatā* such as *Cūḷasakuladāyi Sutta* (MN 79). Tan Ajahn extensively explains *idappaccayatā* and *paṭiccasamuppāda* in Buddhadāsa Bhikkhu, *Under the Bodhi Tree: Buddha's Original Vision of Dependent Co-arising* (Boston: Wisdom Publications, 2017).

13 In the modern West, we have similar fears that seem rational to many, even though they lack evidence, such as the antivaccination movement.

14 Ajahn Buddhadāsa made use of both modern Western medicine and traditional Thai medicine.

Chapter 7: A Systematic Overview of Life's Development

1 *Khwam-thuk-tong* (correctness, rightness, appropriateness) and *thuk-tong* (right, fitting, proper, correct) are important terms in Ajahn Buddhadāsa's vocabulary, equivalent to *sammatta* and *sammā* in Pali. The factors of the noble eightfold path are primary examples of *sammā*, rightness. We employ all of the above translations as best fits the context.

2 Here, Ajahn Buddhadāsa refers to the common understanding that actions performed in previous lives bring results in this life.

3 Paraphrasing *Brahma Suttas* (AN 3.31, 4.63).

4 "Rebirth" is often used in this context. Ajahn Buddhadāsa, however, preferred "birth" as a more honest translation of the Pali *jāti*. The Pali term closest to

rebirth is *punabbhava* (further becoming, renewed existence) rather than *jāti*. Ajahn Buddhadāsa felt that popular usage has obscured the subtleties of the early terminology. See *Under the Bodhi Tree* for more on this.

5 Here and below, Ajahn Buddhadāsa refers to the technical terminology of Theravada meditation teachings to illustrate his perspectives on mental cultivation for a Thai audience that was familiar with those teachings. Various interpretations of this terminology and its practice are now circulating. Ajahn Buddhadāsa followed the mainstream Theravada monastic interpretation.

6 In Thailand, *bhava* and *bhūmi* often appear together and sometimes interchangeably or confusedly. Here, Tan Ajahn notes a subtle difference in the use of these two terms.

7 The distinction between *saṅkhata* and *asaṅkhata* will be explored thoroughly in chapter 13.

8 *Saññā* is one of the Pali terms whose meaning can vary widely depending on context. Most often translated "perception," other terms are a better fit in some cases. In contexts such as here, Ajahn Buddhadāsa explained it in terms of recognizing, naming, regarding, and apprehending, which often involve value judgments. He emphasized how we tend to regard things as truly being how we recognize and name them; we assume that's how they actually are, which overlooks the limitations of recognition and labeling. Such *saññā* verges on delusion and fosters clinging.

9 While *anupubba-sikkhā* (graduated, progressive training), *anupubba-nirodha*, and *anupubba-vihāra* are found in the suttas, Tan Ajahn coined *anupubba-ābādha* to apply the perspective of progression to the obstacles (illnesses, oppressions, *ābādhas*) that are worked through on each stage of practice.

Chapter 8: All-Round Observation of Life

1 Pali and Thai don't have lower- and uppercase. Here, we use English capitalization to distinguish Dhamma in the broad sense from particular *dhammas*—qualities, perspectives, insights, and practices.

2 In the suttas, *vaṭṭa* (circle, round) is largely synonymous with the more common *saṃsāra* (moving or wandering on continuously, circulating), mostly as passing references. "Rebirth" may be implied at times, but not always obviously. Elaboration came in the later literature. Thai usage combines the two, as Ajahn Buddhadāsa does in this chapter, doubly emphasizing the revolving, spinning, rotating movement. The original Latin meaning of *career* is an interesting parallel.

3 Ajahn Buddhadāsa used the Thai *waang* for the Pali *suñña*. *Waang* is an adjective that means both "free" and "empty," such as when describing a chair or time.

4 This large concrete box of a building is covered on the outside with copies of early relief sculptures from India telling the Buddha's life story. All of the inside walls and pillars are covered with paintings from eclectic sources—Thai, Chinese, Tibetan, Zen, Christian, Aesop—to inspire Dhamma reflection.

5 These terms are important in Theravada *vipassanā* teachings. Usually *viññāṇa* is consciousness of a sense object via one of the six senses, which makes conscious experience possible. Ajahn Buddhadāsa translates *nāmarūpa* (lit., name-form) as "body-with-mind," meaning the actively functioning body-mind complex. Sometimes, *viññāṇa* describes something less active, though not quite dormant. Here, Ajahn Buddhadāsa takes it to be the consciousness interacting with living, functioning body-mind.

6 The *cakka* was a discus-like weapon with sharpened blades protruding from its edges. Lotuses symbolize purity and peace.

7 We will return to *saṅkhata* and *asaṅkhata* in the penultimate chapter.

Chapter 9: The Trees of the Complete Dhamma Life

1 Nowadays, we would add therapy, self-help workshops, and the like.

2 *Kevalaparipuṇṇaṃ parisuddhaṃ brahmacariyaṃ pakāsetha.*

3 *Kesaputta (Kālāma) Sutta* (AN 3.65).

4 *Sammāsambuddhas* awaken through discovering the final quenching of *dukkha* on their own and go on to teach others. *Paccekabuddhas* are also self-awakened but don't aid others in full awakening. *Anubuddhas* awaken with crucial guidance from a teacher.

5 *Yogā ve jāyate bhūri.*

6 See *Cakkavatti Sutta* (DN 26). The Sanskrit *Maitreya* is often used in Thai Dhamma teachings.

Chapter 10: Everything in Life Is Solely Matters of Mind

1 *Dhammapada* 160: *Attā hi attano nātho.* Other verses in the *Attavagga* have similar references to *attā*.

2 *Dhātuvibhanga Sutta* (MN 140).

3 In Pali, *purisa* (person) and *puggala* (individual) are synonyms for *attā*.

4 *Pabhassara Suttas* (AN 1.50–53).

5 *Parisuddhi*, purity, is associated with final awakening through which there's no chance of further *kilesas*.

6 *Mahātaṇhāsankhaya Sutta* (MN 38).

7 *Saññā* is usually translated as "perception." Ajahn Buddhadāsa's understanding of *saññā* includes recognition and how experiences are regarded. See chapter 7 for more examples.

8 *Anattalakkhaṇa Sutta* (SN 22.59).

9 *Tuaton* and *attā* are as much about how we see objects as how we see ourselves (subject). This isn't clear with English "self."

Chapter 11: The Journey to Bodhi Mind without Self

1 *Anusayas* were discussed in chapter 4, and *āsavas* in chapter 5.

2 Chapter 7 distinguishes these realms with many more gradations.

3 *Aniccaṃ*, *dukkhaṃ*, and *anattā*.

4 *Suññatā*, *tathatā*, and *paṭiccasamuppāda*.

5 *Nibbidā-ñāṇa*, *muñcitukammayatā-ñāṇa*, and *vimutti-ñāṇa*.

6 *Dhammapada* 160.

Chapter 12: Anything and Everything Are Merely Natural Elements

1 The four material absorptions, which were discussed in chapter 3.

2 For Ajahn Buddhadāsa, "naturally" means through natural law, *idappaccayatā*. Current notions of "natural" in consumerist societies may be another matter, especially in how that word has been appropriated in advertising.

3 The reflection is applied to the four primary requisites: food, clothing, shelter, and medicine.

Chapter 13: Contemplating *Saṅkhāras* and *Visaṅkhāra*

1 The difference in spelling reflects Thai pronunciation. Many of the Thai words derived from Pali terms mean something different than the original—for example, *upādāna* (clinging) became *upathan* (hysteria) and *sati* (mindfulness) became *sati* (conscious).

2 *Mahāparinibbāna Sutta* (DN 16).

3 The Thai phrase in this passage—*plong ayu sankharn*—is usually taken to mean the Buddha determining the date of his *parinibbāna*, which, in the general understanding, means determining the date of his physical death, the relinquishing of his body. Ajahn Buddhadāsa's understanding is more nuanced.

4 Ignorance, concocting, consciousness (sense cognition), mind-body, sense media, contact, feeling tone, craving, clinging, being, birth, and suffering.

5 "Concocting" is an excellent translation for *saṅkhāras* and Thai *karn-prung*, as Ajahn Buddhadāsa uses them. "Concoct" comes from Old French, "to cook together." *Karn-prung* is used so frequently in this chapter that we've employed the synonyms *fabricate*, *create*, and *produce*, all of which render *saṅkhāras* and *karn-prung*.

6 As noted in the editor's preface, the Pali terms used in Thai talks pose challenges when translating into English. Generally, anglicized plural is used here for *saṅkhāras* (but never *visaṅkhāra*). The adjective forms are *saṅkhata* and *asaṅkhata*.

7 *Dhammapada*, Sukha Vagga (Dhp 203).

8 The strong language here encourages cutting to the chase and looking more carefully at the nature of our suffering and reactions to it.

9 The words *impermanence*, *suffering*, and *not-self* are well known to devout Buddhists, especially *aniccaṃ*. Mindfully applying them in real time is something else.

10 This might be translated "non-self," but "no self" confuses the Pali meaning.

11 *Mahāparinibbāna Sutta* (DN 16).

12 *Vepullapabbata Sutta* (SN 15.20).

13 From a verse uttered by the newly awakened Buddha, *Dhammapada* 154.

Chapter 14: The End of the Journey

1 *Winyan* is the Thai pronunciation of *viññāṇa*. *Winyan* is popularly understood in the way Ajahn Buddhadāsa critiques here.

2 "Seer" (Thai, *puu-hen*) could also be translated "one who sees." The same applies to "hearer" and "the one who" of other senses. In some Indian traditions, *the seer* is another name for the *ātman*.

3 The *jhānas* were discussed in chapter 7.

4 *Saupādisesa-nibbāna* and *anupādisesa-nibbāna* refer to the coolness when no *kilesas* burn. In the former, the fuel of pleasure and pain remains. In the latter, no such fuel remains. Both are the perfect *nibbāna* of *arahants*.

INDEX